Discovering
HTML 4

LIMITED WARRANTY AND DISCLAIMER OF LIABILITY

Discovering
HTML 4

Bryan Pfaffenberger

AP Professional
AP Professional is a division of Academic Press

San Diego   London   Boston
New York   Sydney   Tokyo   Toronto

Academic Press
a division of Harcourt Brace & Company
525 B Street, Suite 1900, San Diego, California 92101-4495, USA
http://www.apnet.com

Academic Press
24-28 Oval Road, London NW1 7DX, UK
http://www.hbuk.cc.uk/ap/

Library of Congress Catalog Card Number: 98-3867
Pfaffenberger, Bryan, 1949-
   Discovering HTML 4 / Bryan Pfaffenberger.
     p. cm.
   Includes index.
   ISBN 0-12-553167-2 (paperback : alk. paper)
   1. HTML (Document markup language) I. Title.
QA76.76.H94P488 1998
005.7'2-dc21
                98-3867
                CIP

Printed in the United States of America
ISBN 0-12-553167-2
98 99 00 01 02 IP 9 8 7 6 5 4 3 2 1

For Suzanne, always

Contents

Part One	**A Quick Introduction to HTML 4**	**1**
1.	**First Things First (Things You Really Need to Know)**	**3**
	What Is Hypertext?	4
	The Good Things About Hypertext	6
	The Not-So-Good Things About Hypertext	7
	Where Did the Web Come From?	8
	SGML (Standard Generalized Markup Language)	10
	HTML (HyperText Markup Language)	12
	Editors, Just The Way You Like Them	13
	HTTP (HyperText Transfer Protocol)	15
	My, How You've Grown	17
	HTML 4.0 and Cascading Style Sheets (CSS)	21
	Summary	22
2	**HTML Basics (Learning the Lingo)**	**25**
	The Syntax Attack: Why?	26
	Exposed to the ELEMENTS	27
	Building a Nest	31
	Entity Is Just a Fancy Name for Character	32
	Assigning Values to Attributes	35
	Specifying Colors as Values for Attributes	40
	Specifying URLs as Values for Attributes	42
	Adding Comments to Your Code	45
	Writing Dates and Times in the ISO 8601 Format	46
	Summary	47

3 Your First Web Page in One Easy Lesson (Really!) **49**

Give Me Structure 50

Taking a Look at the Global Structure 51

Type It Up 51

Avoiding Common Typing Errors 53

Check It Out 54

The HTML Version Statement 54

The HTML Element 56

The HEAD Element 58

The TITLE Element 58

The BODY Element 60

Give Me Direction 62

Give Me Content 64

Controlling Line Breaks 69

Give Me Links 72

Give Me Beauty 74

Do It With Style: The STYLE element 78

Summary 82

4 Go Public! (Publishing Your Page) **83**

How Much Will This Cost? 84

The Do-It-Yourself Route 87

It's Sort of Like Remote Control: Using FTP 91

FTP Lingo 93

FTP Login Types and Transfer Types 95

Configuring Your FTP Client 95

Connecting to the FTP Server 96

Changing Directories 97

Sending Your File 98

Creating Directories 98

Maintaining Files on the Remote System 99

Finding Out Whether Anyone's Taken Your Domain Name 99

Summary 100

Part Two   Digging Deeper: More About HTML 4 .... **101**

5 Secrets of Successful Web Page Design **103**

Why Are You Doing This? 104

Specifying Your Intent 106

What's Your Audience? 107

What's Your Approach?   107
How Should You Lay Out Your Page?   108
Looking at Web Pages Critically   111
Summary   113

6   Making Document Design Choices   **113**
Design Follows from Purpose   114
Colors and Mood   114
Instant Typography Course   115
Getting the Background You Need   116
Fun with Fonts (Sort Of...)   125
Grouping Properties for Quick Coding   132
Choosing Document-wide Presentation Formats for Non-CSS Browsers 133
Using an External Style Sheet   135
Summary   136

7   Developing Your Document's BODY   **139**
The Stylish Approach   140
Go to the Head of the CLASS   142
Please Show Your ID   143
Getting Control of Block Element Layout   144
A Quote By Any Other Name Is Still a QUOTE   147
Making and Breaking Rules (Horizontal Lines)   149
Adding Rules with Style Sheets   150
DIVvying Up Your Document   156
Specifying Block Formats for Non-CSS-Capable Browsers   158
Summary   160

8   Making a List and Checking It Twice   **163**
Creating an Ordered List   164
Nesting Ordered Lists   168
Specifying Bullet Types with Styles   169
Using an Image as a Bullet   169
Combining Ordered and Unordered Lists   170
Adding Explanatory Text Within a List   171
Creating a Definition List   172
Controlling Your List's Presentation   174
Defining List Styles for Non-CSS-Capable Browsers   174
Summary   176

9   Lay It on the Line (Inline Elements)   **179**
Elements for Character Formatting   180
Elements for Technical Documents   182
Spelling Out Abbreviations and Acronyms   183
Adding a Short Quotation   184
Showing Insertions and Deletions   185
Styles for Character Emphases   187
Creating Inline Styles   191
Summary   192

10   The Art of the Hyperlink   **195**
Terminology: Links and Anchors   196
Take the <A> Train   197
Anchors Away!   203
The Mailto URL   203
Getting to First BASE   204
The LINK Element   206
Summary   206

11   Finishing Touches   **207**
The META Element: Coming of Age?   208
Using the META Element   209
Telling Search Engines What's in Your Document   210
Keep Your PICS Clean (Using PICS Rules)   213
What's Your ADDRESS? Signing Your Page   214
Creating a "We've Moved!" Page   215
Summary   216

Part Three   Lay It Out With STYLE   **217**

12   Creating Magazine-Quality Layouts   **219**
Box It Up   220
What Can You Put in the Box?   223
CSS Box Properties: Margins   224
CSS Box Properties: Padding   226
CSS Box Properties: Controlling Element Size   227
Let Me Float This By You   229
Please Get into Position—Absolutely!   230
CSS Positioning Properties   232
Using Relative Positioning   233

Creating Newspaper Columns   236
Summary   237

13   Using (and Slightly Abusing) Tables   **239**
Are Tables Worth Doing Manually?   240
Putting Your Cards on the TABLE (Table Basics)   241
Defining Your Table's Appearance   244
Creating a Row   249
Locking Up Data In Their Cells   251
Table Header Cells (TH)   254
How About a Caption?   254
Grouping Rows and Columns   256
Doing Tables with STYLE   262
Summary   263

14   It's a FRAME-Up   **265**
Mixed Feelings about Frames?   266
Introducing Frames   266
Ready, SET, FRAME!   267
Hanging Pictures on the Wall with FRAME   272
We Do Not Like Frames   278
Adding an Inline Frame   279
Summary   280

15   Making a Really Big Site with Lots of Pages   **281**
When One Page IS Enough   282
The Semantic Cloud   282
The Forced March   284
The Guided Cloud   285
Multi-Level Guided Clouds   286
Creating a Style Sheet for Your Entire Site   286
Summary   287

Part Four   Adding Visual Excitement and Interactivity   **289**

16   Getting Your IMG into Focus   **291**
Picture This!   292
Ways to Get Graphics for Your Web Page   293
A Not-So-Small Matter of Copyright   295
Understanding Graphics File Formats   296
The Big Three : GIF, JPEG, and PNG   299

Graphics Processing for Non-Artists   303
Positioning Images with STYLE   306
Formatting Images for Non-CSS-Capable Browsers   309
Creating an Imagemap   310
Summary   315

17   True to FORM   **317**
What Is a Form?   318
The FORM Element   320
Get Control! (Creating Controls with INPUT)   323
Single-Line Text Boxes   324
Password Text Boxes   326
Check Boxes   326
Radio Buttons   328
File Uploading Boxes   329
Hidden Input Fields   329
Drop-Down Menus and List Boxes   330
Text Entry Areas   334
Creating Submit, Reset, and Other Buttons   336
Providing Easier Access to Form Fields   339
Grouping FORM Elements   341
Summary   342

18   Getting Pushy with the Channel Definition Format   **343**
How CDF Channels Work   344
Creating a CDF Channel   346
Specifying the Schedule with CDF   348
Creating Subpages with CDF   350
Adding Items with CDF   352
Directing CDF Content to the Desktop, Screen Saver, or E-mail   353
Creating a Netcaster Channel   354
Summary   355

19   What's Your OBJECT?   **357**
If There's No OBJECT, What Are You Missing?   358
Take a Sip of Java   362
OBJECT—In Its Element   365
What's Your PARAMeter?   367
Inserting ActiveX Controls   368
Using Plug-Ins   368

Adding Multimedia	369
Adding Applets with the APPLET Element	370
Summary	371
20	**Stick to the SCRIPT**	**373**
Introducing Scripting	374
Adding Scripts with the SCRIPT Element	377
OOPs! Where's My Object?	380
Some Simple Examples	382
More Advanced Examples	384
Hiding HTML within SCRIPT Elements	387
Incorporating HTML Markup	387
The Function Junction	388
Handle This Event, Would You?	389
Introducing Event Handlers	390
Using Event Handlers in Forms	393
Isn't It Dynamic?	394
Summary	397

Appendices

| **A** | **HTML Entities Quick Reference** | **399** |
| **B** | **Color Codes** | **403** |

| **Index** | **409** |

Acknowledgments

Many thanks to everyone who helped me bring this book to completion, including editors Stefan Grunwedel, John Bozeman, and Linda Hamilton. Special thanks are due to Tom Stone for believing in this book's mission, namely, to create an entirely new approach to HTML based on the unification of HTML 4 and Cascading Style Sheets (CSS). Very special thanks are due to my family for putting up with lengthy work hours and periods of crankiness when I couldn't get various computer programs to cooperate. And as always, thanks to my agent, Carole McClendon and all the great folks at Waterside Productions.

Introduction

The HyperText Markup Language (HTML) enables anyone to create documents for the World Wide Web (WWW). With the release of the HTML version 4.0 specification, HTML seems poised to help the Web realize its full potential as a publication medium. The key to HTML 4's promise lies in its close relationship with Cascading Style Sheets (CSS), a formatting language that gives Web page designers unprecedented control over document layout, fonts, and the position of elements on the page.

Because CSS unlocks the full potential of HTML, you should learn both—and what's more, you should learn them at the same time. But you won't be able to do this with most books on HTML, which are rehashes of books written about earlier versions of HTML.

This is the first book to present HTML 4 and Cascading Style Sheets (CSS) as a unified body of publishing know-how. It's not a repeat of an earlier book about HTML. It's written fresh, starting from Page 1, with a single, clear approach, called the HTML 4 way. And it's the future of the Web.

Why Should You Read This Book?

This book is for anyone who wants to learn the future of Web publishing, rather than yesterday's technology. It teaches HTML 4.0 and Cascading Style Sheets (CSS) as a unified subject. By reading this book, you'll learn how to unlock the full power of HTML as a language for determining the *structure* of your Web pages, and of CSS for determining your page's *presentation*.

It's important to understand the difference between structure and presentation. Ideally, a markup language such as HTML should be used only to identify the structural components of a page, called elements. Examples of elements are titles, headings, lists, paragraphs, and block quotations. The presentation of these elements—the way they're formatted to appear on-screen—is supposed to be left up to the browser.

Unfortunately, earlier versions of HTML didn't stick to structural markup. A lot of presentation crept into HTML as Web designers (and browser publishers) tried to make the Web look spiffier. But these additions to HTML—called *extensions*—were introduced haphazardly. They result in messy, complicated code that quickly becomes an expensive nightmare to produce and maintain. Making one font size change throughout a document, for instance, might have required an HTML page designer to make dozens or even hundreds of changes.

HTML 4 takes the presentation out of HTML, and puts it into CSS, where it belongs. CSS provides a much more elegant approach to Web document formatting. It's easy to learn. CSS enables you to centralize formatting choices. In fact, you can create a CSS *style sheet* that applies to dozens, or even hundreds of documents. With one little change to the underlying style sheet, you can affect the appearance of all the documents to which the style sheet is linked.

By learning HTML 4 and CSS as a unified subject, you learn powerful Web page design skills that HTML authors could only dream about a year ago. You'll learn how to create Web pages that rival the quality of the Web's very best sites.

What about Browser Support?

HTML 4 and CSS are new to the Web publishing scene, so it's natural to wonder whether people using older browsers will be able to see your Web page designs. The bad news: Older browsers (version 3 and earlier) don't support Cascading Style Sheets, so they'll ignore your presentation choices. The good news: CSS is well supported by version 4 browsers (Netscape Communicator and Microsoft Internet Explorer), which are already in use by millions of Net surfers. In the years to come, anyone using a non-CSS-capable browser will realize that it's time to upgrade.

For now, we're in a transition period, a point that's expressly recognized in the HTML 4 specification. In the *strict flavor* of HTML 4, you do not use any of the presentation extensions that crept into previous versions of HTML, and rely instead on CSS to control formatting. In the *transitional flavor* of HTML, you combine the two approaches, including CSS formatting for CSS-capable browsers, and sneaking those bad, old extensions into your code, so that your page looks good to people using non-CSS-capable browsers. This book doesn't force you to choose the strict flavor of HTML; if you're concerned about narrowing your audience until there's more support for CSS, you'll find all the information you need to format your documents using the transitional flavor of HTML. Without tying you down to a "purist" HTML 4 approach, this book nevertheless teaches HTML the right way, and it will put you out in front of the pack when CSS support becomes nearly universal.

How Is This Book Organized?

Approaching HTML 4 and CSS as a unified field of study, this book begins with a mini-tutorial (A Quick Introduction to HTML 4) that walks you through the entire process of Web publishing. Just by reading the first 100 pages of this book, you'll learn enough to create a great-looking Web page, and what's more, you'll also know how to successfully upload your page to your Internet service provider's Web publishing space. In the space of a few day's study, you'll be on the Web, and you'll do it in style.

Part Two, "Digging Deeper: More About HTML 4," you go back over the methods and concepts introduced in Part I, but in greater detail. You'll learn how to exploit the full power of HTML 4 structure and CSS presentation, while at the same time learning how to format your page for older browsers. By the time you finish Part II, you'll possess most of the knowledge that accomplished Web authors use every day.

Part Three, "Laying It Out with STYLE," pushes your Web publishing skills into the realm of sophisticated document design. You go more deeply into the underlying philosophy of Cascading Style Sheets, learning an approach to Web page design that will enable you to emulate the high-quality layouts you see in newspapers and magazines. The skills you learn here are truly cutting edge, and will help you create pages that really stand out against the drab background of Web publishing mediocrity.

In Part Four, "Adding Visual Excitement and Interactivity," you learn how HTML and CSS provide powerful new tools for incorporating and positioning visual and interactive elements on your pages, including graphics, image maps, movies, sounds, forms, Java applets, JavaScript, and much more. You'll even learn how, in the space of an afternoon or two, you can write simple but powerful JavaScript programs that bring unprecedented interactivity to your Web pages. As you'll see, it's almost ridiculously easy, thanks to the programming "hooks" that HTML 4 makes available.

Where Should You Start?

If you're new to the Internet and everything else about HTML, start with Chapter 1. You'll find a full explanation of all the important, basic terms and concepts that this book discusses, including hypertext, HTML, and CSS.

If you've done a little previous work with HTML, start with Chapters 2 and 3, which provide a mini-tutorial encompassing all the fundamentals of HTML 4 and CSS.

Are you already fluent in a previous version of HTML? Skip directly to Part Two, and sink your teeth into the exciting new possibilities of approaching HTML 4 and CSS as a unified field of study.

A Note From the Author

I hope this book enables you to express yourself in the exciting new medium of Web publishing, and what's more, to do so in the way that all Web authors will write in the not-too-distant future. Whether you choose to write strict HTML 4 or transitional HTML 4, this book will teach you how to approach Web publishing the right way. You'll avoid mistakes that are costing Web publishing houses millions of dollars in unnecessary, tedious page maintenance costs.

As you're learning HTML 4, bear in mind that the language's authors hoped to do more than separate presentation from structure; they also hoped to make the Web more accessible for people with special needs. In this book, you'll learn ways that you can create HTML pages that are much easier to use for people with physical limitations, including repetitive stress injuries (RSI) that limit their use of a mouse. Join me in taking the extra effort to incorporate these needed features into your pages.

Part One

A Quick Introduction to HTML 4

1

First Things First
(Things You Really Need to Know)

In this chapter, you will learn the following skills:

- Understanding basic hypertext concepts
- Finding out how the Web developed
- Discovering what HTML is and where it came from
- Figuring out which version of HTML to use

You've browsed the Web. It's really easy, and fun too. And now you've decided to publish your own content on the Web. Suddenly, it doesn't seem quite so simple. There's a whole new language to learn, for one thing, full of impenetrable jargon such as *hypertext, hyperlink, URL,* and *HTTP.* Also, there's this HTML thing. Is it difficult to learn? Will this take weeks out of my life?

Let's get started with some reassurances. Anyone can learn HTML. Anyone can create really cool-looking Web content. And, it won't take too long. You can

3

read this book and master everything in it just by spending an hour or two with it in the evenings for a couple of weeks. And, when you're done, people will think your pages were created by some kind of Web authoring pro.

It helps, though, to get started on the right foot. In this chapter, you'll find an introduction to basic Web concepts—and with them, to the basic issues of Web authorship. After reading this chapter, you will have an appreciation for just why Web publishing is so special, why it so often goes awry, and how you can make sure you're doing things the right way. So even if you've heard of some of the material this chapter discusses and you think you know what it's all about, I would encourage you to start here. Of course, if the subject matter is all new to you, this is definitely the place to start. Let's begin by examining the most fundamental concept of all, the concept of hypertext.

What Is Hypertext?

The Web is a global hypertext system. The global part is easy to explain—the Internet, after all, is currently available in 132 countries. But what is hypertext?

A Definition of Hypertext

In brief, *hypertext* is a way of organizing information so that its sequencing—the order in which the information is read—is left up to the reader.

Hypertext is nonlinear or nonsequential text in the sense that the reader is free to explore the information it contains by selecting which document, or portion of a document, to read next.

Books do this to a certain extent. For example, I have called this "Chapter 1." You're perfectly free to ignore everything that I say in this chapter and start with Chapter 2, but you'd do so at the risk of missing out on some important preliminary information. To prevent this horrible thing from happening, I could begin a chapter such as this one with the stern moral admonition that you really ought to at least skim this stuff.

In hypertext, authors usually encourage readers to access material in a definite sequence by providing links to related information as often as possible. Thereby, they enable readers to pick their own way through the material.

An Example of Hypertext

Here's an example to make the point about hypertext being nonsequential.

Suppose I want to tell you about—well, hypertext. And it turns out that I think that everyone in the world should know that hypertext is actually a very old idea dating back to the medieval era. So I'd hit you with medieval history, and tell you about how the hypertext concept goes all the way back to the scholarship of medieval monks, who annotated scripture and drew connections between disparate passages. Maybe you came to my lecture to find out how to use hypertext and HTML in your business, and had to listen to this whole long boring thing, with your eyes glazing over.

Hypertext doesn't drag you through anything you don't want to go through. A hypertext starts with a welcome page that indicates the range of topics covered, and lets you select the ones you want to peruse. Pretend for a minute that the following paragraph is on the Web, and that you could click the underlined text to display more information about the underlined topic:

> Hypertext has an interesting history, stretching all the way back to the <u>scholarship of medieval monks</u>, who created richly-illustrated manuscripts (called <u>illuminated manuscripts</u>) that were jammed with cross-references. This history is interesting, but most people just want to know how one goes about <u>creating an effective hypertext</u>, one that avoids the pitfalls of hypertext and gives the reader maximum access to the information the hypertext contains.

See how this version frees the reader? If the ancient history of hypertext fascinates you, fine—click the links that explore this topic. If it leaves you cold, that's fine too. Click the links that give you useful information.

In order to do this right, an author must give up control fixation, the urge to lecture and structure information in a rigid presentation. Among the wizards of hypertext, there is actually a phrase for this. It's called *surrendering authorial privilege*. And if you're willing to do it, you're on your way to creating a fantastic Web site.

Figure 1.1 shows one of my Web publishing efforts, the Catalina 34 Home Page. It's a page that serves as an Internet focal point for owners of Catalina 34s, a production sailboat manufactured by Catalina Yachts, Inc. As an owner of a Catalina 34, I have a lot to say about the subject, but this page doesn't push my

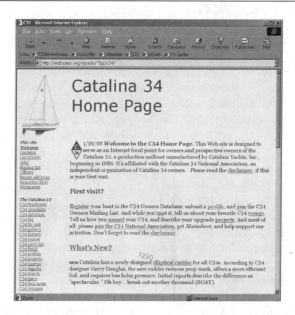

Figure 1.1 Hypertext enables readers to choose their own way

spiel in the face of somebody accessing the site. The navigation links (on the left column) provide a variety of ways to access the material.

The Good Things About Hypertext

Most people really like to access information by means of hypertext. They enjoy the freedom. They like being able to explore only the information they are interested in, without being dragged through a presentation they don't want or need. In the Catalina home page (Figure 1.1), you're free to explore whatever information you like.

Some experts think that hypertext presents information much more like the mind does than conventional means do. People learn by seeing connections between things. By allowing readers to explore connections actively, or so this argument goes, hypertext facilitates learning and engagement. This has never been proven, though, so don't take it as scientific fact.

The Not-So-Good Things About Hypertext

Hypertext is cool, hypertext is now, but it isn't perfect. Brainy researchers at the world's leading universities have identified three problems with hypertext.

Problem #1: Developing Adequate Content

So you're ready to surrender authorial privilege. Great! But it comes with a lot of responsibility. Basically, if you're willing to let people zoom off on whatever tangent they want, you have to develop content for them. This is the number one problem of hypertext.

Here's an example. Suppose I begin a hypertext with the following content:

> Investing in mutual funds is rewarding, but you should match your <u>investment objectives</u> with the right <u>type of fund</u>. You should also consider the fund's <u>risk level</u> and <u>costs</u>.

Simple enough? As a hypertext, though, the job of writing this up gets a heck of a lot bigger. Consider that you'll have to develop rich, fulfilling content for all these links:

- investment objectives
- fund types
- risks of mutual fund investing
- mutual fund costs

This is a big job, right? You'll see in a minute how the Internet solves this problem—but in a way that raises some concerns.

Problem #2: Pulling People to Your Site

Giving up authorial control makes it very difficult to get a certain point across. In order to get people to read your message, you must pull them to a certain page within the hypertext. But maybe they don't want to go. Maybe they're quite happy to ignore your message and read something else.

Hypertext may not be the best medium in the world for making sure that readers get a certain message. This raises the question of whether hypertext is really all that well suited to becoming a public medium supported by advertising. It's just too difficult to get people to access your page (and skip the other 54 million). As you'll see later, this problem has led many commercial content providers to seek a *push* version of the Web, one that delivers content to users' desktops instead of asking them to find it and access it themselves.

Problem #3: Getting Lost

Hypertext gives readers the freedom to explore, but this freedom comes at a price: They may get lost. In controlled experiments, researchers find that users frequently complain of disorientation and a "lost in hyperspace" feeling when using large, poorly-organized hypertexts.

This problem can be reduced by creating sites with good navigation tools, such as a row or column of links that provides users with a quick overview of your site's contents. If you're not aware of this problem and how severe it can be, you're not likely to create a good Web site.

Where Did the Web Come From?

The idea of hypertext was kicking around in the 1970s and 1980s and some people tried to create hypertexts. The computer made hypertext possible because it automates the page flipping that goes on when somebody follows a link. Numerous hypertexts were created that ran on a single computer. But they all experienced problem number one: The enormous job of creating enough content to satisfy readers who might go off in who knows what direction. Based on a single computer, a hypertext is no more than an interesting toy.

There is a solution to this problem, though: Why not distribute content creation tasks among dozens, hundreds, or even millions of people? Instead of having to develop all the linked content yourself, you can link to other people's content. This idea was first hit on by a computer visionary named Ted Nelson in 1965. Nelson coined the term hypertext, and envisioned a world-wide hypertext system called Xanadu. Nelson's system would have been a proprietary network with dialup connections, but it never took off.

The World Wide Web (WWW) stems from the very brilliant idea of using the Internet, instead of a single computer, as the transport mechanism for a huge hypertext of global proportions. The following section recounts the history of the Web's development—and along the way, provides some very important clues about the nature of Web publishing and the problems you'll encounter when you create your own Web content.

The Web's Origins

In Switzerland, there's a physics research institute called CERN (the acronym comes from the institute's French name). CERN was one of the first European research centers to go whole hog for the Internet. By the mid-1980s, CERN was a hotbed of Internet computing. The institute was using the Internet to enable current research fellows to stay in close contact with researchers located elsewhere, including previous fellows of CERN.

At CERN, one of the computer people, Tim Berners-Lee, had heard of hypertext. He then looked at the Internet. Suddenly, the idea struck him. Why not use the Internet to create a distributed hypertext system? In a *distributed hypertext system*, you develop just one topic, the one you know about. Other people develop content based on their knowledge. You all link to each other's pages. Presto! With relatively little effort, this community has created an unbelievably rich hypertext. And as people keep adding to it, it keeps getting richer. Cool, huh?

At the time (1989), Berners-Lee and his colleagues thought that their distributed hypertext system would facilitate communication within the physics research community. But they seemed to recognize that it had wider implications. They called it the World Wide Web, or WWW for short.

Markup Languages

From this initial insight, Berners-Lee and his colleagues quickly realized what would be needed to make this work. The first thing was a content creation method that would enable non-computer specialists to contribute their content to the distributed hypertext.

Why not just let these researchers contribute word processing files? This would not work because word processing files contain special formatting characters that cannot be read by computers other than the one designed to run the word processing program. These formatting codes specify exactly how the document is supposed to look when it's printed. You can't use one of these files unless you have the same program (and, generally, the same type of computer as the one on which it was created). The people at CERN knew all about these file incompatibility problems due to their experiences with the Internet. At CERN, the network included numerous different kinds of computers. These computers could exchange data only if the data contained nothing but the standard *ASCII characters* (the ones found on an ordinary computer keyboard).

It's Elementary, Watson

Berners-Lee had learned about *markup languages*, and he thought such a language might help WWW users. A markup language provides codes (called *tags*) that enable users to identify the *elements,* or parts, of an ASCII text document. Since the codes are made up of ASCII text characters, the marked-up document can be transmitted via a network with no difficulties.

The term "element" sounds obscure, but the concept is simple. This book has a number of elements, including text paragraphs (like this one), headings, figure captions, tables, and so on. When you mark up a text with a markup language, you identify the parts of a document. You say, in effect, "This is a title," or "This is a major heading." The markup doesn't contain any specific formatting instructions.

Structure Versus Presentation

To view a marked-up document, users open the document with a *browser*. A browser reads the tags, identifies the various components of the document, and formats them on-screen. The important point here is that the browser does all the formatting. Markup identifies the *structure* of the document (which parts are which); the browser makes decisions about *presentation* (how the parts look).

The distinction between structure and presentation that makes markup languages work nicely in a networked environment. For each type of computer you have, you create a browser that knows how to take full advantage of whatever fonts or graphics display capabilities the computer might have. Authors mark up their document's structure; the browsers take care of presentation. As a result, every document can be read by everyone on the network, and the documents always look nice.

SGML (Standard Generalized Markup Language)

How do you create a markup language? Happily, there is a formal descriptive language available for doing just that. It's called SGML, short for *Standard Generalized Markup Language*. You don't have to learn SGML to write HTML, but it helps to understand a little of where SGML fits into the picture.

SGML isn't actually used to mark up documents. Instead, it's a *metalanguage*, a computer language for creating other computer languages. Specifically, SGML is a set of rules for defining a particular markup language for a particular purpose.

This is done by creating a *document type definition (DTD)* that lists all the tags that are legal for this markup language to use.

That's really all you need to know about SGML. Berners-Lee and his colleagues used SGML to write the first document-type definition for HTML, back in the CERN days. Table 1.1 lists the HTML versions, each of which exists as a standardized document type definition.

Table 1.1 Versions of HTML

Version	Description
HTML 1.0 (1989)	This is the original version of HTML, created by Tim Berners-Lee for an obscure European research lab. It couldn't do a lot of the things that current versions of HTML can do, such as tables, frames, Java, and all the other snazzy things that we've come to expect of the Web. But it could display inline graphics (pictures mixed with text), and it enabled Web authors to create hyperlinks. And that's what got the ball rolling, big time.
HTML 2.0 (1994)	This version, officially ratified as an Internet standard, captured prevailing practice at the time, but was quickly outpaced due to the Netscape extensions (including tables).
HTML 3.0 (1996)	Never formally approved by the World Wide Web Consortium (WC3), headquartered in Cambridge, MA, or ratified by Internet standards bodies, this standard attempted to capture prevailing practices (such as tables and font tags) but was abandoned due to its internal inconsistencies.
HTML 3.2 (1996)	An updated version of the 2.0 standard, HTML is the work of the W3C. HTML formalized many of the popular extensions to HTML 2.0, including tables and text wrapping around images. Formally approved as a standard in January, 1997, HTML 3.2 is the current baseline version of HTML; most Web authors continue to write assuming that people are using HTML 3.2-capable browsers.

| HTML 4.0 (1997) | First published in the summer of 1997, the proposed HTML 4.0 specification has now been issued as a World Wide Web Consortium Recommendation. |

HTML (HyperText Markup Language)

Since Berners-Lee wanted to create a distributed hypertext system, he and his colleagues called their markup language HTML—short for *HyperText Markup Language*.

HTML enables authors to mark up their document so that the browser knows which part of the document is a title, an author's name, a heading, a paragraph, and so on. But it also contains support for hypertext. Using HTML, you can mark certain text so that, when clicked, it takes the reader to another document. That document might be located on the same computer as the one that was just clicked—or halfway around the world.

Most HTML tags have two parts, an opening tag and a closing tag. The text in-between is the marked text. Here is how you would mark the opening few lines of a novel:

```
<H1>Chapter 1</H1>

<P> Robin gazed into the cold, foggy darkness. The
waves came crashing up the steep, boulder-
covered shore far below. Wearing her dark green
cloak, she would have been completely invisible,
were it not for her white sweat socks. They gleamed
eerily in the moonlight.</P>
```

There are two tags used here, <H1> (first-level heading) and <P> (text paragraph). Note that the closing tag is the same as the opening tag, except for the slash mark. The slash mark is always used in closing tags.

Just how these elements appear depend on how the browser has been configured. The browser strips the tags from the text, and shows the text on-screen, with whatever formatting it has been programmed to display.

The browser might display the text like this:

Chapter 1

Robin gazed into the cold, foggy darkness. The waves came crashing up the steep, boulder-covered shore far below. Wearing her dark green cloak, she would have been completely invisible, were it not for her white sweat socks. They gleamed eerily in the moonlight.

Note that the line breaks are not the same as those found in the original. The browser formats the text so that it fits within the current window. Also, note that the browser displays <H1> and <P> text differently; both the font size and type-face are different. The basic idea, in sum, is this: just mark up the parts of the text, and let the browser decide how to display these parts.

To demonstrate how HTML could make life easier for physicists, the CERN team created the first Web browser in 1991. This was a text-only browser, but it could read HTML and display the text using some simple on-screen formats, and you could jump from document to document using the embedded hyperlinks.

Editors, Just The Way You Like Them

You can use a variety of programs to write HTML, as explained in Table 1.2. But you shouldn't shell out big bucks for a top-of-the-line HTML program—at least, not yet.

When you're learning HTML, there's a very good argument for starting out with a *text editor*, a simple word processing program that programmers use to write programs. If you're using a Macintosh, you can use the freebie Simple Text editor; Windows users can use the Notepad accessory.

With a text editor, you can learn the fundamentals of HTML. Once you've got these down, you can use a WYSIWYG editor (WYSIWYG is an acronym for "what you see is what you get") to sketch out your page's basics. Chances are pretty good, though, that you'll need to go into the HTML file to do some clean-up and to add advanced features, and then your HTML coding experience will really help you.

Table 1.2 HTML editor options

Type of editor	Description
text editors	These are simple programs that enable you to enter and edit text. Most computers come with one. Windows computers come with NOTEPAD.EXE, while Macs come with Simple-Text. You can use these programs to write both your content and the HTML tags. The good thing about text editors is that you get total control over how the HTML is entered. The bad thing is that you don't get any help, and there is usually no spelling checker.
HTML editors	These are text editors that have a few spiffy add-ons. For example, they enable you to click the tags you want to enter, and then put them in your document automatically. The better ones include spelling checkers, and give you a way to preview your document's appearance, the way it will look on the Web. A lot of people create their Web documents using these programs. Examples include Hot Dog Professional for Microsoft Windows, and HTML Editor for the Macintosh.
WYSIWYG editors	These programs enable you to create HTML documents without actually typing any HTML tags. You just create your document using word-processing-type commands; you see your document on-screen the way it will look on the Web. Examples include Netscape Page Composer (for Windows and Mac OS systems) as well as Microsoft Front Page Express (for Windows systems).
site managers	These programs combine WYSIWYG editors with tools for managing multi-document Web sites. They are expensive and definitely overkill if you're just beginning to use HTML. Examples include NetObjects Fusion (for Mac OS and Windows) and Microsoft Front Page.

HTTP (HyperText Transfer Protocol)

The CERN team needed something more to make the World Wide Web function: A set of standards to handle the transfer of Web documents via the Internet. Such standards, called *protocols*, already existed for other Internet services, such as the File Transfer Protocol (FTP) for transferring files. So the CERN team developed the *HyperText Transfer Protocol (HTTP)*.

Basically, HTTP defines the format that a computer can use to request a resource, such as a graphic or an HTML document, from another computer. It does this by means of Uniform Resource Locators (URLs), discussed in the next section. Also, HTTP defines the session that is created between the client (the browser) and the server (the program that intercepts client requests and supplies the requested document). This session involves the sequence shown in Table 1.3.

Table 1.3 Sequence of events in an HTTP connection

Event	Description
connection	Somebody clicks a hyperlink, and the browser initiates an HTTP request. The browser examines the URL, determines the location of the computer on which the requested resource is stored, and attempts to contact the computer. When you're using a browser, you can see this happening by looking at the browser's status bar: It will say something like "attempting to connect to www.microsoft.com..."
request	Once a connection is made to the distant server, the browser requests the specific resource that it is looking for.
response	After the server receives the request, it attempts to locate the resource. If the resource is found, the server sends the resource to the browser. If it isn't found, or if the server can't comply with the request for some other reason, an error message is sent.
close	After the browser receives the requested data (or the error message), the connection is terminated.

URL (Uniform Resource Locator)

As defined by HTTP, a *Uniform Resource Locator (URL)* provides a standard means by which a World Wide Web client program (specifically, a browser) can request information from a World Wide Web server, which makes Web documents available. A complete URL has the parts shown in Table 1.4.

Table 1.4 Components of a URL

Component	Description
protocol	This specifies the Internet standard to be used to access the document. For the Web, it's HTTP, the HyperText Transfer Protocol.
path	This specifies the exact location of the document on the Internet. It contains the domain name of the computer that's running the Web server. Also included is the exact location of the document on this computer, including the names of sub-folders (if any).
resource name	This gives the file name of the resource you're accessing. A resource is a computer file, which might be an HTML file. It might also be a sound, a movie, a graphic, or something else. The resource's extension (the part of the file name that goes past the period) indicates the type of resource. HTML documents get the extension .html, or .htm.

As you just learned, HTML is pretty much a generic markup language except for its ability to create *hyperlinks*, which retrieve another document when users click them. You will learn how to do this later in this book, but essentially a hyperlink hides a URL under a highlighted word or phrase. When you click the word or phrase, the browser originates a request for the information. This request is picked up by a Web server.

Web Servers

What's a Web server? Basically, a *Web server* is a program that sits there, patiently waiting for information requests to come in via the Internet, and then distributes the requested information as specified by a URL. In Unix, a program that waits for something to happen is called a daemon, so the first Web server was called CERN HTTPd—the little "d" is short for daemon. CERN HTTPd still exists, but there are plenty of other (and more advanced) Web servers these days.

These requests come in via the Internet, and they basically request, "Give me such-and-such document." The server meekly complies, and uploads the page. If it can't find the requested page, it sends back an error message. (I'm sure you've seen plenty of these—they usually read, "Error 404—Not found.")

My, How You've Grown

The Web grew slowly at first, and it wasn't much to write home about initially. In 1993, the first year of the Web's operation, there were only 130 Web sites. You had to use a text-based browser to access these sites. That's right—all text, no graphics. No wonder the Web didn't find popular appeal immediately. To become a public mass medium, the world needed graphical browsers, which display pictures as well as text. Here's how it all happened.

Graphical Browsers: NCSA and Mosaic

The Web story now moves from Switzerland to the United States. At another research institute, the U.S. government-funded National Center for Supercomputing Applications (NCSA) housed at the University of Illinois, efforts were underway to enhance scientific collaboration using the Internet. Programmer Marc Andreesen and his co-workers believed that text-only interfaces wouldn't cut it, so they created the first graphical browser—that is, a browser capable of displaying images as well as text. They called it Mosaic, and the first version was released in 1993.

Made available for Unix, Macintosh, and Microsoft Windows systems, and distributed for free over the Internet, Mosaic transformed the Web from an obscure Internet service into a new public medium, all in the space of just two years. Millions of copies of Mosaic were distributed, and the number of active Web servers grew by leaps and bounds. By 1994, it was clear that the Web was a very big deal indeed. Andreesen left NCSA to co-found Mosaic Communications, later renamed Netscape Communications.

The Rise of the Web as a Commercial Medium

Today, the World Wide Web is in use by an estimated 45 million people world-wide, and the global hypertext has grown to an astonishing 50 million documents. Both figures—the number of people using the Web and the amount of available content—continue to grow at a very high rate, with millions of new users each year. It is clear that the Web is well on its way to becoming the first major new public communications medium to appear in some time, and will eventually take its place among television, radio, telephones, and print media as one of the chief ways that virtually everyone acquires information.

The Web is no longer an anarchy. The task of maintaining Web standards (including HTML) and advancing the Web is in the hands of the World Wide Web Consortium (W3C). W3C is a consortium of industry practitioners, academics, and content providers, including Adobe Systems, Hewlett Packard, IBM, Microsoft, Netscape Communications, Novell, SoftQuad, Spyglass, and Sun Microsystems; content specialists at HotWired, PathFinder, and Verso; and experts in the fields of accessibility and internationalization. Figure 1.2 shows the Consortium's home page, which is a great source of recent information about HTML. You can find this page at www.w3c.org.

The Web is big business, too. For example, according to a recent *Wall Street Journal* article, Web advertising increased to approximately $140 million in 1998. That's still a pittance, compared to the money companies spend on advertising in other media, but this figure is growing steadily. The days when unknown research labs contributed to the Web's evolution are long gone. In their place are the giants of the computing industry, such as Microsoft Corporation, and aggressive new companies, such as Netscape Communications. And what complicates things for a student of HTML is that these powerful players are trying to push HTML in differing directions.

The Extensions Game

Early HTML forced the markup language distinction between structure and presentation. But commercial Web authors want precise control over the appearance of their company's Web sites. They want tags that will enable them to create complex, magazine-style layouts, with fonts, multiple columns, and other eye-catching formats. They also recognize the "pull" problem discussed in this chapter's earlier survey of the shortcomings of hypertext. They want to "push" information at you.

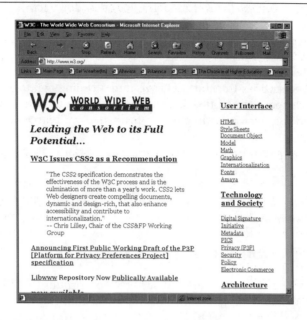

Figure 1.2 The W3C Home Page has the latest news about HTML

This creates an opportunity for browser publishers. If a browser publisher uni-laterally introduces a non-standard HTML tag that gives formatting control or enables authors to push content in your face, and supports it in their browser, the company might be able to get everyone or almost everyone to use its brows-er. These new tags are called *extensions*.

For example, Netscape added a number of new HTML tags to Version 2.0 of Netscape Navigator. They were features that Web authors really wanted. At the time (1995), these features weren't present in the standard version of HTML (1.0). Web authors used these features, and put messages on their welcome pages that said, "This site looks best with Netscape Navigator." The result was free advertising for Netscape, and too bad for you if you were using another brows-er! This effectively knocked many of the smaller browser players out of the pic-ture, unless they had the money to update their product so that it could display the new Netscape tags (called the Netscape extensions). More recently, Netscape introduced a proprietary "push" technology called NetCaster, which enables users to subscribe to Web sites so that they appear in a "Webtop" window.

Microsoft plays this game, too. For example, Version 2.0 of Microsoft Internet Explorer introduced new tags for creating marquees (scrolling text banners) as well as watermarks (background graphics that don't scroll with text). The company has also introduced its own "push" technology, which is not compatible with Netscape's.

What's wrong with the extensions game? By putting presentation aspects into HTML, extensions transform HTML into a coding nightmare, difficult to write and very expensive and time-consuming to maintain. Here's an example of what is needed to center a heading that is formatted with large Helvetica type:

```
<CENTER><FONT face = "Helvetica" size="7">A Head-
ing</FONT></CENTER>
```

All the presentation tags transform what should be a simple expression into an editing and maintenance nightmare.

The Standardization Process (Such As It Is)

It would be nice if the World Wide Web Consortium (W3C) could step in and force companies to stop introducing extensions to HTML. But W3C has absolutely no enforcement power. And besides, this probably wouldn't be desirable. Both Netscape and Microsoft have introduced useful new extensions to HTML—extensions that might not have existed were the task of HTML standardization left up to some academically-oriented committee.

W3C recognizes this point, to its credit. Currently, the standardization process consists, essentially, of bringing all the industry participants to the table, and getting them to agree on new standards that reflect the best and most widely accepted innovations—and everyone agrees to support the new, standardized version once it is approved and published.

The HTML standardization process is best characterized as follows:

1. The W3C publishes a standard, and the leading browsers support it. But, by the time it appears, it's already out of date, and people want to push the Web in new directions.
2. Browser publishers introduce new, non-standard tags (extensions) in the hope of gaining market share for their product. Other publishers, miffed, refuse to recognize the tags and fight back with their own, which are not compatible.

3. Some of the new tags win out, and W3C incorporates them (with modifications to make sure they conform to HTML principles) in the next HTML standard.
4. The W3C publishes a standard, and the leading browsers support it. But, by the time it appears, it's already out of date...

And so on. But maybe not ad infinitum, as I will explain in a moment.

The Dilemma for Web Authors

The way the HTML standardization process works causes a dilemma for a would-be Web author, which boils down to this:

- If I use any of the new tags (extensions) to do something really cool and fancy, my site will be fully accessible only by people using the browser that supports the new tags.
- If I don't use any of the new tags, and instead use only the tags from the last standard version of HTML, then almost every browser will be able to access my site—but it won't be as snazzy.

In short, there's a trade-off between coolness and accessibility. If you use the cool new extensions, you shut people out. If you use standard HTML so that everyone gets in, your site isn't as cool as competing ones.

Most Web authors agree that it is safest to write to the standard. You get the biggest audience that way.

HTML 4.0 and Cascading Style Sheets (CSS)

It's wise to write using standard HTML. But which standard?

Most HTML authors are now writing to HTML 3.2. But there's a new version, called HTML 4.0. Essentially, HTML 4 tries to put a stop to the extensions game by restoring the distinction between structure and presentation.

In HTML 4, you transfer all the presentation to *style sheets*, in conformance to the Consortium's Cascading Style Sheets (CSS) Standard. Style sheets enable you to choose presentation styles for HTML tags. For example, you can choose 18-point Helvetica for H1 headings, if you wish. Because the style sheet is kept away from most of the HTML code (and even in a separate document, if you prefer), your HTML code is cleaner and much easier to maintain.

Does HTML 4 solve the coolness vs. accessibility trade-off? Not yet, but it will. Currently, HTML 4 and CSS are well supported by Version 4 of the leading browsers (and partially by Version 3 of Microsoft Internet Explorer), but not the previous versions. What this means is that people using earlier versions of Netscape Navigator and Microsoft Internet Explorer won't be able to see the HTML 4/CSS aspects of your site. (They'll still be able to access it; it just won't look as pretty.) However, people will gradually upgrade their browsers to HTML 4/CSS-capable versions.

Recognizing that HTML Version 4 will require time to gain full acceptance, the consortium specifies HTML 4 in three "flavors," as shown in Table 1.5.

Table 1.5 The three flavors of HTML 4

Flavor	Description
strict	This is the "pure" version of HTML 4, in which you transfer all of the presentation to Cascading Style Sheets.
transitional	This version of HTML 4 includes support for HTML 3.2-era presentation tags and extensions, so that your pages look good when accessed by non-CSS-capable browsers.
frameset	This version includes support for frames, which enable you to split the browser window into two or more independently-scrollable panels.

Summary

A nonsequential medium for presenting information, hypertext is popular with readers, but it's a lot of work to create content for every possible direction in which a reader might explore. Also, hypertext makes it difficult to "pull" people to your page, and many users complain of disorientation. By distributing a hypertext across the Internet and allowing millions of people to generate content, the World Wide Web solves the content-generation problem—you can link to content that other people have created.

To create Web content, Web authors use HTML, a markup language that's not supposed to include formatting instructions. However, commercial Web designers want formatting control, and they also want to push content in people's faces. In an attempt to gain market share, browser publishers give this control in the form of non-standard extensions, which other browsers cannot read. This fragments the Web audience until the next published HTML standard appears. To make sure your Web pages reach the widest possible audience, you should write to Web standards. Currently, most Web authors write to the HTML 3.2 standard. To reach the widest audience, use the transitional flavor of HTML 4, but learn how to use the strict flavor. Soon, most Web browsers will fully support the strict flavor of HTML 4.

2

HTML Basics
(Learning the Lingo)

In this chapter, you will learn the following skills:

- Understanding the various parts of an element and telling them apart
- Reading an element definition
- Nesting elements
- Entering non-standard characters (entities)
- Specifying values (including colors, URLs, and more) for attributes

The basic building block of an HTML document is the *element*, each of which has a name (such as TITLE or BLOCKQUOTE). Basically, an element marks a unit of text so that the browser can tell what part of the document it is displaying. Text marked with the TITLE element, for example, appears on the browser's title bar.

There are dozens of elements in HTML 4.0. Learning HTML amounts to learning how to use the elements so that your document takes shape the way you want. As you'll see, many elements have properties called attributes. (For example, the IMG element—the element that enables you to add a graphic to your document—has a width attribute, which enables you to determine the width of the graphic as it is displayed by the browser.) As you learn how to type elements and choose options for attributes, you begin to get a handle on HTML's expressive potential.

To use elements correctly, you need to learn HTML's syntax rules. Syntax specifies precisely how you should mark text with elements, and how you should supply values (settings) for attributes. This chapter provides a solid foundation by clearly explaining just what these rules are and how they work. Admittedly, this chapter's material is about as much fun as reading the Manhattan phone book, but it is really important, and I'll try to make it as brief and painless as possible. Don't skip it!

The Syntax Attack: Why?

When you're dealing with any type of computer language, you're going to have to face a painful thing called *syntax*. Basically, syntax refers to all the rules specifying just how you're supposed to write something in the language so that the computer will understand it. Above all else, it's a matter of getting the various parts in the right order and using the correct symbols. We have syntax in everyday human languages, too—which is why "? out person last Thanks go to turn would lights. The!" doesn't really come across as "Would the last person to go turn out the lights? Thanks!"

The good news is that HTML syntax is fairly simple. Almost everything you need to know about HTML syntax is revealed when you grasp what goes into an element, as discussed in the next section. Still, you have to make sure to type everything carefully.

As you will see when you start experimenting with HTML, the least little typing mistake will probably produce unwanted results when you look at your document with a Web browser.

Remember, too, that if a browser can't figure out your HTML, it just skips it—so your work might not show up at all! If this happens, go back and check your typing. Chances are you'll find a missing angle bracket, quote mark, or end tag (you learn more about these things in the next section).

Here's one very basic rule of HTML syntax: Don't introduce spaces where they don't belong. For example, you can't include spaces within the name of an element, such as TITLE. If you type TI TLE or TITL E, the element won't work. This is pretty obvious, but it's still worth mentioning, because one little mistake like this will keep your page from appearing the way it's supposed to.

Exposed to the ELEMENTS

As you've learned, a markup language enables you to mark the parts of a document, such as a title, a heading, or paragraphs of text. In HTML, you use *elements* to do this. An element is a named markup unit that describes one of a document's structural components, such as a title or heading.

Block Elements and Inline Elements

You'll encounter two types of elements:

- **Block elements** A block element defines a paragraph construed broadly (including headings, lists, and ordinary text paragraphs).
- **Inline elements** An *inline element* defines a character style, such as bold or italic, or some other element that fits within a line.

What's In an Element?

Whether you're talking about block or inline elements, they consist of the parts listed in Table 2.1.

Table 2.1 Components of an element

Name	Description
start tag	This tells the browser, "Hey! Wake up! There's an element coming! A start tag begins with a left angle bracket (<), and always includes the element name. It may include one or more attributes, separated by a space. It closes with a right angle bracket (>).

element name

This is a code name such as TITLE or H2. Note that you don't have to type element names in capital letters—almost all of HTML is case-insensitive. (You could type it tItLe if you want.) But it's easier to read HTML code if you capitalize element names. That's what this book does, and I encourage you to do so, too.

attributes

Sizes etc

Many elements have their own, special attributes, which are the properties of whatever element you are working with. For example, the IMG element enables you to insert a graphic in your document. A special attribute of the IMG element is the src attribute, which enables you to specify where the graphic is stored.

value

Each attribute has a value, which is usually surrounded by quotation marks and preceded by an equals sign (for example, SRC="sail34.gif" specifies the image source and gives the file name). For clarity, attribute and values are usually typed using lowercase letters. Note, though, that some values are case sensitive (such as Unix file names).

content

Every element that accepts content has a content model that specifies what can be included. Generally, you can include elements as well as text within the element. Some elements are empty, meaning they don't accept any content. An example is the <BR> element, which introduces a line break.

end tag

The end tag repeats the element name. It surrounds the name with angle brackets, like a start tag, but there's an extra mark—a slash mark—that comes after the first angle bracket (like this: </TITLE>). This tells the browser that the element is over now.

Remember that not every element has all these parts. Some elements don't have attributes. Some don't even have content or end tags. You'll learn more about this when we look at specific elements.

Looking an Element Over

Look at a block element to see how all the parts fit together:

```
<H1 align="center">This is a centered heading</H1>
```

OK, quick now. Can you tell which part is which? Here's a guide.

- ∞ **<H1>** This is the start tag for a level one heading.
- ∞ **align = "center"** This is an attribute. It governs the alignment of the title text. Here, the value is set to center, and is surrounded by quotation marks. Note that the attribute fits within the start tag (<H1 align="center">).
- ∞ **This is a centered heading** This is the content. This is what the user sees on-screen. The browser shows this text using the formatting that it's programmed to display when it encounters a level one heading, except that it takes the attribute align = "center" into account.
- ∞ **</H1>** This is the end tag.

A lot of what goes into learning HTML involves figuring out which attributes you can use (if any), and what values they can take. To figure out what's allowed in an element, it helps to know how to read an element definition, covered in the next section.

Reading an Element Definition

When an element pops up for the first time in this book, you'll see an *element definition*, such as the following one for the <H1> element. This succinctly summarizes what you can and can't do with the <H1> element.

ELEMENT NAME	H1
PURPOSE	Marks the enclosed text as a heading, ranging from most prominent (H1) to least prominent (H6)
TYPE	Block
NESTED WITHIN	BODY element
START TAG	Required
END TAG	Required
CONTENT	Contains HTML elements and text
ATTRIBUTES	**Strict DTD**:

id = "name" (optional)
class = "name" (optional)
style = "CSS style definition" (optional)
title= "name" (optional)
lang = "language code" (optional)
dir = (rtl, ltr) (optional)

Transitional DTD:
align = "left, center, right, justify" (optional)

EXAMPLE	<H1>This is a major heading</H1>
TIP	The H1 element appears to be the document's title, so it's wise to use it for this purpose. Note that heading levels H4 through H6 are very rarely used.

Table 2.2 shows you how to read this definition.

Table 2.2 Reading an element definition

Component	Description
element name	The name of the element, which you'll type within angle brackets.
purpose	What the element is for.
type	Block or inline.
nested within	Where the element goes in your HTML document's global structure, about which you'll learn more in Chapter 3.
start tag	Two possibilities here are optional or required.
end tag	Two possibilities here, too, are optional or required.
content	What you can enclose within the element.
attributes	The attributes you can use, along with the values that are permitted. This chapter discusses values in a later section and shows you how to use them. When you see a series of values separated by commas, you can choose one of them. Note that the list of attributes shows which ones are accept-

ed under the strict flavor, and which ones are *deprecated* (but supported by the transitional flavor).

example | What the element looks like in an HTML document.
tip | Something useful to use or remember.

Obsolete and Deprecated Elements

As HTML has evolved, it has become clear that a few of the elements introduced in previous versions or extensions have either fallen into disuse, or should be scorned because they violate the underlying symmetry of the language.

HTML has a special language to refer to these poor elements. Elements that have fallen out of use are called *obsolete elements*, while elements scorned by HTML 4.0 are called *deprecated elements*. For example, the <MENU> element is obsolete—nobody could ever figure out just what it was for. Meanwhile, the <FONT> tag is deprecated, because it violates the principles of how HTML 4.0 handles formatting.

I'll mention the various obsolete and deprecated elements when they come up in context. By the way, note that the obsolete elements aren't being supported in HTML 4.0, but the deprecated elements are—and it's a good thing, since about 95% of the Web documents out there are using them currently. When you write according to the *transitional flavor* of HTML, you'll use certain deprecated elements—but don't let that stop you. If you don't use them, very few people will be able to see all the interesting things you have done with your page.

Building a Nest

When you place an element within another element, you create a *nested element*. For example, suppose you mark some text with the <BLOCKQUOTE> element, which creates an indented quotation:

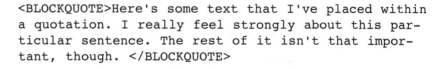

```
<BLOCKQUOTE>Here's some text that I've placed within
a quotation. I really feel strongly about this par-
ticular sentence. The rest of it isn't that impor-
tant, though. </BLOCKQUOTE>
```

Now I'll create a nested element by using <STRONG>. This forces the browser to display the element's content in boldface type:

```
<BLOCKQUOTE>Here's some text that I've placed within
a quotation. <STRONG>I really feel strongly about
this particular sentence.</STRONG> The rest of it
isn't that important, though. </BLOCKQUOTE>
```

Here's what this will look like when your browser displays it:

> Here's some text that I've placed within a quotation. **I really feel strongly about this particular sentence.** The rest of it isn't that important, though.

There are limits to what you can nest within certain elements—and sometimes nesting just doesn't make sense. For example, there's no real point to nesting <STRONG> within <H1>, since most browsers format <H1> text using boldface emphasis. However, nesting is what gives HTML its expressive power. As you learn how to nest elements, you discover how you express some very complex document structures.

Entity Is Just a Fancy Name for Character

Enough about elements—now we're on to *entities*. An entity is basically a character code. Before explaining how characters are coded, though, you'll find it helpful to understand why character codes are needed.

128 Characters Aren't Enough

To make sure that just about any computer can handle an HTML document, HTML is written using a basic set of 128 keyboard characters. This is sufficient for English, although just barely—the 128 characters don't include a number of widely-used symbols, such as © and ®. And this limited character set is hopelessly deficient for most foreign languages—let alone those that don't use Latin characters (such as Tamil, Chinese, or Japanese).

The Document Character Set

To support the internationalization of HTML, HTML 4.0 supports the *Universal Character Set (UCS)*, also known as *Unicode 2.0.* Capable of representing characters from most of the world's written languages, Unicode 2.0 can handle a maximum of 65,536 characters, of which roughly half have been defined thus far.

Character Encodings

Unicode defines many characters—too many, in fact, to be kept in memory without slowing down processing times. To make HTML work more efficiently, it is possible to specify a *character encoding*. Essentially, a character encoding is a subset (a partial list) of the Unicode characters—just enough of them to represent a particular language. For example, the default character encoding used by most HTML 4.0-compliant Web browsers is called *Latin-1*. This encoding contains enough characters to handle most European languages. Other encodings exist for Cyrillic (Russian), Arabic, Chinese, and other languages.

Using Entities

Here's where entities come into the picture. If you want to use a Unicode 2.0 character other than the standard 128 characters recognized by HTML, you need to use a code. You can write the code in the three different ways explained in Table 2.3.

Table 2.3 Three ways of typing entity codes

Name	Description
decimal code	To type the Scandinavian character å, for instance, you type the numerical code 229. This code must be preceded by &# and followed by a semicolon, so the correct code is å.
hexadecimal code	Another way to type an entity is to type the character's hexadecimal code. Hexadecimal numbers use a 16-bit base, and are familiar to programmers. The hexadecimal code xE5 is the same as decimal 229, so you can also represent å by typing å.
mnemonic codes	Because the decimal and hexadecimal codes are difficult to remember, a limited number of characters can be entered using abbreviations. For example, & is the *mnemonic* (easily remembered) code for an ampersand.

These codes don't look very good in your source HTML document, but browsers should display them on-screen without any trouble.

Table 2.4 lists some useful mnemonics. See Appendix A for a complete list of HTML 4.0 mnemonics for character entities.

The mnemonic codes for entities are case-sensitive. For example, Å enters a different character than å. This is one of the few exceptions to the general insensitivity of HTML to case.

Table 2.4 Some useful mnemonics for entities

Entity	Decimal code	Mnemonic
Pound sterling	&#163	&pound;
Copyright	&#169;	&copy;
Registered trademark	&#174;	&reg;
1/4	&#188;	&frac14;
1/2	&#189;	&frac12;
3/4	&#190;	&frac34;
Left arrow	&#8592;	&larr;
Right arrow	&#8594;	&rarr;
Square root	&#8730;	&radic;

As you can see, the ampersand (&) is used to flag an entity. For this reason, you'll be wise to escape the ampersand when you're using this symbol in ordinary text. (To escape a character means to enter its code instead of typing the character on the keyboard.) For example, suppose you want to type, "Mary & I went the Bahamas for our winter vacation." To avoid confusing a browser, type this as follows: "Mary & I went to the Bahamas...."

Here's an example of an entity in action:

```
Copyright &#169; 1998. All rights reserved.
```

And here's how it looks in a browser:

```
Copyright © 1998. All rights reserved.
```

Assigning Values to Attributes

Most attributes require a value, as you've learned. Sometimes an attribute's value options are specific to just that one attribute. For example, the align attribute, mentioned earlier, can take any of the following values: left, center, right, or justify.

Other attributes use values that fall into various categories, such as CDATA, colors, URLs, numbers, percentages, and pixels. These different kinds of values are called *data types*. Table 2.5 provides a quick explanation of what this is all about.

Table 2.5 HTML 4 valid data types

Data type	Description and example

attribute-specific	Some attributes take values that no other attribute uses. For example, the dir attribute governs text direction. It has only two possible values: ltr (left to right) and rtl (right to left). The following example shows how to one option:
	
	`<HTML dir="ltr">`
	`  [A document in French]`
	`</HTML>`

boolean	Some attributes have simple yes/no values, which are controlled by the presence or absence of the attribute's name. For example, the UL element has a deprecated attribute called compact, which you can use in the transitional flavor of HTML 4. This attribute tells browsers to render the list in a more compact form, if possible. To turn on this attribute, you type its name with no other value, as in the following example: `<UL compact>`

```
[Here's a bulleted list]
</UL>
```

CDATA

Essentially, CDATA just means text, but with a bit of a twist: The text must be made up of characters from the document's current character set. Normally, as long as you stick to ASCII characters for English documents, you're fine. Note that CDATA *can* contain spaces. Here's an example of an attribute that takes CDATA; it's the alt attribute of the IMG element, which inserts a graphic into your document. The CDATA you type appears if the user has switched off graphics (or is using a text-only browser).

```
<IMG alt="This shows a pretty pic-
ture of a sunset">
```

color

You can specify colors in two different ways: an RGB (red-green-blue) code, or a mnemonic (easily remembered word):

```
<BODY bgcolor = "#FFFFFF> or
<BODY bgcolor = "black">
```

character

Some attributes ask you to supply a character from the document's character set. Here's an example:

```
accesskey = "k"
```

charset

In addition to language codes, some attributes enable you to specify a *character set* (abbreviated *charset*). The character set definition differs from the language code in that the charset specifies which subset of the Unicode 2.0 character set the browser should use. The default charset for most browsers sold in English-speaking countries is Latin-1 (iso-8859-1).

```
charset = "iso-8859-1"
```

date/time

You type this using a YYYY-MM-DDThh:mm:ssTZD format. You'll learn more about this later in this chapter, but here's an example:

```
1997-09-08T11:54:20+5:30
```

language code

Virtually every HTML 4 element enables you to specify a *language code* (abbreviated *langcode*) by means of the lang attribute. See Table 2.6 for a list of commonly-used language codes. Here's an example of a language code specification:

```
langcode = "EN"
```

media descriptors

This is a new feature of HTML 4, and not well supported. You can use it to specify the output media (screen, tty, tv, projection, handheld, print, braille, aural, or all).

```
media = "print"
```

length

Some attributes enable you to type a length (which could mean width or height). For this attribute, you can choose between specifying a length in pixels or a percentage of screen width. To specify a pixel length, just type an integer (whole number). To specify a percentage of screen width, type the percentage followed by a percent sign (%). Always enclose these values in quotation marks. Note the following examples:

```
<OBJECT border = "1">  Specifies a
border width of one pixel.
```

```
<OBJECT width = "50%"> Specifies a
width of 50% of the available win-
dow space.
```

name

A name is made from text (no spaces). Note that names are case sensitive, and they must begin with an alphabetical character (A to Z or a to z). After you begin with an alphabetical character, you can add numbers, hyphens, underscores, colons, and periods, but no spaces. Here's an example:

```
<H1 class="majorheading">Here's a
major heading</A>
```

number   Type an *integer* (a whole number). For example, when you're setting up a table, you use an attribute called cols to define the number of columns. To specify three columns, you type:

```
cols="3"
```

pixels   Some attributes ask you to specify a width or height in screen pixels (dots). For a standard 640 by 480 display, there are 640 pixels horizontally and 480 vertically. To specify the number of pixels, type a whole number. In the following example, the height of an element is set to 200 pixels:

```
<IMG height = "200">
```

MIME type   Some attributes ask you to specify a *MIME type*. MIME stands for Multipurpose Internet Mail Extensions, but it's more accurately defined as a list of Internet data types. Table 2.7 lists some of the common MIME types; Appendix F provides a more complete list.

style   This data type requires you to specify a style using Cascading Style Sheet (CSS) specifications.

```
style = "font-weight: bold"
```

URL   Be sure to enclose the URL within quotation marks completely, as in this example:

```
href = "contents.html"
```

The following tables provide a handy reference to the most frequently-used language codes and MIME types.

Table 2.6 Commonly-used language codes

Code	Description
en	English
fr	French
he	Hebrew
hi	Hindi
ja	Japanese
ru	Russian
zh	Chinese

Table 2.7 Commonly-used MIME types

Type	Description
application/pdf	Adobe Acrobat file
audio/wav	WAV sound
image/gif	GIF graphic
image/jpeg	JPEG graphic
image/png	PNG graphic
text/css	CSS style sheet
text/html	HTML document
video/mpeg	MPEG video
video/quicktime	QuickTime video

Specifying Colors as Values for Attributes

To dress up your document, you'll want to assign colors to various elements. We'll get into just how you do this later, but for now, learn the syntax for specifying colors as values for attributes.

Table 2.8 Specifying color numbers

Name	Description
RGB code	This code enables you to specify the precise combination of the primary colors (red, green, and blue) that go into making up a color.
mnemonic codes	RGB codes don't mean much of anything to the human eye, so HTML supplies a set of 16 mnemonics for popular colors. Table 2.9 lists the 16 basic color mnemonics you can use (and their corresponding color codes).

For each color, you can specify 256 values (in hexadecimal, ranging from 00 to FF); since there are three colors, this means that you can choose from a palette of more than 16 million colors.

Before you get carried way with this, though, note that most people are using monitors that display only 256 colors, and it's almost anyone's guess how a given RGB code will look on a given monitor.

Be forewarned: It's very difficult to predict just how your color scheme is going to look when it's viewed on varying systems. On one computer, it might look great, but on another, it may look like radioactive fruit salad.

To use an RGB code, you need to precede the code with a hash mark (#). To use one of the mnemonics, just type the color name. The color mnemonics aren't case-sensitive. In either case, be sure to enclose the color code or mnemonic in quotes (for example, bgcolor = "aqua" or bgcolor = "#00FFFF").

Note that in the RGB code, those are zeros, not the letter O.

Table 2.9 The Sixteen Basic Colors

Color name	RGB code
Aqua	#00FFFF
Black	#000000
Blue	#0000FF
Fuchsia	#FF00FF
Gray	#808080
Green	#008000
Lime	#00FF00
Maroon	#800000
Navy	#000080
Olive	#808000
Purple	#008080
Red	#FF0000
Silver	#C0C0C0
Teal	#008080
White	#FFFFFF
Yellow	#FFFF00

Here's an example of a color code in action. In a table, you can specify the background color of a cell using the <TD> element and its bgcolor attribute, as in the following example:

```
<TD bgcolor="#C0C0C0">
```

This cell will have a silver background.

Although you can specify millions of different colors with color codes, it's safe to stick to the colors that will be correctly displayed on most computers. These colors, the 216 colors originally defined in Netscape Navigator's color palette, are listed in Appendix B.

Specifying URLs as Values for Attributes

As you'll learn in the next chapter, where you'll write your first hyperlinks, you create links by using the <A> tag.

The <A> tag's most important attribute is HREF, which takes a URL as its value. You can supply a completely fleshed-out (absolute) URL, a fragment URL, a relative URL, or a mailto URL, as the following sections explain.

Absolute URLs

This is a URL that contains all three of the components discussed in the previous chapter: the protocol, the machine name, and the name of the requested resource (including the path information needed to find it). Here's a completely fleshed-out URL:

        http://watt.seas.virginia.edu/~bp/c34/faq.html

Here are a few things to note about typing URLs:

- ∞ **Case sensitivity** Some parts of the URL are case sensitive, while others aren't. The protocol name (such as http://) and machine name (here, watt.seas.virginia.edu) aren't case sensitive, but the path and resource names are. Because it's often hard to tell the difference between the machine name and path name, it is best to treat the whole thing as if it were case sensitive.
- ∞ **Spaces** No spaces!
- ∞ **Quotes** When you're supplying a URL as a value for an attribute, be sure to enclose it all in quotes (for example, href= "http://www.me.com/hi.html").

Fragment URLs

As you'll learn later in this book, you can define *targets* within a document. A target is like a bookmark. Once you've defined a target, you can write a URL that jumps to the bookmark. This is a great way to give people a way to move around within a single document.

If the document you're linking to contains targets, you can write a *fragment URL* that jumps right to the target (instead of displaying the top of the referenced page).

A fragment URL has the target glued on to the end of the URL with a hash mark, as in the following example:

```
http://bag-end.hobbiton.shire/birthday-
party/party.html#guest-list
```

When the user clicks a link that uses this URL as a value, the browser opens party.html, and jumps down to the target called guest-list.

Like any other URL, you need to surround the whole thing with quotes if you are using it as a value.

Relative URLs

Unlike a completely fleshed-out URL, a relative URL doesn't contain any protocol or machine information. Relative URLs are often used to link to documents on the same system. A hyperlink that uses HREF="welcome.html" directs the server to look for welcome.html in the same directory as the page in which the hyperlink is found.

To put this point in somewhat more technical language, the server assumes that welcome.html has the same *base URL*. A base URL is the assumed reference point from which other documents are located.

Suppose the link to welcome.html is found within the following document:

```
http://bag-end.hobbiton.shire/birthday-
party/party.html
```

To determine the base URL, the server strips the resource name (party.html) off the document that contains the link, and replaces it with the name of the referenced resource. (This is called resolving the URL.)

Once the URL is resolved, the server goes after the following document:

```
http://bag-end.hobbiton.shire/birthday-party/wel-
come.html
```

Although relative URLs don't include the protocol or machine names, they can include path information:

∞ To reference the directory directly above the current directory (the one in which the linking document is stored, type .. (two periods) followed by a slash mark (../).
∞ To reference a directory below the current directory, type the directory name followed by a slash mark (subdirectory/).

Here's an example. Suppose your Web server's computer has the following directories:

```
Chesapeake-rivers
      southern
            Potomac
            Rappahannock
                  marinas
                  restaurants
            James
```

In the directory called Chesapeake-rivers/southern/Rappahannock, you place a document called welcome.html. Now suppose you placed the following relative URLs within this document. Here's what they'd refer to:

∞ **../southern.html** Refers to Chesapeake-rivers/southern/southern.html
∞ **../../default.html** Refers to Chesapeake-rivers/default.html
∞ **marinas/marina-list.html** Refers to Chesapeake-rivers/southern/Rappahannock/marinas/marina-list.html

---

If you use relative URLs with additional path information, please bear in mind that bad things can happen if you move the document that contains these URLs to some other directory that doesn't have the same subdirectory structure. In the document's new location, the URLs may not map to the new directory structure, unless you've taken pains to change all of them. It is best to keep things simple. Most experienced HTML authors keep graphics in a subdirectory called /images, and keep all other HTML documents together in a single directory.

Mailto URLs

The last type of URL that you can supply as a value is called a mailto URL. This provides you with a way of enabling reader feedback without having to do any scripting or programming. When users click a hyperlink that contains a mailto URL, they see a mail composition window that enables them to send e-mail to the page maintainer.

It's easy to write a mailto URL. Just type mailto: followed by the e-mail address of the person who should receive the mail. For example, the following sends e-mail to Frodo:

```
mailto:frodo@bag-end.org
```

As with any URL used as a value, you need to enclose mailto URLs in quotation marks, as in the following example:

```
<A HREF="mailto:frodo@bag-end.org">Send mail to
Frodo!</A>
```

Adding Comments to Your Code

Experienced computer programmers know that it's a great idea to add comments when you're writing code. Comments are ignored, but they really come in handy when you're looking at your code, months later, and trying to figure out what something does. You can add comments to your HTML documents, too, and it's a great idea to do so. To create a comment, you begin the comment with <!-- and close it with -->. Here's an example:

```
<!--This is a comment.-->
```

If you would like to write a comment that takes up more than one line, you don't need to type the closing symbols (-->) at the end of each line. Just wait until you finish typing the whole comment, and place the closing symbols there, as in the following example:

```
<!--This is a comment. Wow, it's a really long com-
ment. I don't think I'll be able to get it on one
line.-->
```

Writing Dates and Times in the ISO 8601 Format

If you specify a date and time using a recognized syntax, programs can recognize that you've typed a date and time, and they can process this information automatically. It's a bit painful to learn how to do this, but once you get the idea, it's easy.

The World Wide Web Organization specifies the ISO 8601 format as the date and time format of choice. Here's a shorthand version of the ISO 8601 date and time syntax:

```
YYYY-MM-DDThh:mm:ssTZD
```

Table 2.10 shows what all these symbols mean.

Table 2.10 Specifying the date and time (ISO 8601)

Symbol	Explanation
YYYY	The year, using all four digits.
MM	The month, using two digits (01 is January, 02 is February, etc.).
DD	The day of the month, using two digits (01, 02, etc.).
T	Don't change this; it indicates where the time part starts.
hh	The hour, using a 24-hour clock (am and pm aren't allowed). Use two digits (01, 02, etc.).
mm	The minute, using two digits (01, 02, etc.).
ss	The second, using two digits (01, 02, etc.).
TZD	The time zone relative to Coordinated Universal Time (Greenwich Mean Time), expressed by the number of hours and minutes to add or subtract (use either +hh:mm or -hh:mm).

Here's a valid ISO 8601 date and time:

```
1997-09-08T06:00:20+5:30
```

This is September 8, 1997, at 11:30 am my time (+5:30 from Greenwich).

Summary

It's easy to learn HTML syntax. Start by learning the parts of an element—the start tag, the element name, the attributes, the attribute's values, the content, and the end tag. Much of the control you will gain over HTML comes from knowing which values are available for a given attribute, and how to use these values effectively. To supply values correctly, learn the special techniques you use to type color codes, URLs, numbers, pixels, and lengths. In the next chapter, you'll learn how to apply this knowledge as you create your first HTML document.

3

Your First Web Page in One Easy Lesson (Really!)

In this chapter, you will learn the following skills:

- Creating the global HTML structure
- Adding headings to improve your document's readability
- Adding text and controlling line breaks
- Creating a bulleted list
- Incorporating in-line graphics
- Using a style sheet to control your document's appearance

Now that you've learned the basic lingo, take a stab at your first HMTL 4.0 page. In this chapter, you'll learn how you begin an HTML document with an overall structure, and you'll also learn how to deal with the basics of text entry (including line and paragraph break control). Along the way, you'll create a simple Web page—nothing fancy, mind you, but enough to convince you that this really isn't rocket science. You could create a home page for yourself, or an informational document on a hobby or interest of yours. By the time we get done, it will look pretty spiffy.

This chapter doesn't go into all the details concerning each element you'll learn; that's the job of Part Two. In fact, you should view this chapter as an introduction to Part Two. As you create your first page, you will also get your first experience with everything that's covered in Part Two of this book. The Part Two chapters go back into each of these topics, and cover them in much more detail. For example, in Part Two, you'll learn about all the attributes you can use with each of the elements this chapter introduces.

Even though this chapter is strictly introductory, it differs a lot from anything you'll find in other HTML books. That's because it adheres to the HTML 4.0 way, about which you'll learn more as the chapter progresses.

Give Me Structure

Every HTML document should have an overall structure, which is called the global structure. Table 3.1 lists the components of the global structure; you'll learn more about each of them in the sections to come. Note that subsequent chapters examine them in more detail.

Table 3.1 Components of the global structure

Component	Description
version statement	Indicates the version of HTML that you're writing in.
HTML element	This element encloses all the HTML (and associated text).
HEAD element	This element encloses the header information in the document, including the title.
BODY element	This element contains all the HTML and associated text that appears when the page is viewed in a browser.

Taking a Look at the Global Structure

Here's what this basic structure looks like. It is the starting point for every English-language HTML document you create:

```
<!DOCTYPE HTML PUBLIC "-//W3C/DTD HTML 4.0 //EN"
"http://www.w3.org/TR/REC-html40/loose.dtd">
<HTML lang = "EN">
     <HEAD>
          <TITLE>Your document's title goes
          here</TITLE>
     </HEAD>
     <BODY>
     </BODY>
</HTML>
```

The HEAD and BODY elements are nested within the HTML element. Notice how the indentations capture the nesting structure. For example, the HEAD and BODY elements are nested within the HTML element (that's why they're indented). The TITLE element is nested within the HEAD element, and it's indented even more, in order to show this.

You don't have to type your HTML this way—not every Web author does this—but it's especially wise to do so while you're learning. The indentations help to clarify your page's overall structure.

The following sections unpack what these various components do. For now, don't worry about what all this means.

Type It Up

Fire up your text editor, and type the basic, global structure. Keep the points shown in Table 3.2 in mind.

Table 3.2 Points to remember when typing HTML

Item	Description
quote marks	No "smart quotes." If you're using a word processing program, make sure to turn off "smart" quotes (a feature that automatically enters beginning and ending quote marks with differing shapes. These will really mess up your coding. It's much better to use a plain text editor (such as the Windows NOTEPAD utility) that doesn't have fancy features like this.
title	Don't forget the TITLE text. You can replace the TITLE text with something more to your liking, such as "My First Home Page" or "Dungeon of Nightmares."
elements	Type element names in caps. HTML is not case sensitive (apart from a very few exceptions), but experienced HTML authors like to type the element names in caps. This makes your HTML easier to read.
indents	Use indents to indicate nesting structure.
typos	Proofread, proofread, proofread. Carefully proofread your work to make sure you have included both the opening and closing angle brackets in each tag. Also, make sure you have typed quotation marks around values. As Chapter 2 explained, a few values don't require quotation marks, but to be on the safe side, just get into the habit of typing them for every value. (If they are not needed, browsers just ignore them, so you've nothing to lose by supplying them even when they're not necessary.)
plain text	Save as plain text. Make sure you save your document as plain text. If you're using a word processing program, choose the text (or ASCII) file format. In Microsoft Word, the format of choice is called Text only with line breaks.

extension	Use the extension *.html or *.htm. Save your file with the extension .html. (An extension is a three- or four-letter code that comes after the file-name, and it is always preceded by a dot.) If you are using an early version of Microsoft Windows (such as Windows 3.1) that can't handle four-letter extensions, use .htm (browsers recognize this extension too).

Consider making a template that contains the basic HTML structure. A template is a stored file that contains some basic text, which you can use as the starting point for creating a finished document. Call it something like template.html. As you learn about additional elements and attributes that you want to add to every new HTML page you create, you can flesh this document out. You'll save a lot of time that would be otherwise spent typing all this stuff in every time you want to start a new page.

Avoiding Common Typing Errors

It's really easy to forget to type one of those quotation marks or angle brackets. *None* of the following is correct!

```
<H1 align = "center>This is a centered heading</H1>
(missing quotation mark)
```

```
<H1 align = center">This is a centered heading</H1>
(missing quotation mark)
```

```
<H1 align = "center"This is a centered heading</H1>
(missing angle bracket)
```

```
<H1 align = "center">This is a centered heading/H1>
(missing angle bracket)
```

```
<H1 align = "center">This is a centered heading</H1
(missing angle bracket)
```

None of these will work correctly. If you are having trouble getting an element to look right (or show up at all), the first thing to check is whether you've included all the necessary angle brackets and quotation marks.

Check It Out

Try opening your page using your browser. In both Microsoft Internet Explorer and Netscape Navigator, do this by choosing Open from the File menu, and click the Browse button to locate your file.

Don't be surprised if nothing shows up—it shouldn't! If you see anything in the browser window, chances are you've forgotten to include one or more angle brackets. But there's something to see. If you look at the browser's title bar, you see your title.

> *The TITLE element doesn't really provide what most people would see as the document's title, which they look for in the browser window. Not many people notice what's on the title bar. To create what looks to most people like a title, you use the H1 element, as explained below.*

The HTML Version Statement

The very first line of your page should include a version statement. This is not in HTML – it's in SGML. Don't let that worry you, though – you don't have to learn SGML. This is the only SGML you have to enter, and you can just copy one of the examples given in this section. The version statement performs the functions listed in Table 3.3.

Table 3.3 Functions of the version statement

Function	Description
DTD identification	Indicates which version of HTML you're conforming to.
DTD location	Indicates where the version's document type definition (DTD) is stored.

| DTD language | Indicates the language of the DTD (EN is short for English). |
| DTD availability | Indicates whether the DTD is publicly available or not. |

Choosing the Version Statement

You can choose from three HTML 4 version statements, each corresponding to one of the "flavors" of HTML 4:

- **Strict** Use this version statement for the strict flavor of HTML 4, in which you refrain from using deprecated presentation attributes or elements and instead add presentation with CSS style sheets.
- **Transitional** Use this version statement for the transitional flavor of HTML 4, in which you use some deprecated elements in order to increase the audience that can fully enjoy your pages.
- **Frameset** Use this version statement if you plan to use the frameset flavor of HTML 4. This version statement is the same as the transitional statement except that it adds the frames tags.

Which should you use? For most of your Web publishing, you'll use the transitional version statement. If you plan to also use frames, use the frameset version statement.

Text of the Three Version Statements

The following table lists the three version statements for HTML 4.

Table 3.4 Version statements

Flavor	Version statement text
strict	`<!DOCTYPE HTML PUBLIC "-//W3C/DTD HTML 4.0 //EN" "http://www.w3.org/TR/REC-html40/strict.dtd">`

| transitional | `<!DOCTYPE HTML PUBLIC "-//W3C/DTD HTML 4.0 //EN" "http://www.w3.org/TR/REC-html40/loose.dtd">` |
| frameset | `<!DOCTYPE HTML PUBLIC "-//W3C/DTD HTML 4.0 //EN" "http://www.w3.org/TR/REC-html40/frameset.dtd">` |

Why bother typing the version statement? If you include the version statement, browsers can read this to figure out which version of HTML you're using, and so can readers. Also, you can run a program called a parser (also called a validation checker) on your document in order to validate your HTML usage. A parser checks your HTML coding against the DTD, and lets you know if you've made any errors.

The HTML Element

The HTML element contains all the HTML code and associated text within your document. Strictly speaking, it is optional, as you can see from the element definition; you can create an HTML document that omits these tags, and your browser can still read it and display it. (In other words, if you omit the HTML element, it's implied, or assumed.) Still, it is always good form to include the start and stop tags. Here's the element definition:

ELEMENT NAME	HTML
PURPOSE	Demarcates the portion of the document containing HTML..
TYPE	Block
NESTED WITHIN	None (encloses all other elements)
START TAG	Optional
END TAG	Optional
CONTENT	Contains HTML elements and text
ATTRIBUTES	lang = "language-code" (optional)

	dir = (ltr, rtl) (optional)
EXAMPLE	<HTML>
	[all other elements]
	</HTML>
TIP	Although the HTML element is optional, it is good form to include it.

You *must* include the HTML element if you'd like to take advantage of the attributes, lang and dir. Table 3.5 tells what these attributes do.

Table 3.5 Language attributes

Attribute	Description
lang	This attribute specifies the language you are using to write your document. Browsers can use this information to display the correct character encoding. For now, use the lang= "EN" attribute, assuming you're creating your page in English. If you don't include a lang specification, it's set to "Unknown."
dir	This attribute enables you to specify whether the language in which you're writing is to be read left-to-right, like English, or right-to-left, like Hebrew. Note that this is separate from the lang specification; if you're writing in Hebrew, it's not enough to use the lang code for Hebrew. You must also specify the text direction. If you leave this blank, browsers default to the left-to-right (ltr) option.

As you look at additional element definitions in this chapter, you'll notice that you can also use the lang and dir attributes with many other elements. When you specify the lang and dir with the HTML tag, you set the language and direction for the whole document. If you would like to add a bit of text in some other language, perhaps in a quotation, you can flag this by adding a different lang and dir specification to the element surrounding this text. In this way, a document written predominantly in French can have a short quotation in Spanish.

The HEAD Element

After the HTML start tag, you should include the HEAD element. Within it, you find the TITLE element, which you should include in every HTML document you create. Here is the element definition:

ELEMENT NAME	HEAD
PURPOSE	Demarcates an area containing elements describing the document's contents, including the TITLE.
TYPE	Block
NESTED WITHIN	HTML element
START TAG	Optional
END TAG	Optional
CONTENT	Can contain the SCRIPT, STYLE, META, LINK, OBJECT, TITLE, and BASE elements
ATTRIBUTES	profile = "url" (optional) language attributes (lang, dir)
EXAMPLE	<HEAD> <TITLE>Cruising the Rappahannock River</TITLE> </HEAD>
TIP	The most important function of the HEAD element is to provide a home for the TITLE element.

This element introduces only one new attribute, profile. The profile attribute enables you to specify the URL of a document containing information about this document. It's not widely used and not supported by most browsers.

The TITLE Element

As you've just learned, the TITLE element displays text on the browser's title bar. Here's the element definition:

ELEMENT NAME	TITLE
PURPOSE	Enables you to specify title text that appears on the browser's title bar (but *not* in the document itself).

TYPE	Inline
NESTED WITHIN	HEAD element
START TAG	Required
END TAG	Required
CONTENT	Character data only (including entities); no elements.
ATTRIBUTES	None
NOTE	All other elements are excluded. You can't add character formatting (such as boldface) or any other presentation within the TITLE element.
EXAMPLE	<TITLE>Cruising the Rappahannock River</TITLE>
TIP	Use substantive title words to maximize retrieval.

Note that the TITLE element has an important restriction: You can only use it once. This makes sense, because browsers only have one title bar! Also, note that you cannot include anything in the title besides characters (CDATA), including character entities. You can use the entities to provide a foreign-language title, if you wish.

Devote some thought to your page's title. Search engines typically give more weight to the words found in the document's title than they do to words buried in the midst of the document. Therefore, if you choose your title words carefully, you increase the chance that your page will be retrieved by a search. Be as specific and descriptive as possible, and omit commonly-used words and phrases, such as "home page" or "introduction."

Here's what your HTML code looks like so far, after adding a title:

```
<!DOCTYPE HTML PUBLIC "-//W3C/DTD HTML 4.0 //EN"
"http://www.w3.org/TR/REC-html40/loose.dtd">
    <HTML lang = "EN">
    <HEAD>
        <TITLE>Sailing the Southern Chesapeake
        Bay</TITLE>
    </HEAD>
    <BODY>
    </BODY>
</HTML>
```

The BODY Element

Within this element, you'll find everything that appears on-screen when your page is accessed by means of a browser. Let's take a look at the element definition. Note that this element has a lot of deprecated attributes, to be used only if you're using the transitional flavor of HTML 4.

ELEMENT NAME BODY	
PURPOSE	Provides a container for all the text and elements that appear on-screen within the browser window.
TYPE	Block
NESTED WITHIN	HTML element
START TAG	Optional
END TAG	Optional
CONTENT	Block elements
ATTRIBUTES	**Strict DTD**: language attributes (lang, dir) id = "name" (optional) class = "name" (optional) style = "CSS style definition" (optional) title= "name" (optional) **Transitional DTD** (deprecated): background = "url" (optional) text = "color" (optional) link = "color" (optional) vlink = "color" (optional) alink = "color" (optional)
NOTE	Although the BODY tags are optional, you shouldn't omit them.

EXAMPLE	`<BODY>`
	    `<H1>Rappahannock River Gazette</H1>`
	 `</BODY>`

TIP	Don't use BODY if you're creating a document with frames.

The BODY start and end tags are not required, but you should still include them so that your page is easier to proofread. There's one important exception to this rule, though: If you're creating a document with frames, you can't use the BODY element. For more information, see Chapter 14.

The BODY element introduces a lot of new attributes, which fall into two categories: the core attributes (id, class, style, and title), which you can use in almost any HTML element, and some deprecated presentation elements, which you can use in the transitional flavor of HTML 4. The core attributes come in very handy for scripts and style sheets, as you will learn later in this book. If you're writing to the strict flavor of HTML, you'll avoid the deprecated presentation attributes (Table 3.7); however, you'll need to include them if you suspect that your page might be accessed by people using non-CSS-capable browsers. You'll learn more about this point later when this book delves into style sheets.

Table 3.6 Core attributes

Attribute	Description
id	Enables you to assign a unique name to an element. The name can be referenced in scripts and style sheets.
class	Enables you to specify a name for a class of elements, which can then be grouped together for action by scripts or formatting by style sheets.
style	Enables you to insert Cascading Style Sheet (CSS) specifications to define the presentation aspects of the element.
title	This attribute enables you to specify some text that is associated with the element. Browsers may display this as a tool tip (a little yellow box that appears when you move the mouse over the element).

Table 3.7 Deprecated BODY attributes

Attribute	Description
background	Specifies the URL of a document containing a background graphic.

text	Specifies the color of normal text.
link	Specifies the color of link text (text that has been defined to function as a hyperlink).
vlink	Specifies the color of visited links (hyperlinks that the user has already clicked).
alink	Specifies the color of the active link (the link the user is clicking now).

Give Me Direction

Get your reader oriented by providing some text that looks like a title. The best way to do this is by means of the H1 element, which defines a first-level heading. You can then add some additional subheadings to your document by using additional heading tags.

A Title Except in Name: The H1 Element

The H1 element looks like a title—and that's exactly what most Web authors use it for. Unlike the TITLE element, which defines text that appears in the title bar of most browsers, the H1 text appears within the browser window. And what's more, it is usually formatted in bold, with extra-large type, to boot.

Here's the element definition:

ELEMENT NAME	H1
PURPOSE	Marks the enclosed text as a major heading.
TYPE	Block
NESTED WITHIN	BODY
START TAG	Required
END TAG	Required
CONTENT	Contains HTML elements and text
ATTRIBUTES	**Strict DTD:** language attributes (lang, dir) core attributes (id, class, style, title)

	Transitional DTD:
	align = "left, center, right, justify" (optional)
EXAMPLE	<H1>This is a major heading</H1>
TIP	The H1 element looks like a document title.

In your test document, try typing the following (except type in your own text in place of "Sailing the Southern Chesapeake Bay," if you wish). Be sure to put this within the BODY tags, or it will not show up.

```
<!DOCTYPE HTML PUBLIC "-//W3C/DTD HTML 4.0 //EN"
"http://www.w3.org/TR/REC-html40/loose.dtd">
<HTML lang = "EN">
        <HEAD>
                <TITLE>Sailing the Southern Chesa
                peake Bay</TITLE>
        </HEAD>
        <BODY>
                <H1>Sailing the Southern Chesa
                peake Bay</H1>
        </BODY>
</HTML>
```

Save your document, and open it in your browser (see Figure 3.1). I wasn't kidding about this element's prominence!

If nothing shows up in your browser when you try to see what your H1 element looks like, check your code. First, did you re-save your document? Your browser reads your page from the disk file, not from your text editor's memory. Before you can see the changes, you must re-save your page, and then open it using your browser. If this doesn't work, carefully check to see whether you've used all the angle brackets. If you leave just one out, you'll see some fragments of the HTML on-screen and your H1 heading won't have any special formatting.

Adding More Headings

Try adding some additional headings with the <H2> tag. By doing so, you'll provide your readers with visual clues to your document's contents. The H2 element has the same definition as the H1 element, so it's not necessary to repeat the definition here.

Although HTML defines 6 heading levels, the headings lower than H3 are very rarely used.

Give Me Content

It's text time. You've created the basic, global structure for your HTML document, and you've created a framework that consists of a page's title and some major headings. Now it's time to add text.

In this section, you will learn some peculiarities about HTML that make text entry a lot different than using a word processor. You will also learn how to deal

Figure 3.1 The H1 heading looks like a document title

with the worrisome fact that a browser might break lines in ways that make your document look strange. There are solutions, though, as you'll discover!

This Isn't a Word Processor!

If you're used to using word processing programs, get ready for a paradigm shift: Typing text in an HTML document is a very different matter. Here's why:

- **Browsers ignore extra spaces** You can't format text by pressing the spacebar—for example, to align text in columns. Browsers ignore any additional spaces you type, and compress the text as if the spaces didn't exist. For example, you can type "I l o v e l o t s o f s p a c e," but the browser will display, "I love lots of space."
- **Browsers ignore your line and paragraph breaks** This is the really weird part. You can press Enter all you want to create line and paragraph breaks, but they won't show up when you display the document with the browser. In order to control line and paragraph breaks, you must use elements such as P and BR. You learn about these in this section.

You can see for yourself how this works. In a text editor such as Windows NOTEPAD, type some text that you format with spaces and Enter keystrokes. For an example, see Figure 3.2—and check out what happens when this nice formatting is displayed by a browser (see Figure 3.3).

Line Breaks the Way You Want Them: The PRE Element

If you're typing a poem or something else that requires total control over spacing and line breaks (such as a sample computer program), you can use the PRE element. Within a PRE element, browsers preserve the spaces you enter as well as your line breaks.

Here's the element definition:

ELEMENT NAME	PRE
TYPE	Inline
PURPOSE	Preserves spaces and line breaks as you type them.
NESTED WITHIN	BODY
START TAG	Required
END TAG	Required

CONTENT	Contains HTML elements and text (but see the note, below).
ATTRIBUTES	core attributes (id, lang, style, title) language attributes (lang, dir) width = "number" (optional)
NOTE	You can't use IMG, OBJECT, BIG, SMALL, SUB, or SUP within a PRE element.
EXAMPLE	\<PRE\> This text will preserve its bizarre spacing\</PRE\>
TIP	To align characters correctly, consider using a monospace font.

You can use the width attribute to specify the amount of space that the browser should set aside for the preformatted text. This is important, because the browser may not show the line breaks correctly if the browser's window isn't large enough.

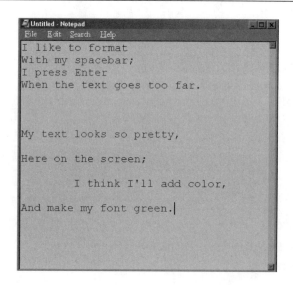

Figure 3.2 Text editors let you add line breaks and spacing

If you specify a width attribute, the browser will size the font so that it appears within the available space. To specify a width attribute, supply the number of characters on the longest line of your text (for example, width = "80" makes sure that lines of at least 80 characters will appear within the browser window, without being broken up). Note that this attribute is not widely supported yet.

Don't press the Tab key to align text in a PRE format—there's just no guarantee how the text will be displayed by browsers, not all of which recognize tab characters. Use spaces instead.

Ordinary Text Paragraphs: The <P> Element

Normally, you use PRE only when you really need to preserve line breaks exactly the way you've typed them. For most of the body text in your page, you should use the P element.

With the P element, you can tell the browser where a given paragraph of text begins and ends; it is up to the browser to decide how and where to break lines.

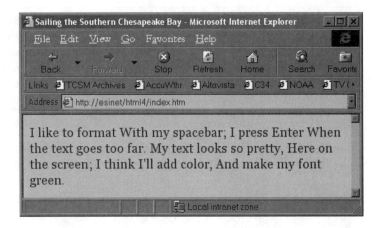

Figure 3.3 **All the spacing is lost when the browser displays the text**

Here's the element definition:

ELEMENT NAME	P
TYPE	Block
PURPOSE	Defines a paragraph of body text (generally with a blank line above the paragraph).
NESTED WITHIN	BODY
START TAG	Required
END TAG	Optional
CONTENT	Contains inline elements and text; cannot contain block elements.
ATTRIBUTES	**Strict DTD:** core attributes (id, class, style, title) language attributes (lang, dir) **Transitional DTD:** align = "(left, center, right, justify)"
EXAMPLE	<P>This is a text paragraph</P>
TIP	For good form, begin each paragraph with <P> and close with </P>. Do not use <P> to enter blank lines.

As you can see from the element definition, the P element requires a start tag, but does not require an end tag. This is because when you add <P> to your document, the browser skips a line and starts a new paragraph. When the browser encounters another <P> tag (or any other start tag for a block formatting element, such as a bulleted list or quotation), the browser assumes that you meant to include a </P> tag.

Even though the </P> tag (the end tag) is not required, it's good form to use it. The following example shows the correct way to mark a paragraph of body text:

```
<P>This is a paragraph of body text. The browser
will insert a blank line before the paragraph. The
browser will also format the line breaks so that
they fit the window width.</P>
```

Controlling Line Breaks

When browsers display text formatted with the P element (or any other block text element), they dynamically adjust line breaks to fit the width of the window. In a really wide window, you see really long lines of text. In a narrow window, you see short lines.

Thanks to this feature, your text is always visible, even if the person using the browser has chosen a weird window size. However, you can control line breaks, both by preventing them where you don't want them, and inserting them where you do. The following sections explain.

Many Web authors create blank lines in their Web pages by entering empty <P> tags. But this is deprecated in HTML 4.0, and may not be supported by future browsers. To enter blank lines, use the BR element, as discussed later in this chapter.

Preventing Line Breaks

It's nice that browsers size line lengths dynamically. It's not so nice when they introduce a line break where there shouldn't be one.

Here's an example. Two-word proper nouns should not be broken up by a line break, as in the following example:

```
Among emerging markets, an interesting one is Sri
Lanka, a tiny Asian country with a solid commitment
to a free economy.
```

To prevent the browser from breaking a line between "Sri" and "Lanka," you can use the non-breaking space entity ( ), as follows:

```
Sri Lanka
```

Inserting Line Breaks: The BR Element

What happens when you want to break a line at a specific point? You can, thanks to the BR element. The BR element is empty—it doesn't take any content at all. If it is placed at the end of some text, it forces a line break (but without adding a blank line, like the P element does). Here's the element definition:

ELEMENT NAME	BR
TYPE	Inline
PURPOSE	Inserts a line break at the element's position.
NESTED WITHIN	BODY
START TAG	Required
END TAG	Forbidden
CONTENT	Empty (no content permitted)
ATTRIBUTES	**Strict DTD:** core attributes (id, class, style, title) **Transitional DTD:** clear = "(none, left, right, all)"
EXAMPLE	Wouldn't it be nice to have a line break here.
TIP	Enter blank lines with , not <P>.

The deprecated clear attribute specifies how text lines wrap when BR is used next to floating objects, such as images. If an image is positioned flush to the left margin and you break a line with BR, the next line begins normally. If you add the clear = "left" attribute, however, the next line begins below the floating object, flush to the right margin. To begin the next line below a floating object positioned flush right, use clear = "right."

Here's how BR works. Note the BR tag in the following paragraph:

```
<P>If you really want to control the precise <BR>
point where the browser breaks the line, you can.
The secret lies in the BR element.</P>
```

Here's how browsers render this paragraph:

> If you really want to control the precise
> point where the browser breaks the line, you can. The secret lies in the
> BR element.

You can also use the BR element to add blank lines to your document. Just place one or more BR tags where you want blank lines to appear.

Using Hyphens

HTML 4.0 recognizes two types of hyphens:

- **Ordinary hyphens** These are entered when you press the hyphen key. An ordinary hyphen is treated just like any other character.
- **Soft hyphens** You can enter a soft hyphen by using the named entity ­. When a browser encounters a soft hyphen, it may use the hyphen to even out the line breaks. If this is done, a hyphen appears in the document and the line is wrapped at that point. If not, the hyphen doesn't appear.

Hyphenated proper nouns (such as Radcliffe-Brown or Evans-Pritchard) should not be broken up by a line break. To prevent this from happening, use the   entity, as in the following examples:

```
Radcliffe - Brown
Evans - Pritchard
```

In HTML, an *entity* is essentially a character code that enables you to insert foreign language characters. See Appendix A for a list of codes you can use.

Adding Text to Your Page

Add some text to your page. Beneath the H2 elements, add text surrounded by <P> and </P>.

Figure 3.4 shows how my page is shaping up. Without any attention to presentation, it looks a little boring Don't worry; we'll fix it, in the section called "Give Me Beauty." But first, let's throw in a hyperlink or two.

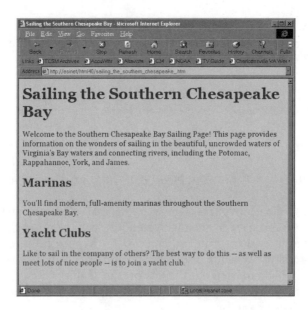

Figure 3.4 Adding text beneath the H2 headings

Give Me Links

A Web page just isn't a Web page without hyperlinks. And what's more, they are really easy to add. You just need to learn a few terms and a few basics about the A element. To be sure, there's much fancy work you can do with hyperlinks, but we'll get to that in Chapter 10.

Getting Hyper: The A Element

To insert a hyperlink into your document, you use the A element. Here's the element definition:

ELEMENT NAME	A
TYPE	Inline
PURPOSE	Inserts a hyperlink.
NESTED WITHIN	BODY

START TAG	Required
END TAG	Required
CONTENT	Contains inline elements and text.
ATTRIBUTES	core attributes (id, class, style, title)
	language attributes (lang, dir)
	accesskey = "character" (optional)
	charset = "charset" (optional)
	href = "url" (optional)
	href = "langcode" (optional)
	rel = "link-type" (optional)
	rev = "link-type" (optional)
	tabindex = "number" (optional)
EXAMPLE	<A href="http://www.yahoo.com">Yahoo!</A>
TIP	Make sure you've surrounded the URL with quotation marks.

This element has numerous attributes, but don't worry about them right now. Very few of them are commonly used. Just focus on the most important one, the href attribute.

To increase the accessibility of your documents for users with special physical needs, you can specify a "hot key" for a hyperlink by using the accesskey attribute (as in this example: <A href="http://www.yahoo.com" accesskey="y">). The user can press the Y key to activate this link.

Defining an Absolute Link with Href

The href attribute enables you to define a link to another document on the Web. In order to insert a link, you need to type the document's address: its Uniform Resource Locator (URL). You will also supply the text that appears when the browser displays the link. A fully-spelled-out URL (including the http:// part and everything else) is called an *absolute URL*. Here's an example with an absolute URL (a URL that fully specifies the protocol and location of the referenced resource):

```
<A HREF = "http://www.dilbert.com">The Dilbert
Zone</A>
```

To make sure you type the URL correctly, use a browser to access the page to which you're linking. In the browser's address (location) box, select the text, and copy it to the clipboard. Then paste the URL into your document.

Go For It!

Try placing a link in your HTML document now. Save your document, open it with your browser, and click the link. If the link doesn't work for some reason, the following table contains a list of likely causes.

Table 3.8 Likely causes of hyperlink errors

Error	Description
typo	You typed the URL incorrectly. Remember, URLs are case-sensitive. I strongly recommend that you use a browser to access the site; then copy the URL from the address (location) box to your clipboard; then paste the URL into your document.
missing bracket	You forgot to include one of the angle brackets. Your browser can't process the link correctly unless the start and end tags are fully formed.
missing slash mark	You forgot the slash mark on the end tag. This is easy to do, particularly if you type a lot of link text.
missing end tag	You forgot the end tag. This has ugly results, because it turns the rest of your document into one huge link.
missing quote marks	You forgot one or both of the quotation marks around the URL. It is particularly easy to forget the closing quote mark.

Give Me Beauty

You've got a functioning Web page! You've added structure, direction, content, and links. But there's only one problem: It's ugly.

More to the point, what you've created is known (derogatorily) to Web authors as an Early Mosaic page. (Mosaic was the first popular graphical browser.) An Early Mosaic page is very, very plain—it uses all the background and font defaults. To be sure, Early Mosaic has its merits: Early Mosaic pages download fast, and they're easy to read. But surely you'd like to add some pizazz. You will learn lots of ways to do this in the chapters to come, but let's start with three: a bulleted list, a graphic, and—most important of all—a few STYLE definitions.

As in previous sections of this chapter, bear in mind that there's much more to say about each of the topics that follow. That's what Part Two of this book is for. Here you will find enough of the basics to get you going.

Magic Bullets: The UL Element

Professional document designers have a saying: "Where possible, break up the text on the page." They don't mean that you should scramble it all over the place, just to create an interesting effect. What is at issue here is the effective use of white space. When well handled, it can guide the eye to important material.

One of the best ways to break up text on the page involves creating a bulleted list. A bulleted list is a list of items, each of which is preceded by a bullet. In HTML, bulleted lists are known as unordered lists. To create an unordered list, you use the UL element.

Here's the element definition:

ELEMENT NAME	UL
TYPE	Block
PURPOSE	Creates an unordered (bulleted) list.
NESTED WITHIN	BODY
START TAG	Required
END TAG	Required
CONTENT	LI elements for each line of list.
ATTRIBUTES	**Strict DTD:** core attributes (id, class, style, title) language attributes (lang, dir)
	Transitional DTD (deprecated): type="(disc, square, circle)" (optional) compact (Boolean)

EXAMPLE	`<UL>`
	`<LI>`Here's the first item in the list.
	`<LI>`Here's the second item in the list.
	`<LI>`Here's the third item in the list.
	`</UL>`
TIP	Define each line with the LI element. With the LI element, you don't have to enter an end tag at the end of each line.

As you can see from the definition, an unordered list must contain LI elements, so let's take a look at LI.

List Your Items: The LI Element

The LI element enables you to mark the items in your bulleted list. Here's the element definition:

ELEMENT NAME	LI
TYPE	Block
PURPOSE	Defines an item in a list.
NESTED WITHIN	UL, OL, DIR, MENU
START TAG	Required
END TAG	Optional
CONTENT	LI elements for each line of list
ATTRIBUTES	**Strict DTD:** core attributes (id, class, style, title) language attributes (lang, dir) **Transitional DTD (deprecated):** type = "(disc, square, circle)" (OPTIONAL)
EXAMPLE	`<UL>`
	`<LI>`Here's the first item in the list.
	`<LI>`Here's the second item in the list.
	`<LI>`Here's the third item in the list.
	`</UL>`
TIP	The end tag is optional.

Like the P element, the LI element doesn't require an end tag—and you really don't need to use it. Here's how the unordered list should look:

```
<UL>
        <LI>This is the first item in the list
        <LI>This is the second item in the list
        <LI>This is the third item in the list
</UL>
```

Getting Graphic: The IMG Element

What's a Web page without a picture? In HTML 4.0, you add a graphic to your document by means of the IMG element.

You'll learn a lot more about images (including the types of graphics files you can use) in Chapter 16. For now, here are the essentials.

Here's the element definition for IMG:

ELEMENT NAME	IMG
TYPE	Inline
PURPOSE	Inserts a graphic at the tag's location.
NESTED WITHIN	BODY
START TAG	Required
END TAG	Forbidden
CONTENT	Empty
ATTRIBUTES	**Strict DTD:** core attributes (id, class, style, title) language attributes (lang, dir) alt = "character data" (optional) longdesc = "url" (optional) **Transitional DTD (deprecated):** width = "length" (optional) height = "length" (optional) vspace = "length" (optional) hspace = "length" (optional)

	borders = "pixels" (optional) align = "(bottom, middle, top, left, right)" (optional)
EXAMPLE	<IMG source = "picture.gif" alt = "A picture of my sailboat.">
TIP	Include alternate text (with the alt attribute) so that your graphic will have meaning for people browsing with graphics switched off (or with text-only browsers).

As you can see the IMG element has a lot of deprecated presentation attributes. Chapter 7 discusses them, and shows how to achieve the same (or much better) effects by means of style sheets. For now, the two most important attributes are src (the source of the image) and alt (alternate text), which are discussed here.

To add a graphic to your Web page, you need some sort of graphic file that is stored in the JPEG or GIF format. I'm sure you have a few of these on your disk; if not, you can easily download one from the Web (check out Microsoft's Multimedia Gallery at www.microsoft.com/workshop/design/mmgallry/).

To add the graphic, position the cursor where you want the graphic to appear, and add an IMG element such as the following:

```
<IMG src="picture.gif" alt="A picture of my sail-
boat.">
```

The alt text appears while the browser is downloading the graphic, and stays on-screen only if the browser can't display the graphic. Don't forget to include this; some people still use text-only browsers, and lots of people browse with graphics switched off.

Do It With Style: The STYLE element

In previous versions of HTML, there wasn't any logical way to control the appearance of elements on-screen. Sure, you could use a number of extensions (such as Netscape's FONT tag), but you wound up with a mish-mash, such as the following:

```
<H1 align = "center"><FONT color = "red" face =
"Helvetica"><I>My Title Is Here</I></FONT></H1>
```

This code formats a centered H1 heading with a red Helvetica font and italics, but what a mess! It borders on the unreadable. Imagine having formatting tags such as these all over your document—you'd be lucky to be able to read it at all. Even worse, if you want to use another H1 heading and give it the same formatting, you have to type all this information all over again. And if you make a mistake, the headings look different.

Formatting the HTML 4.0 Way

With HTML 4.0, there's a clear, logical separation between structure (the marking of elements) and presentation (formatting). As far as possible, you place the formatting within the STYLE element, which you type within the HEAD. Here's how the same formatting looks with HTML 4.0:

```
<HEAD>
      <STYLE type = "text/css">
      H1 {text-align: center; font-family:
      Helvetica; color: red; font-style: italic}
      </STYLE>
</HEAD>
<BODY>
      <H1>My Heading is Here</H1>
</BODY>
```

Within the STYLE element, you find a full definition of the formats for the H1 heading to follow: centered alignment, Helvetica font, red text, and italics. What's more, this definition affects all the H1 elements throughout your whole document. (This is called *inheritance*.)

Note that the style definition (within the STYLE tags) uses a different syntax than HTML. The syntax is that of Cascading Style Sheets (CSS). You'll learn more about CSS syntax in Chapter 7.

The STYLE Element

Here's the STYLE element definition:

ELEMENT NAME	Style
TYPE	Inline

PURPOSE	Defines the style to be associated with an HTML element throughout the document.
NESTED WITHIN	HEAD
START TAG	Required
END TAG	Required
CONTENT	Character data (style sheet)
ATTRIBUTES	type = "CDATA" (required) media = "MIME type" (optional)

EXAMPLE	`<STYLE type = "text/css">`
	`      H1 {text-align: center;`
	`      font-family: Helvetica;`
	`      color: red;`
	`      font-style: italic}`
	`</STYLE>`

TIP	Define the type as text/css.

Of the two attributes mentioned, the type attribute is required. In the type attribute, you specify the Internet data type of your style sheet; here, you type "text/css" to indicate that you're creating a Cascading Style Sheet (CSS), as discussed in Chapter 6.

In the media attribute, you indicate what type of device you've written your document for. Because many Web documents can and will be written for specialized display devices, you should indicate that yours is designed for screen display; this will enable specialized browsers (for example, speech-synthesizing browsers) to ignore all but those documents specially created for that device. In this way, you can contribute to the Web's accessibility for people with physical limitations.

Try It!

Chapter 7 examines styles and style sheets in more detail. For now, try typing a STYLE element into your document, so that it picks up the elements you've created and gives them distinctive formats. Be sure to place the STYLE element within the HEAD.

When you type in the STYLE values, be sure to name fonts that are resident on your computer system; otherwise they won't appear. For more information on the issues of fonts on the Web, see Chapter 19.

Here's an example to try:

```
<HEAD>
     <STYLE type = "text/css">
          BODY  { background-color: white }
          H1    { text-align: center; font-family:
          Helvetica }
          H2 {font-family: Helvetica }
          P { font-family: Garamond; text-
          align: justify; text-indent: 0.25in;
          font-size: 12pt }
          UL {font-family: Garamond; text-
          align: justify; font-size: 10 pt}
     </STYLE>
</HEAD>
```

As you're typing the STYLE element, note the following:

- There's a list of elements here, followed by a style definition for each.
- The definition must be enclosed within curly braces.
- Within the curly braces, you find *properties*. These are like attributes, but note that the syntax is different. After the property name, you type a colon, followed by the value. You *don't* have to put the value in quotation marks.
- You can include more than one property in a style definition, as long as you separate the properties with semicolons (;).

The results are pretty impressive. Wow! Justified paragraphs, with a first-line indentation; a nice distinction between the display type (headings) and body type (paragraphs); and even a white background. No more Early Mosaic!

Bear in mind that older browsers don't support style sheets. The good news is that both of the leading ones do, beginning with Version 3.0 of Microsoft Internet Explorer and Version 4.0 of Netscape Navigator. Browsers that don't support style sheets won't display your formatting, though, so you're back to Early Mosaic with anyone who's using an out-of-date browser. However, you can use the deprecated presentation tags in the transitional style sheet to add presentation for users of older browsers.

Summary

In this chapter, you have learned the fundamentals of creating HTML documents. You begin with the global structure (version statement, HTML element, HEAD element, and BODY element). You continue by adding text and additional structural elements, such as headings and lists. Finally, you choose formatting for the elements you've used by adding a STYLE element to your HEAD.

By now, you've created your first HTML document. What's more, you did it the HTML 4 way. The HTML 4 way can be summed up very simply: Don't try to control presentation when you mark up your document. Instead, add a STYLE element that creates global styles for the various elements you've used. The result makes your HTML code much easier to edit. It's more efficient, too, requiring a smaller size for the amount of presentation control that you get. In the next chapter, you learn how to publish your Web pages using the FTP protocol.

4

Go Public! (Publishing Your Page)

In this chapter, you will learn the following skills:

- Figuring out where to publish your page
- Deciding how to publish most cost-effectively
- Judging whether to run your own server or not
- Using FTP to upload files so that other Web users can access them
- Maintaining your Web pages with FTP

You've created a Web page. That's great, but it's more or less meaningless if it is accessible only on your own system. The whole point of Web publishing involves making your page available to others. In this chapter, you learn how this is done. You'll complete the journey you began at the beginning of Part One—namely, to create and publish your own page as quickly as possible.

How Much Will This Cost?

The answer is anywhere from nothing to a lot. In this section, you learn how to get your Web page published inexpensively—and maybe for nothing.

Publishing on Your Company's or School's Server

If your company or school has an Internet connection and a Web server, chances are that you can publish your Web page there. But there are bound to be restrictions on this. After all, you're publishing on somebody else's computer equipment. As the courts have had to explain patiently time after time, there is no First Amendment right to free speech using somebody else's printing press!

What's allowed on a company or school server? It all depends on policies (if there are any). Ask your network administrator what's acceptable for employee or student publication. Often, there is no objection to publishing a professional-looking home page, especially (in companies) one that makes it easier to get in touch with you and explains what you do that's so special. It may be OK to publish a page concerning a hobby or a politically correct social issue. Ask!

Getting Free Web Publishing Space with Your Internet Connection

Here's one of the few remaining great deals of this increasingly stingy world. Some Internet service providers (ISPs) will throw in a megabyte or two of storage space on their Web server for free, in exchange for your signing up for a premium connection (about $25 per month). Unfortunately, this is getting harder to find. Also, there are some restrictions. Too many service providers found that, after offering this deal, they'd get some 17-year-old with a scanner who posted several megabytes' worth of Playmates of the Month, resulting in 600,000 hits (accesses) per day and threatening letters from Playboy, Inc. So read the fine print carefully—you may find that there is a per-byte charge that kicks in after a certain number of external accesses. This can get very expensive, very fast. And it's designed to.

Maybe this isn't completely free. But you're paying for Internet access anyway, aren't you? Why not shop around for an Internet service provider who throws in some Web publishing space as a freebie?

The limitation here is that this freebie Web publishing space is often restricted to individuals, and for non-business purposes. Also, it doesn't come with any of the extras that are needed for business Web publishing, such as usage reports, secure servers for online ordering, and other advanced features (see the section, "You Get What You Pay For"). If you want to set up a professional or business Web page, service providers switch you to the commercial rates—and costs go up, as the next section explains.

You Get What You Pay For: Web Publishing Services

If you can get free Web publishing space, that's great, but chances are it won't come with any of the services listed in Table 4.1. You may need some or all of these to create the type of site you want (particularly one with lots of interactive features, such as secure on-line ordering). A Web hosting service can provide these services for you—but for a price, naturally. As explained later in this chapter, you can implement these same services if you set up and run your own server, but you'll need a considerable amount of programming and system maintenance expertise to pull this off.

Table 4.1 Services provided with Web hosting

Service	Explanation
domain names	When you publish your page on a Web server, your page's URL begins with the name of the computer on which the Web server is running. The result could be a really long URL that's hard to remember and full of difficult-to-type characters (like www.your-local-ISP.com/~meirschmidt/business_pages/welcome.html). What you'd really like to have is a URL like this: www.superhot-deals.com. You can have it, but it's going to cost you: Currently, domain name charges run $50 per year. You'll need to pay $100 up front for two years, and expect to pay your ISP a $50 to $75 processing fee.
CGI scripting	You can create pages with forms—you'll learn how in Chapter 17—but the forms don't do anything impressive without some programming to make them work. Often, this program is done according to the Common Gateway Interface (CGI) standard, using perl, a scripting language

known to UNIX programmers. Although it isn't very difficult to learn how to direct form output to existing CGI scripts, writing the scripts is another matter, and you may need custom programming if you want to implement advanced features such as Web-based newsgroups, real-time chatting, or guestbooks.

secure (SSL) ordering	Are you thinking about setting up shop on the Web? You'll need a secure server—and the expertise to set up a "shopping cart" application, which enables users to make selections and see them grouped and totalled on a check-out page.
database searching	Another application that requires programming expertise and experience, database searches enable people accessing your site to locate and retrieve information. Professional Web hosting services have much experience with this and can get the application going in short order.
usage statistics	How many people are accessing your site? Which pages are they looking at—and which ones are they ignoring? These and other important facts require Web site monitoring and reports, which are provided by Web hosting services.

Web Hosting Services

Most Web hosting services are also Internet service providers. They make Web publishing space available at a variety of price levels. Often, you can get the bare-bones hosting for as little as $25 per month for 1 or 2 megabytes of storage space. Costs go up from there, depending on how much space you need, how frequently your page is accessed, and which services you select. Table 4.2 sums up some estimated costs for various levels of service for commercial Web hosting.

Caveat emptor! Watch out for costs per megabyte of data transferred—as much as 10 cents or more per meg. One Web hosting service that charges $25 per month allows 2500MB of transferred data per month for free—but charges 12 cents per megabyte subsequently. This could be a very expensive *trap. Just consider: Suppose your Web page has a lot of graphics, and the typical user downloads 500KB with every access. After 5,000 accesses, you start paying 12 cents per megabyte. If your page gets accessed 10,000 times in a month, you'll get a bill for $600! Not such a great deal, is it?*

Table 4.2 Estimated monthly costs for various levels of Web hosting services

Monthly cost	Type of Web hosting service
$25 - $100	Basic service for lightly-accessed site (1-3MB of storage space, 2500MB of free data transfer per month); up to 1000 accesses per month
$100 - $250	Extended service for lightly-accessed site (1-3 MB of storage space, 2500MB of free data transfer per month), including custom-programmed links to guestbooks, forms processing programs, and monthly or weekly usage reports; up to 5000 accesses per month
$250 - $1000	Premium service for site with moderate access (5-10MB of storage space, 5000MB of free data transfer per month), including custom programming, detailed usage reports, domain name registration; up to 10,000 accesses per month
$1000 - $10,000	Premium service for heavily accessed site (10-25 MB of storage space, 5000MB of free data transfer per month); more than 10,000 accesses per month but less than 100,000

The Do-It-Yourself Route

Let's look at Web publishing from another angle: Doing it yourself. What's involved? It's something like owning a boat—costs come at you from all directions, way beyond what you anticipated. Let's stare them in the face.

Bill 1: Permanent Internet Connection

You cannot set up a Web server on a dial-up, modem connection—at least, not if you want people to be able to access your Web server regularly. Here's why: to connect to the Internet, your computer needs an Internet address (also called an IP address). This is a four-number address, with the numbers separated by dots (such as 128.143.43.7). The problem with a dial-up connection lies in the fact that you get a different IP address every time you log on. That's because your service provider assigns addresses dynamically, depending on which modem you happen to access (out of the dozens or hundreds available) when you dial in.

What does that mean for Web publishing? Bad news, basically. Think of it this way: suppose you want to start a mail order business, and you send out thousands of flyers stating that you're available for business at 125 Spring Street. But that's just today. Tomorrow, you could be at 96 Elm Avenue, 148 Walnut Street, or 3097 Pistachio Circle. Who knows? Chances are, you won't get too much business.

So what does it cost to get a permanent IP address and run your own server? Unfortunately this is a pricey proposition. Table 4.3 summarizes some typical costs. As you can see, this isn't going to be cheap—and this is just the beginning of the costs you will learn about in this section.

Table 4.3 Typical charges for permanent internet connection

Bandwidth	Typical monthly charge
56 Kpbs	56,000 bits per second leased (permanent) telephone line (sufficient for a personal Web server or small business or organization). Costs: $200 from the phone company, or $150 from an Internet service provider. You'll also pay a one-time setup fee ranging from $50 to $100.
128 Kbps	128,000 bits per second ISDN line (sufficient for a small- or medium-sized business or organization). Costs: $75 to $150 from the phone company, or $100-$200 from Internet service provider. Setup fees can run as high as $250, and you'll need about $500 worth of specialized equipment to connect to the ISDN line.

1.5 Mbps	1.5 million bits per second T1 line (sufficient for a medium- to large-sized business or organization, such as a university). Costs: $1000 to $2500 per month (including service provider charges).

Bill 2: Equipment

If you expect your Web page to be popular, you may start getting simultaneous hits (accesses)—and that spells trouble if your computer can't handle the load. Just about any computer can handle a few dozen external Internet accesses per day, but costs mount when you start talking about thousands, or tens of thousands. Federal Express needs hefty mainframe computers to run its popular package-tracking site, which gets thousands of hits per day. At the minimum, you're talking about setting aside a reasonably good Pentium machine—preferably, a Pentium Pro or Pentium II. So add another couple of grand to the bill.

What if your page suddenly becomes so popular that it overwhelms your equipment? You may have to add additional servers. How much are you prepared to spend on this? If your page gets really popular, you may need to go to a hefty Unix-based system, and that almost guarantees that you will need at least a part-time computer technician/programmer to keep the darned thing running right. That's going to cost you plenty—at least $1500 per month. If you need full-time staff, figure on paying up to $4,000 per month, including benefits.

Bill 3: Domain Name Registration

If you're setting up your own Web server, you need a Web address (also called a domain name), such as www.mydomain.org. But this requires obtaining a registration from the current Internet registration authority, InterNIC. Currently, InterNIC charges $35 per year to maintain a registered domain name; you pay $100 up front, and after two years you are billed $35 per year.

Bill 4: Software

Although there are freeware and shareware Web servers out there, chances are you'll want to go with a tried and tested product. It's going to cost you between $250 and $1000 if you want the best software available. Unfortunately, this software is not particularly easy to configure, use, and maintain—so you had better build in some costs for somebody to do this for you.

Bill 5: Maintenance

Here's a cost that most people don't anticipate. Keeping a Web site maintained and fresh is a big job. If you don't have time to do it, you'll have to pay somebody to take up the slack. For a big, complex corporate site, this could cost as much as $25,000 per month! For a small business, figure that site maintenance is going to take two or three days of employee-days per month. That's a significant amount of change, and you'd better figure it in.

And the Bottom Line?

Table 4.4 sums up some rough-and-ready estimates of what it's going to cost to set up your own server. The estimated costs reflect the money you spend for equipment leases, staffing, telecommunications charges, service provider charges, and registration fees.

Table 4.4 Estimated monthly costs of setting up your own Web server

Monthly cost	Type of server
$100 - $500	Very light duty (personal or small business Web server with fewer than 1000 accesses per month)
$500 - $1000	Light duty (personal or small business Web server with up to 5000 accesses per month)
$1000 - $5000	Medium duty (small- to medium-sized business Web server with up to 10,000 accesses per month)
$5000 - $10,000	Medium duty server with complex programming (such as database access), CGI scripts, and other interactive features
$10,000 - $25,000	Heavy duty (large company's Web server with up to 500,000 accesses per month)
$25,000 - $100,000	Very heavy duty (corporation or large university with millions of accesses per month)

Which Way to Go?

There is no magic formula to determine whether you should have your pages hosted by a service provider or try to run your own server. Here are some things to think about:

- **How much interactivity do your want your site to have?** If you want to run interactive features such as forms, guestbooks, database searches, and other advanced goodies, think long and hard about whether you want to run your own server. If you don't possess the necessary expertise, watch out—the skills needed to implement these applications are in very heavy demand, and you'll have to spend some very good money for competent staff. In New York City, accomplished Webmasters with CGI programming expertise command salaries of up to $100,000. You might be better off with a Web hosting service.

- **How many accesses do you expect to get per month?** If you go the Web-hosting route, watch out for those per-megabyte data transfer fees, which kick in after so many megabytes' worth of data have been downloaded from your site. Anyone thinking about creating a very popular site—one that is accessed tens of thousands of times per month or more—will have to think about running their own server.

As the above discussion makes clear, would be Web publishers are caught in a trade-off between, on one hand, the expertise needed to run the complicated servers, and on the other hand, the very real threat of ridiculous data transfer fees should they go the Web hosting route. And that's exactly why Windows NT is fast becoming the Web publishing platform of choice for small- and medium-sized organizations. Windows NT is much cheaper and less complicated to administer and run than Unix systems of comparable power. What's more, Microsoft's server software (Internet Information Server) enables site administrators to create interactive features, including database access and forms processing, without requiring extensive or advanced programming skills.

It's Sort of Like Remote Control: Using FTP

FTP sounds like some sort of flower delivery service, but in reality it is one of the oldest and most useful Internet services available. The really great thing about

FTP is not only that it enables you to send and receive files over the Internet, but that it also enables you to perform file operations (such as copying, deleting, and moving files) on a distant computer. With FTP, you can send your completed pages to the computer where you publish pages, and you can also keep your pages organized, just as you organize them on your own computer. Think of FTP as if it were some kind of remote control system for doing things to files on far away computers.

Getting in Sync with FTP

In order to use FTP, you need the information listed in Table 4.5.

Table 4.5 What you need to upload files via FTP

Item	Description
account information	From your Web hosting service, get your login name (also called user name), your password for FTP access, and the exact location of the directory where you will store your files. On most Web hosting services, your Web publishing directory is located within your home directory (the directory where you store all of your files, including your e-mail mailbox).
FTP server address	You also need the address of the computer where you will store your Web pages. This will be a standard Internet computer name, such as www.coolhost.net. Be sure you get the exact spelling of this computer's name.
FTP client	This is a program that runs on your computer, and enables you to send and receive files via FTP, as well as perform file maintenance operations within your home directory. You can get an FTP client for almost any type of computer, including Macintoshes, Windows systems, and Unix workstations.

Talk to your Web hosting service, and get all of this information before you try uploading your files.

Sending Files over the Net

To publish your Web page, you need to upload them to your Web publishing directory. This may be a directory within your home directory—check with your Web hosting service to find out exactly where to upload pages.

Did you include the graphics in your page? You also need to upload the graphics, as well as any other objects that you have placed within your page. Bear in mind that this is not automatic. If you forget to upload one or more of the images referenced on your page, people accessing your page will see error icons instead of your images. Also, make sure graphics are correctly referenced in your hyperlinks. Did you use relative URLs to reference your images? If you used simple relative URLs which contain only the name of the image file, then you must place the graphics in the same directory that contains your Web page. If you used a relative URL that includes a subdirectory of some type (for example, /images), then you must create a subdirectory on the remote system, using exactly the same name, and copy your graphics files to that subdirectory. Later in this section, you'll learn how you can create subdirectories and perform other file maintenance operations with your FTP client.

FTP Lingo

Like everything on the Internet, FTP has its own, distinctive vocabulary. In case you're new to FTP, here's a quick guide to the terms you will most often encounter when technical people start talking about FTP.

Table 4.6 An FTP glossary

Term	Definition
anonymous FTP	A public FTP service that makes files available for downloading to any Internet user. When using anonymous FTP, you supply the user ID "anonymous" and give your e-mail address as your password. You cannot do anything but download files using anonymous FTP; you can't erase them, alter them, or move them from their stored locations.

ASCII transfer mode   One of two basic transfer modes (the other one is called binary) in which you transfer nothing but numbers, the basic letters of the English alphabet, and common punctuation symbols.

auto detect   A transfer mode in which the FTP client automatically detects the type of data that you're trying to transfer (ASCII or binary), and selects the correct type of transfer mode.

binary transfer mode   One of two basic transfer modes (the other is ASCII transfer mode) in which you can transfer program files, graphic files, and other files that contain non-ASCII data.

directory   A named storage space for your files. A directory can also contain subdirectories. In FTP, directory and subdirectory names are preceded by a forward slash (/), as in the following example: /~janet/home/welcome.html.

download   To retrieve a file from a remote computer.

FTP client   A program that runs on your own computer and enables you to exchange files with other computers by means of FTP.

FTP server   A program that makes file in directory information and remote file maintenance available to external Internet users.

FTP   Short for the File Transfer Protocol, one of the oldest and most useful Internet standards. With FTP, you can upload files to a computer that is running an FTP server. You an also download files and perform file and directory maintenance operations.

timeout   An error that occurs when the remote computer does not respond during a specified interval such as one minute. If you get a timeout message, try executing the command again, and make sure you are still connected.

| upload | To send a file from your computer to a remote computer that is running FTP. |

FTP Login Types and Transfer Types

With FTP, you can access remote computers and transfer files into two different ways:

- **Login types** FTP enables you to log in to remote computers in different ways. You can log in via anonymous FTP, which doesn't require you to have a previously arranged password. Instead you log in with the user name "anonymous," and you supply your e-mail address as your password. In anonymous FTP, you don't have full read/write privileges; you can only download files. The second login type gives you full read/write privileges, but you must supply a user ID and password. It's the latter type of login that you will use to upload files to a Web hosting service.
- **Transfer types** You can transfer files in different ways. With most FTP clients, the default transfer type is called ASCII. In ASCII file transfers, the only thing you can upload or download is a plain text file, one that contains nothing but the characters found on a typical computer keyboard. This is fine for HTML files, which contain nothing but text. If you want to transfer graphics or other objects (such as Java applets), you must use binary transfer mode. In this mode, you can transfer graphics files, program files, or any other type of file that contains non-ASCII characters. The better FTP clients automatically detect which type of data you're trying to transfer, and select the transfer mode accordingly.

When you are working with a Web hosting service, you use regular FTP (as opposed to anonymous FTP), which means that you need a user ID and password. Also, you will be wise to work with an FTP client that has an auto-detect feature; otherwise, you'll sooner or later spend time uploading some huge graphics file, only to find that you've sent it in ASCII rather than binary mode, and that you will have to do the whole operation over again.

Configuring Your FTP Client

To get started with FTP, you need to configure your FTP client to access your home directory. This is a fairly simple process with most programs; for example, in my favorite FTP client, called Cute FTP, there is an FTP Site Edit dialog box (Figure 4.1). This dialog box may look a little complicated, but it's really not; you just need to enter the FTP address of the computer where you're uploading your files, your user ID, your password, and the directory on your local system from which you are uploading files.

Connecting to the FTP Server

Once you configure your FTP client, connecting ought to be as simple as clicking the connect button. Of course, nothing associated with computers is really simple; if you forgot to log onto the Internet, for example, you would get an error message, and you might spend 15 minutes in total confusion before realizing your error. Also, if you made a mistake typing in your user ID, password, or the address of the Web hosting service's computer, you would not be able to log on. If you have trouble making a connection, be sure to check the information in the same dialog box that you used to configure your FTP client. If you still have trouble, don't spend hours sitting in front of your computer trying this and that. Call the Web hosting service and get some help.

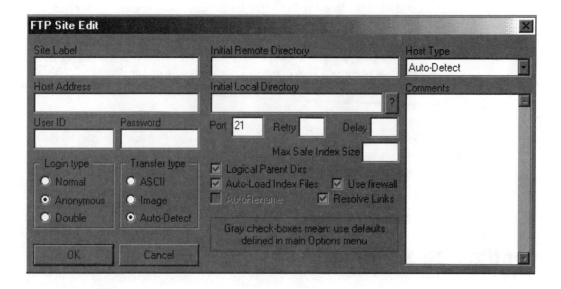

Figure 4.1 To upload your Web pages, you need to configure your FTP client

Assuming all goes well, your FTP client will show you the contents of your home directory on the remote system (see Figure 4.2). The better FTP clients show you this information in a familiar way; for example Cute FTP displays remote directories in the same way that Windows Explorer displays files and folders on a Windows system. Similarly, the better Macintosh clients, such as Fetch, present the remote directory information as if it were no more threatening than a friendly Macintosh folder.

Changing Directories

Chances are that there is more than one directory below your home directory, the one that you see when you connect to the FTP server. In many systems, there is a subdirectory that is supposed to contain all of the Web documents that you want to publish. (You can create additional subdirectories within this publishing directory, if you wish, and the files within the subdirectories will also be available for Web publishing.) Ask the Web hosting service's help people which directory you are supposed to use for publishing your files.

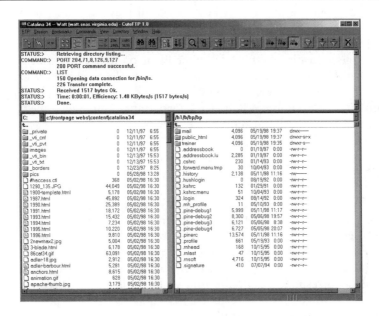

Figure 4.2 Viewing two file directories (local and remote)

If you're using a user-friendly FTP client such as Cute FTP or Fetch, it is easy to change directories. Directories are shown as folder icons. To open your Web publishing directory, just double-click it. Once you've opened your Web publishing directory, you are ready to transfer your files.

Here is another question to ask your Web hosting service: What file name should I use for my default page? A default page is the page that appears if somebody accesses your directory from the Web, but without specifying a specific filename. For example, suppose your Web publishing directory is located at http://www.coolhost.net/~janet/. If you place a default page in this directory, this page will be displayed automatically if somebody accesses your directory without specifying a file name. This is a good thing, because it makes your URL shorter and easier to remember. With most servers, the default page name is index.html. Check with your Web hosting service to find out how to name your default page.

Sending Your File

To send your file, use your FTP client to display the name of the file that you want to send, and choose the command that initiates the file transfer. If your FTP client can automatically detect the file type (ASCII or binary), you can just click the uploading button, and your file is on its way. If your FTP client does not have an auto detect feature, you need to select the correct transfer mode—ASCII or binary—depending on which type of file you are uploading. To upload an HTML file, choose ASCII. To upload graphics or some other object (such as a sound or video clip), choose the binary transfer mode.

Creating Directories

As explained in the preceding chapters, you can use relative URLs in hyperlinks. The simplest relative URL is one that contains only the filename of the HTML page, image, or other object. In order for such a URL to work, you must place the referenced file in the same directory that contains the referenced page. If you included a subdirectory name within the URL (for example, /images), you must create a corresponding subdirectory within your home directory on the remote system. If you do not, the relative URL will not work, and people accessing your page will see an error message.

With the user-friendly FTP clients such as Cute FTP or Fetch, you can create new subdirectories (subfolders) on the remote system as simply as you do on your own computer. Begin by selecting the directory in which you want to create the new subdirectory, and choose the command to create a new directory. After you supply the directory name and click OK, your FTP client sends this information to the FTP server, which then obligingly creates that directory using the name that you supplied. You can then switch to this new directory, and upload the files that belong in it.

Maintaining Files on the Remote System

Once you've uploaded your files, and, if necessary, created the appropriate directory structure on the remote system, you can perform file maintenance tasks just as you would on your own computer. Examples of such tasks include deleting files that are no longer needed, moving files to new locations, or renaming files.

Think long and hard before you delete, move, or rename any file on the remote system that is referenced in a hyperlink. If you change any file's location or name, the hyperlink won't work, and people accessing your site will see an error message ("404 -- not found," or something equally cheery). You must also change the hyperlinks that referenced these files to reflect their new locations or names—and that's a large, messy job, and what's worse, it's prone to error. You might miss one of the hyperlinks buried somewhere in one of the pages you created, and unless you extensively and exhaustively test your site, you won't catch the error. That's why it is best to plan your site's directory structure before you start uploading pages. If this sounds frightening, don't be concerned; unless you are planning to create a really huge site with dozens or hundreds of pages, you can get by with just two directories: one to hold your HTML pages (this is the same as your default publishing directory), and another to hold your graphics.

Finding Out Whether Anyone's Taken Your Domain Name

How could they? Real easy—just fork over $100 to the InterNIC, the organization responsible for registering domain names. To find out whether anyone has taken your pet name, check out the InterNIC's WHOIS Web gateway (ds.inter-nic.net/wp/whois.html). Type the domain name you want—something like pfaf-fey.com—and see whether anyone has it already. When you access the site, you'll see a form that enables you to enter the domain name you're looking for. Try typing "microsoft"—as you will see, this name is taken.

Summary

As you decide where to publish your page, you face a trade-off between Web hosting service's data transfer costs and the costs of running your own server. That's not an issue if you want to publish a simple page that's not going to get a lot of hits—you can probably find an ISP that will give you free Web publishing space in return for a full-service Internet subscription—but costs go up if you want to add interactive features. Once you figure out where to publish, an essential skill is to master FTP; you will do well to pick a program that mimics the functionality of your computer's file system, such as CuteFTP (Windows 95) or Fetch (Mac OS).

Part Two

Digging Deeper:
More About HTML 4

5

Secrets of Successful Web Page Design

In this chapter, you will learn the following skills:

- Defining your publishing purpose
- Understanding your audience
- Framing your approach
- Planning your page
- Evaluating published pages

Now that you have learned the basics of how to create an HTML page, step back for a bit and look at the big picture. Beyond the details of HTML, what's involved in creating a truly fantastic Web page?

If you think about the pages that you really like, you'll come up with a ready answer: The best pages combine much good content, easy navigation, and great looking graphics—and what's more, the whole thing doesn't take a long time to download.

But there's more, really. Lying behind the best Web pages is a formula that is well known to communication specialists: Purpose + audience + approach (or P+A+A, in case you'd like yet another acronym). In brief, this formula says that you communicate best when you clearly define your purpose, know your audience, and develop an approach that is right for your audience. The very finest pages on the Web offer more than content navigability and graphics; they also show a deep grasp of P+A+A.

In this chapter, you will learn how to create your Web page using the techniques used by today's hottest public speakers, Webmasters, and advertisers. It doesn't matter whether you are creating a simple, one-page presentation, or a complex site with dozens of pages. The techniques in this chapter will work for you.

Why Are You Doing This?

Why do you want to create a Web page? You would be surprised to learn how many people publish Web pages without fully thinking through this question. But it is the first important step you should take if you want to create something other than a boring, ordinary Web page. This is true even if your ambitions are as modest as creating a home page—for example, a page on your company's server. What is really the purpose of this page? Is it to convey a positive image of yourself? To make your resume available, so that you can increase your chances for promotion internally? To enable other people in the company to contact you and make use of the services that you can perform? Perhaps some combination of these? If it is a combination, which purpose is the most important? As you'll see, your answers to these questions provide important clues about your document's layout—the way you organize your document's components so that each achieves the maximum effect.

Looking at a Variety of Purposes

There are many, many reasons for creating a Web page, probably as many as the number of pages on the Web! Still, it is possible to categorize Web publishing purposes in a number of ways. See Table 5.1 for a summary of Web publishing purposes.

Table 5.1 Web publishing purposes

Purpose	Explanation
personal	You have some personal reason for creating your page. Perhaps you want to share information about a hobby of yours, express your opinion on a political matter, or share information about yourself in hope of getting into contact with like-minded folks.
social	The focus isn't so much on you, but rather on others—and specifically, helping others. Perhaps you want to provide a tutorial or background information about a subject in which you are professionally knowledgeable, so that others can benefit. Maybe you'd like to make people more aware of a social or environmental issue that you feel is not being adequately recognized.
community	The World Wide Web provides powerful tools for making communities work. Perhaps you belong to local organizations, such as the parents and teachers association, that could use the Web to get the word out about activities, fund raising events, and school issues.
publishing	According to one estimate, more than 100,000 newsletters are distributed using the postal service in the United States alone. It's an expensive proposition to publish a newsletter, even if the mailing list is small. The appeal of using the World Wide Web as a distribution medium for newsletters and other publications is simply this: The distribution costs are zero. Of course, readers need Internet access; in some topical areas, that's very common, while in others it is rare.
professional	The Web can help you advance professionally in many ways. You can make your resume available to potential employers. You can gain recognition for your contributions. You can share working drafts of your professional work, which will help

	you get in touch and network more effectively with others who share your interests. You can reach potential clients. There's a whole world of purposes here.
business	I can't think of a business that shouldn't have a Web page, unless it really doesn't want to have more customers. That said, it is really important to think through exactly what your purpose is. Do you want to market your firm's products and services? If so, do you want to market locally, or would you like to go after a wider market—perhaps an international market? Are you trying to attract and recruit highly qualified people, generate sales leads, reduce paper consumption and waste by publishing manuals and documentation on the Web, provide technical support, explain your services, or even sell goods online?

Specifying Your Intent

Once you determine just where your purpose lies in the spectrum of what you can accomplish on the Web, you need to think more specifically about just what you are intending to pull off. What's your intent? Table 5.2 lists some very common and useful ones.

Table 5.2 Publishing intentions

Intent	Description
To inform	Somewhere, somebody really needs this information.
To question	People really ought to think about this issue.
To educate	Too many people have misconceptions about this.
To persuade	You really ought to see things my way.
To sell	Buy this!

The average person doesn't spend very much time looking at a Web page. You really only have about 20 seconds in order to get your basic point across. If you haven't thought through what that basic point is, it is not very likely that you'll succeed in communicating it. Sure, it would be nice to create a Web page that accomplishes more than one purpose. And, sometimes there are good reasons for doing so. Until you have more experience in Web publishing, though, it's best to make each page serve just one purpose. Of course, this is the most important rationale for creating a site with more than one page. By doing so you can make each page accomplish one purpose and one purpose only. Users can then select the page or pages that meet their needs.

What's Your Audience?

Once you figure out your purpose, the next step is to define the audience for your Web page. Forget the MBA in marketing, this isn't rocket science. It's simply a matter of understanding what your audience wants. When you're ready to define your audience, do so in the following way: Write a one- or two-sentence description of the type of people who will most likely access your Web site and feel rewarded by the content they will find there, and then explain why.

Once you have defined your audience, you have important clues about the next step in the P+A+A method: defining your approach.

What's Your Approach?

Professional communicators know that it's not enough to define your purpose and know your audience. You must also devise an approach. With the right approach, your audience takes interest in what you're saying. With the wrong approach, forget it.

Imagine that you are a college student. If you can only get your grade point average (G.P.A.) up to 3.5, you can qualify for a fantastic scholarship. Standing in your way is Professor Buncombe, who for some reason has consistently refused to recognize what an amazing genius you are. You make an appointment with the professor in order to discuss the totally unfair grade he gave you on your midterm paper.

Here is a lousy approach—I know all about it, because I get at least one of these per week. "Would you please re-evaluate my paper? You gave a B+ to Marty! I read his paper, and mine is much better. But you only gave me a C-." This approach doesn't work. It calls into question just who ought to be judging the quality of papers—the professor or the student. If you use this approach, you are quite likely to get yourself ejected rather grumpily from the professor's office, accompanied with a lot of sour mumbling about how such things could never have happened when he was a student.

Here is a much better approach. "Could we discuss my paper? I wasn't happy with the grade, but that's not the most important thing. I know you said that an A paper begins with a clear opening thesis statement, and goes on to provide evidence and discussion. I would really welcome your advice on how to do this more effectively."

Where did this approach come from? It is the result of a very good audience analysis. This student knows that professors want to be loved, valued, and respected for their knowledge. The student's purpose is served by knowing the audience and developing the right approach. P+A+A!

How Should You Lay Out Your Page?

Once you've thought through purpose, audience, and approach, you possess powerful clues about how your page should be organized. Ask yourself, "What is my audience really looking for? How can I make it easy for my audience to find what they are looking for? Will visitors see immediately that my page has the content they seek?" By answering these questions, you learn how to lay out your page for maximum effectiveness.

Front and Center

Get your message out fast. You have only a few seconds to get your page's purpose across. This does not have to be done solely with text, though. It can also be done with graphics, colors, fonts, and other design elements that convey your understanding of the audience. You can't really see this in the screen shots, of course, but the Catalina 34 National Association Web site (Figure 5.1) has the same colors as Catalina Yacht's logos—and, not coincidentally, of Catalina 34s themselves (red and navy blue against a white background).

Get Organized

What is your audience after? You need to figure this out so you can give it to them quickly. To make your site as useful as possible, you need to organize your

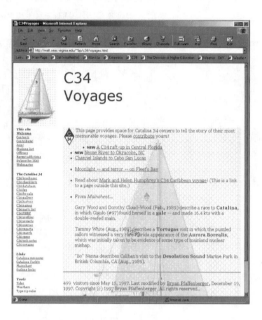

Figure 5.1 The Catalina 34 site mimics the yacht's color scheme

content so that it is easy to use. The way to do this is to choose a method of development that's in line with your audience's interests.

A method of development is a plan for organizing your site's content—a plan with an underlying principle. Table 5.3 presents a brief overview of some of the methods of development that are most appropriate to Web sites.

Table 5.3 Methods of content development

Method	Description
alphabetic	If you have much material to list, this method of development gives users an easy-to-understand means of locating what they want.
analogical	This method of development organizes material by comparing it to something that is more familiar. It is a good choice when you are presenting lots of material in a complex site. In an analogical method of development, a site is compared to

some kind of familiar physical entity, such as a room, a building, a museum, or a map.

division
In this method of development, you divide your material into categories (and, optionally, subcategories). This is a good method to use when you have tons of material. The top-level categories should make immediate good sense to your readers; it should strike them as a refreshingly clear plan for making sense out of the huge variety of goodies you're offering.

general to specific
This method of development begins with the most general information, such as an introduction, and continues with increasingly specific material. This is a good choice when you're dealing with an unfamilar topic.

geographic
This method of development organizes material spatially by region or political division.

most to least
This method of development places the most important material at or near the top of the page; less important material comes later. It is a good choice when you don't have too many top-level items, and you want to make it clear that you've thought through your readers' needs.

persuasive
In this method of development, you arrange material in a logical order, based on what it takes to persuade your reader that you have a good point to make. Because users can access your Web from any of its pages, you should use this method only for material that you can arrange on a single page.

random cool goodies
In this method of development, you list a few interesting items, in no particular order, that you're sure your audience will like.

reverse chronological
In this method of development, you place the most recent item at or near the top of the page; older items come later. This is a good choice when you want to emphasize how fresh your material is

and how often you update your page.

rhetorical	This method of development employs the tried-and-true structure of an engaging public speech. It opens with a hook, continues by providing a statement of purpose, and goes on to specify the scope, and only then gets into the heart of the matter. Obviously, this is an excellent choice for the first page of a site.

You need to think about methods of development whether you're creating a one-page presentation, or one that has many pages, such as the Catalina 34 National Association site. In a single-page presentation, the method of development structures the way you present the material on that page (often, a most-important to least-important method works well for one-page sites).

Looking at Web Pages Critically

Now that you know the basics of the P+A+A system, try visiting Web pages to see how they measure up. Do some surfing and try to rank the pages you visit using the following table.

Table 5.4 Grading Web sites

Grade	Explanation
A	Great page. You can tell the purpose at a glance and the intention is clear (whether it is to inform, question, educate, persuade, sell). The page's author knows the audience, and the page's approach seems like it is right on target. What's more, the design is tied into the purpose in some way that makes the page really enjoyable and appealing.
B	Good page. The purpose and intent are clear enough, but the author didn't put quite enough thought into carrying this through. The approach isn't really compelling—maybe it's focused on the author rather than the audience—and the design doesn't seem to be linked to the purpose as well as

it could be.

C	Average page. There does seem to be some sort of purpose or intent, but there is only a loose and not very compelling connection between the page's purpose and its design elements. There's an approach, but it's clumsy or inappropriate.
D	Awful page. The author doesn't seem quite sure what the purpose and intent of the page are supposed to be, although there is a fumbling attempt to define these. The design is apparently chosen at random, but at least it doesn't get in the way. The author has apparently never heard of the word "approach."
F	Really awful page. It is very difficult to determine just why this page is on the Web. There seems to be a purpose, but it appears to be some kind of joke. Worse, the author apparently thinks that he or she is design genius, and has chosen a very striking background graphic, which unfortunately makes the text impossible to read. But that's just as well, because it is not worth reading. (Note: Unintentionally hilarious pages get a D-.)

Summary

To publish successfully, you need to consider your purpose, your audience, and your approach. From there, you will know just how to develop and organize your content.

Now that you are oriented conceptually, get started with some HTML 4 coding! The next chapter explores basic page design choices. You will continue to develop your document's body (Chapter 7), and you'll fully explore elements such as lists (Chapter 8), inline elements (Chapter 9), and hyperlinks (Chapter 10). And all the while, of course, you'll do it the HTML 4 way.

6

Making Document Design Choices

In this chapter, you will learn the following skills:

- Translating your purpose into design
- Choosing a color scheme
- Adding background colors and graphics
- Using fonts
- Dealing with non-CSS-capable browsers

As you learned in the previous chapter, your design choices ought to reinforce your page's purpose and there are numerous ways you can do this. In this chapter, you'll learn several really interesting ways to express your purpose by making design choices that affect your whole document.

You will learn how to choose a color scheme for your document, one that harmonizes your choices of background colors, background images, text colors, and link colors. You'll go on from there to consider the vital question of fonts and how you can trick the Web into showing the fonts you want, even though the technology is, admittedly, far from perfect right now. As you will see, though, HTML 4.0, when linked with style sheets, provides very powerful tools for gaining control over your document's overall design.

Design Follows from Purpose

You know your page's purpose—you learned how to determine this in the previous chapter. From here, it's simple. Your design choices should, as much as possible, help to communicate your page's purpose.

There is not one best way to do this. It's more like a state of mind, in which you choose design features—colors, graphics, fonts, text alignment tricks—that people would be likely to associate with your page's purpose. There are numerous different ways you could do this, and every one of them depends on the details of what you're doing. Sometimes the association is direct—see an example that follows— and sometimes it's just more a matter of setting mood, as explained in the next section.

Start thinking now about a color scheme for your page. You can define the color of the background (or use a background graphic). You can also define the default text color and font for the entire document, including unvisited links, visited links, and the active link (the one the user is clicking). When you get the whole scheme in harmony with your page's purpose, you are on your way to creating a winning Web page.

Colors and Mood

By choosing default background and text colors, you create an overall mood for your document which helps communicate your page's purpose. Table 6.1 provides a few examples.

Figure 6.1 Some interesting color combinations

Background/text	Mood
black/white	Stark, clean, slightly evil-looking, hip. Suggests that you could just possibly have browsed outside the "normal Web" into something outré.

dark gray/light gray	Cool, refined, not given to outward shows of exuberance or pushy selling. Sophisticated. Slightly aloof.
olive green/yellow	Artsy, but pushing the boundaries a bit; a page trying to get you to notice something by jangling your sensibilities.
salmon/turquoise	Fifties, media-hip, Elvis, fun, music, pastels, California, Florida

Increase your color sensitivity by browsing the Web and looking only at a page's overall color scheme. What words come to mind to describe the mood that's created?

Instant Typography Course

You don't have to be a trained graphic designer to learn how to dress up your Web pages with good font choices. Basically, it boils down to learning some very important distinctions along with some basic rules. Once you have these down, start paying attention to anything that looks like it was professionally designed —magazines, newspapers, professionally-designed Web sites—to see how fonts are handled. As you notice how designers use fonts to achieve effects, you will get lots of ideas concerning ways you can use fonts to enhance your page's message.

There are many types of fonts, but most of them fall into two categories: serif and sans-serif. A serif font has those little finishing strokes (called serifs) at the end of the character's lines, while a sans-serif font does not. (Sans serif means "without serifs.")

Now that you know the basic distinction between serif and sans-serif, Table 6.2 presents a few things you should know about using these two basic font types.

Table 6.2 Using serif and sans-serif fonts

Font type	Best use
serif fonts	*Body type* (the type that's used for the body paragraphs of your document). Serif fonts are easy to read, but they look like schoolbook text.

sans-serif	*Display type* (the type that's used for headings). Sans-serif fonts are more noticeable and often have funky designs.

From what you just learned, you'll probably realize why professional graphic designers hate the way the Web looks. Most browsers display almost all of the text, body type and display type alike, using a serif font such as Times Roman. This gives a formal, academic, overly serious look to these pages.

Here's a quick, general rule for most documents: Use a sans-serif font for display type (headings) and use a serif font for the body text. However, consider using a sans-serif font for the whole document, especially if the text is relatively brief (remember, sans-serif fonts are harder to read) and you want to convey a clean, modern image.

Getting the Background You Need

Are you ready to create your document's overall presentation formats? You can get started by examining how to choose background colors and images with Cascading Style Sheets (CSS).

Background Options

Basically, you have two choices:

- **Background color** Background colors can do wonderful things for your document, as long as you give some thought to how they will look with the other colors you've used. You will need to devote some thought to default text colors so that everything works harmoniously.
- **Background image** Background images add depth and beauty to your document, but they can make your document difficult to read. If you're planning to use a background image, make sure it is something that won't interfere with your text's legibility. And again, you will need to think about text color so that the overall color scheme works harmoniously.

Browsers don't display background images and background colors at the same time. You can define both for a given document, but the background image takes precedence. In case the browser cannot load the background image for some reason, it displays the background color. If you use a background image, you should also define a background color, just in case the graphic isn't available for one reason or another.

Adding a Background Color

To add a background color to your document, use the CSS background-color property to define the BODY element. (You can actually use this property for any element, but we're working on document-wide issues in this chapter.)

PROPERTY	background-color
PURPOSE	Specifies the background color of an element.
INHERITED	Yes
VALUES	Color code or mnemonic
DEFAULT	Defined by browser
USED IN	All elements
SUPPORT	MSIE 3.0/Win95: Yes
	MSIE 4.0/Win95: Yes
	NN4.0/Win95: Yes
	MSIE 3.0/Mac OS: No
	MSIE 4.0/Mac OS: Yes
	NN4.0/Mac OS: Yes
EXAMPLE	{ color: #C0C0C0 } or { color: red }
DON'T FORGET	You can specify values using color codes or color mnemonics.

Here is how to add a background color to your document. In the HEAD element (as shown), add the following style definition:

```
<HEAD>
     <STYLE type="text/css">
     BODY {background-color: color}
     </STYLE>
</HEAD>
```

In place of the value "color" in the above example, use any valid way of referring to a color (see Chapter 2), such as a color name (purple) or a color code (#FFF000). Here's a completed example, which creates a black background:

```
<HEAD>
      <STYLE type="text/css">
      BODY {background-color: black}
      </STYLE>
</HEAD>
```

Don't forget that style sheet syntax differs from the rest of your HTML document. To define the properties of an element, you list the properties within curly braces. You type the property name, followed by a colon, a space, and the value. Note that you don't have to put quote marks around the value. Confusing, isn't it? If for some reason your STYLE statements don't work, check to make sure you used the right syntax. Remember, if you want to add more than one property to an element's definition, be sure to use a semicolon to separate them.

Understanding Inheritance

In the background-color property definition, you may have noticed that this property is inherited. What does this mean?

Essentially, *inheritance* means that the property passes its setting down to elements at a lower level. For example, if you choose a background-color for the BODY of your document, all the elements contained within the BODY element will "inherit" the same color.

In Version 4 browsers, inheritance is a bit buggy. Take a look at your document to make sure that contained elements really do inherit the property you defined. If not, you may need to repeat the style within the contained elements. For example, suppose you choose a background-color for BODY, but the BLOCKQUOTE element doesn't inherit it for some reason. To fix the bug, define the same background-color property for BLOCKQUOTE.

Adding a Background Image

Adding a background image to your document is just as easy as adding a back-ground color, but there are many more options. Here's the background-image property definition.

PROPERTY	background-image
PURPOSE	Inserts a graphic in an element's background.
INHERITED	Yes
VALUES	url
DEFAULT	Defined by browser
USED IN	All elements
SUPPORT	MSIE 3.0/Win95: Yes MSIE 4.0/Win95: Yes NN4.0/Win95: Yes MSIE 3.0/Mac OS: No MSIE 4.0/Mac OS: Yes NN4.0/Mac OS: Yes
EXAMPLE	{ background-image: url(picture.gif)}
DON'T FORGET	Note the syntax for including URLs. It differs from the way you include URLs in HTML statements. Use caution with this property as current implementations are very buggy.

Here is the basic STYLE statement for adding a background graphic to the BODY element:

```
<HEAD>
     <STYLE type="text/css">
     BODY {background-image: url(picture.gif)}
     </STYLE>
</HEAD>
```

To specify the URL, you type url, and then enclose the absolute or relative URL within parentheses, as in the example that follows. The syntax is a bit weird, so take special note of this example (which uses a relative URL):

```
background-image: url(sailboat.jpg)
```

Please remember that it is not a very good idea to use an absolute URL to reference a graphic on somebody else's server. This places an additional and unexpected load on the server. What's more, it increases the chance that your image will not appear. What if the server goes down?

To Tile or Not to Tile, That Is the Question

By default, most browsers tile the background image. They make enough copies of it to completely fill the space within the window. Tiling is actually a wonderful thing because it enables you to use a rather small GIF or JPEG graphic, which doesn't take very long to download. Nevertheless, the graphic fully covers the whole background of the window. What's more, if the user enlarges the window, the browser fills in the additional space with more copies of the graphic.

To control background tiling, use the background-repeat property. Here's the property definition.

PROPERTY	background-repeat
PURPOSE	Specifies how a background image is repeated.
INHERITED	Yes
VALUES	repeat, repeat-x, repeat-y, or no-repeat. *Repeat* repeats the image both horizontally and vertically. *Repeat-x* repeats the image horizontally, while *repeat-y* repeats the image vertically.
DEFAULT	repeat
USED IN	All elements
SUPPORT	MSIE 3.0/Win95: No MSIE 4.0/Win95: Yes NN4.0/Win95: Yes MSIE 3.0/Mac OS: No MSIE 4.0/Mac OS: Yes NN4.0/Mac OS: Yes
EXAMPLE	{ background-repeat: repeat-x }
DON'T FORGET	If a browser doesn't recognize this property (but does handle others), you'll get a repeated graphic whether you like it or not.

Do you prefer not having the background image tiled? If so, include the following property and value: background-repeat: no-repeat

Specifying Background Position

If you are going to turn off tiling, you can specify a position for the graphic. To do so, use the background-position property. Here's the property definition:

PROPERTY	background-position
PURPOSE	Specifies the position of the background graphic within an element.
INHERITED	Yes
VALUES	You can specify the position in several different ways. The easiest way uses keywords (top left, top center, right top, left center, center, right center, bottom left, bottom center, and bottom right). You can also type two percentages to express the distance from the left and the distance from the top, respectively; 50% 100% is the same as bottom center. You can also type measurements for an absolute position from the left and top, respectively (see the examples).
DEFAULT	Defined by browser
USED IN	All elements
SUPPORT	MSIE 3.0/Win95: **No** MSIE 4.0/Win95: Yes NN4.0/Win95: **No** MSIE 3.0/Mac OS: **No** MSIE 4.0/Mac OS: **No** NN4.0/Mac OS: **No**
EXAMPLE	{ background-position: top center } { background-position: 50% 0% } { background position: 48pt 60pt }
DON'T FORGET	This property is not supported by Netscape Navigator 4.

Here is an example. I'm going to omit the HEAD elements for now; just remember that the STYLE element belongs within the HEAD of your document.

```
<STYLE type="text/css">
      BODY {background-image:   URL(sailboat.gif);
      background-position: center center)}
</STYLE>
```

Note that the duplication of "center" is not an error. The syntax of the background-position property looks like this:

```
background-position: x y
```

Here you substitute something for x to specify the horizontal position, and something for y to specify the vertical position. See the following examples:

```
background-position: left center
background-position: right top
background-position: center bottom
```

Table 6.3 lists the horizontal and vertical background position values you can use.

Table 6.3 Background image horizontal and vertical position values

Value	Aligns the image to the:
left	Left of the containing element
right	Right of the containing element
center	Horizontal center of the containing element
top	Top of the containing element
bottom	Bottom of the containing element
center	Vertical center of the containing element

Making the Background Image Stay Put

With Version 2.0 of Microsoft Internet Explorer, Microsoft introduced an attribute called a *watermark*. This attribute enabled Web authors to "anchor" a background image so that it stayed put when users scrolled. The way Microsoft handled this attribute is deprecated—and worse, unsupported by any other browser besides Internet Explorer, but a revised version of the idea has found its way into style sheets.

To make a background graphic not scroll with the text, use the background-attachment property. Here's the background-attachment property definition.

PROPERTY	background-attachment
PURPOSE	Determines whether the background image scrolls with the content or remains fixed.
INHERITED	Yes
VALUES	scroll or fixed
DEFAULT	Defined by browser
USED IN	All elements
SUPPORT	MSIE 3.0/Win95: No MSIE 4.0/Win95: Yes NN4.0/Win95: No MSIE 3.0/Mac OS: No MSIE 4.0/Mac OS: Yes NN4.0/Mac OS: **No**
EXAMPLE	{ background-attachment: fixed }
DON'T FORGET	This property is not widely supported, but it isn't risky to use. If a browser doesn't recognize it, it will scroll the image with the text. This property is not supported by Netscape Navigator 4.

Here is an example of how this property and the "fixed" value (no scrolling) look in a complete background image statement:

```
<STYLE type="text/css">
     BODY {background-image: URL(sailboat.gif);
     background-repeat: fixed)}
</STYLE>
```

In this chapter, you are using the properties explored in this section to define a background image for the BODY element, but you can also use these for any other element that functions as a container. That includes text paragraphs, tables (and components of tables), and many more. With this much freedom, you could go completely wild, and have different images in back of paragraphs, lists, table cells, etc., creating a completely illegible, horrifying mess. What fun!

Background Tips for Would-be Graphic Artists

Can you see yourself doing computer graphics? You don't have to be artistic to pull off some amazing things. All it takes is a great graphics program, such as the shareware Paint Shop Pro or the commercial program Adobe PhotoShop. Both of these programs enable you to process images in a number of interesting ways, and some of them are especially useful for background graphics. The following table lists some of the effects you can use.

Table 6.4 Special graphics effects

Effect	Explanation
tessellation	A tesselated image is adjusted so that the image tiles seamlessly in all directions. You can use this process to make background graphics.
embossing	An embossed image is one that has been transformed from a full-color image into a gray-scale image with apparent raised areas. The effect works for text, too. For example, you can take your company's name, emboss it, fade it a bit, and then rotate it at an angle. When tiled, the image repeats all across the page.
transparency	If you are creating a GIF graphic, you can modify it so that one of the colors in the graphic is set to be transparent. The color you've marked to be transparent doesn't show up in the browser; instead, you see the background color. This is a great way to make an image apparently "float" over a colored page background. You can create transparent GIFs with lots of graphics programs.

interlacing   Here is another great GIF capability. If you save a GIF graphic using the interlacing option, the image downloads gradually, rather than line-by-line; it's as if the image is out of focus initially, and then takes on additional detail.

Fun with Fonts (Sort Of...)

One thing is certain: The Web needs fonts, and they're long overdue. Desktop publishing would still be a hobbyist's pastime if you could only create newsletters with the Courier (typewriter) font. Unfortunately, there are two huge, interconnected problems concerning fonts on the Web:

- **Intellectual property concerns**   Font designers are not particularly enthusiastic about giving their design work away for free. You can't just take a font from your computer, put it on your server, and let people download it with your page, unless you really want to get into big trouble. Of course, there are some public domain fonts where this wouldn't be a concern.
- **Lack of a downloading mechanism** Even if you could provide a public-domain font with your page, there is no single, standard method for downloading the font along with your page. Several schemes have been proposed, but at this writing no clear standard has yet emerged. At this writing, the CSS Level 2 proposal is still under discussion. We will examine this later.

Since Netscape unilaterally introduced the now-deprecated BASEFONT and FONT elements with their *face* (typeface) attribute, it has been possible to define fonts for Web documents. What's more, Microsoft Internet Explorer supports this element, so you can define fonts with the knowledge that both of the major browsers support it. But that does not necessarily mean that the user will see the fonts on your page. In order for the fonts to appear, they have to be installed and present on the user's system.

Unfortunately, there are no "universal" fonts that are installed on everyone's system. To be sure, most Windows users have the standard Microsoft TrueType fonts, such as Arial and Times New Roman. On Macintosh systems, though, the closest fonts to these are called Helvetica and Times Roman. Even the lowly, monospace Courier is called New Courier on some systems. You can't win this one.

If this sounds grim, take heart. With CSS Level 1, you can use some tricks to get around some of the current shortcomings of fonts on the Web: You can use generic font names, and you can also supply a list of fonts to try, to see whether any of them are present on the user's system. Coming soon is downloadable font support from the newly-approved CSS Level 2 specification, which is not widely implemented (yet)—but it will be. This section shows you how to use the Level 1 tricks, which almost always generate something other than the hum-drum default fonts.

The Generic Route

When you specify a generic font name (Table 6.5), the browser looks for an installed font that has the font's characteristics. For example, suppose you format an element with the sans-serif generic font. If somebody is browsing your page using a Mac, she will see Helvetica. If, instead, she's using Windows 95, she will see Arial.

Table 6.5 Generic font names

Generic font name	Looks like
cursive	Script
fantasy	Comic
monospace	Courier
sans-serif	Helvetica or arial
serif	Times Roman

The only downside here is that you can't get too specific about which font you would like the browser to use, and that takes a lot of the fun and artistry out of designing your document using fonts. Still, this is a lot better than the default font situation, in which browsers display documents using the same, old, boring default fonts.

The "Take Your Pick" Route

There is another way to solve the font problem: Give the browser a list of font options so that it can check to see whether any of them are installed on the user's system. You can use the font-family property to do this.

Here's the font-family property definition:

PROPERTY	font-family
PURPOSE	Defines font typeface and alternates (in order of preference)
INHERITED	Yes
VALUES	Font names or font family names, in a comma-separated list (in order of preference). Font family names: serif, sans-serif, cursive, fantasy, monospace
DEFAULT	Determined by browser
USED IN	All elements
SUPPORT	MSIE 3.0/Win95: Yes MSIE 4.0/Win95: Yes NN4.0/Win95: Yes MSIE 3.0/Mac OS: Yes MSIE 4.0/Mac OS: Yes NN4.0/Mac OS: Yes
EXAMPLE	{ font-family: Helvetica, Arial, "sans-serif" }
DON'T FORGET	If the font name requires two or more words (such as Times Roman), place the name in quotes.

See the following example of the font-family property applied to a BODY style definition. This defines a family of related system fonts (fonts installed on the user's system), any one of which can be used for the *base font* of the document (the font that is supposed to be used unless there is some specific instruction to the contrary):

```
<STYLE type="text/css">
     BODY {font-family: font-family: Helvetica,
     Arial, "Avant Garde"}
</STYLE>
```

In this property definition, you see a list of fonts (two of them), separated by commas. It tells the browser to look for the Helvetica font. If that's not found, the browser looks for the Arial font. If Arial is not found, the browser looks for Avant Garde. Only if the last font isn't found does the browser fall back on the default font.

The Best of Both Worlds

To increase the likelihood that users will actually see something like the fonts you would like them to see, you can combine both of these methods, as shown in the following example:

```
<STYLE type="text/css">
      BODY {font-family: Helvetica, Arial, "Avant
      Garde",  sans-serif}
</STYLE>
```

If none of the named fonts are found, the browser uses whatever font happens to be currently registered in the user's font registration database as a sans-serif font. Only if there is no such font does the browser fall back on the default font. This is a good way to make sure that a lot of users—not all, but a lot—will see something like the font design you intended.

Choosing a Font Size

You can choose a font size that will affect all the text in your Web page, save where you have selected some text to have a different size. Most browsers use a 12-pt. font size by default, so there's no need to do this unless you want to use a smaller or larger font size throughout your document for some reason.

To specify font size, you need to use one of the measurement formats shown in Table 6.6. You add font size specifications with the font size property. Here's the property definition:

PROPERTY	font-size
PURPOSE	Defines font size.
INHERITED	Yes
VALUES	Absolute sizes (xx-small, x-small, small, medium, large, x-large, or xx-large); relative sizes (larger or smaller), font size measurement in pts, in, cm, px, or em), or percentage in relation to parent element.
DEFAULT	Medium
USED IN	All elements
SUPPORT	MSIE 3.0/Win95: Yes MSIE 4.0/Win95: Yes NN4.0/Win95: Yes

	MSIE 3.0/Mac OS: Yes
	MSIE 4.0/Mac OS: Yes
	NN4.0/Mac OS: Yes
EXAMPLE	{ font-size: 14pt }
TIP	Because of inconsistent browser support, avoid using em, ex, or percentage measurements.

Here is an example of a BODY style definition that sets the default font size for the whole document:

```
<STYLE type="text/css">
     BODY {font-size: 14pt}
</STYLE>
```

Table 6.6 Specifying font size (recommended formats only)

Measurement	Description	Example
pt	Printer's points	14pt
in	Inches	.125in
cm	Centimeters	2cm

Specifying Text Colors

You can define colors for the types of text shown in Table 6.7.

Table 6.7 Text types

Text type	Description
document text	Affects all the text in the body of your document, unless you change this for a specific element or a specific portion of the text in your document.
link text	Affects hyperlink text. This should be brighter or noticeably different from the body text.
visited link text	Affects visited links, those that the user has visited recently. (Browsers vary in how they handle

this, and users can also change the settings for how long the browser stores a record about which links have been visited.) This should probably be darker than the link text.

active link text   Affects the color of the text that the user is in the midst of clicking. Normally, this should be brighter than the link text color.

To define body text color, you use the font-color property. Here's the element definition:

PROPERTY	font-color
PURPOSE	Specifies text color
INHERITED	Yes
VALUES	Color code or mnemonic
DEFAULT	Determined by browser
USED IN	All elements
SUPPORT	MSIE 3.0/Win95: Yes
	MSIE 4.0/Win95: Yes
	NN4.0/Win95: Yes
	MSIE 3.0/Mac OS: Yes
	MSIE 4.0/Mac OS: Yes
	NN4.0/Mac OS: Yes
EXAMPLE	{ font-color: #C0C0C0 }
TIP	You can use font color mnemonics too (such as black, red, silver, navy).

You can use the font-color property to create a BODY element definition such as the following:

```
<STYLE type="text/css">
      BODY {color: blue}
</STYLE>
```

You can use a color name, as in the above example, or a color code (such as #000FFF).

To define unvisited link, visited link, and active link colors, you need to create STYLE definitions for the A (hyperlink) element, as in the following example:

```
<STYLE type="text/css">
      A:link {color: red)
      A:visited {color: maroon}
      A:active {color: yellow}
</STYLE>
```

As in the previous example, you can use color codes instead of color names, if you wish.

Downloading Fonts with CSS Level 2

The just-released Cascading Style Sheets Level 2 specification provides much better support for fonts, including font downloading. However, browsers don't yet support most CSS Level 2 properties. With those caveats in mind, this section tells you about a third way to specify fonts in your document—a way (finally) that makes sure *everyone* can see the fonts you've chosen.

The key lies in the CSS Level 2 property called @font-face (the @ sign tells the browser it's supposed to import some data). Here's the @font-face property definition:

PROPERTY	@font-face
PURPOSE	Indicates name and location of a downloadable font.
INHERITED	No
VALUES	Include a font-family descriptor and the url of the downloadable file, as shown in the example below.
DEFAULT	Determined by browser
USED IN	All elements
SUPPORT	Microsoft Internet Explorer Version 4

EXAMPLE	@font-face {
	  font-family: Verdana;
	  src: url (http://www.fictitious.org/verdana.eot)
	  }

TIP	This property is not expected to come into widespread use until Version 5 browsers appear.

In order to use this element, you need to be able to specify the location of a font definition file. Just exactly how these files will be created, what they will contain, and how this whole thing will work is still under discussion at this writing.

Grouping Properties for Quick Coding

To help you choose background and font properties quickly, you can use the background property and the font property. These properties enable you to group properties in a single statement by listing them, separated by spaces. Here is an example:

```
<STYLE type="text/css">
     BODY  {      background: url(picture.gif) blue
                  no-repeat fixed; font: sans-serif
                  12pt

           }
```

The background property definition follows:

PROPERTY	background
PURPOSE	Provides a shorthand method for grouping background. properties.
INHERITED	Yes
VALUES	You can specify any of the values used for background-color, background-image, background-repeat, background-attachment, or background-position.
DEFAULT	Not defined
USED IN	All elements
SUPPORT	MSIE 3.0/Win95: Yes MSIE 4.0/Win95: Yes NN4.0/Win95: Yes MSIE 3.0/Mac OS: Yes MSIE 4.0/Mac OS: Yes NN4.0/Mac OS: Yes
EXAMPLE	{ background: url(picture.gif) repeat fixed }
TIP	This is a handy way to set background properties without a lot of typing.

The font property definition appears below:

PROPERTY	font
PURPOSE	Provides a shorthand method for indicating two or more font properties.
INHERITED	Yes
VALUES	List font properties in a list.
DEFAULT	Not defined
USED IN	All elements
SUPPORT	MSIE 3.0/Win95: Yes
	MSIE 4.0/Win95: Yes
	NN4.0/Win95: Yes
	MSIE 3.0/Mac OS: Yes
	MSIE 4.0/Mac OS: Yes
	NN4.0/Mac OS: Yes
EXAMPLE	{ font: 14pt Arial bold}
TIP	If the font name requires two or more words (such as Times Roman), place the name in quotes.

Choosing Document-wide Presentation Formats for Non-CSS Browsers

You can do this in two ways: the deprecated way and the HTML 4 way. "Deprecated" sounds bad, but it may be the way to go if you want everyone to see your page. As you know, the deprecated elements and attributes are still supported in the transitional flavor of HTML 4. This section examines the deprecated BODY attributes that enable you to choose a document color scheme, as well as the BASEFONT element that enables you to choose a default font for your document.

Deprecated BODY Attributes

HTML 4.0 expressly deprecates (but continues to support, by means of the transitional flavor) the many extensions made to the BODY element concerning background graphics and background colors.

For example, in previous versions of HTML, you created background graphics and colors by using BODY tags such as the following:

```
<BODY background="parchment.gif" bgcolor= "white">
```

Should you use the deprecated attributes, such as background? No, if you would like to adhere to the basic premise of HTML 4.0, which is that HTML has become so cluttered with presentation (formatting) extensions that it can't be handled very easily by text-only browsers, speech synthesizers, and other programs that could greatly extend the accessibility of the Web. But be aware that somebody browsing with a non-CSS capable browser will not be able to see your color choices. Instead, they'll see something very basic.

If you are worried that somebody won't see your color scheme because they are using an older browser that doesn't support style sheets, consider creating an alternative version of your site for these users.

Table 6.8 Deprecated attributes of the BODY element

Attribute	Specifies
background= "url"	Background graphic for document
bgcolor= "color"	Background color for document
text= "color"	Document text color
link= "color"	Hyperlink text color
vlink= "color"	Visited hyperlink text color
alink= "color"	Active hyperlink text color

Here is an example of a BODY element that defines document colors (black background, white text, and silver links):

```
<BODY bgcolor = "black" text = "white" link = "sil-
ver" vlink = "silver" alink = "silver">
```

Choosing Fonts for Your Document

Other deprecated elements enable you to specify document fonts. See the element definition for the deprecated BASEFONT element that follows.

ELEMENT	BASEFONT (Deprecated)
PURPOSE	Sets the default font, font size, and color for the entire document.
TYPE	Inline
NESTED WITHIN	BODY
START TAG	Required
END TAG	Forbidden
CONTENT	Empty
ATTRIBUTES	id = "name" (optional) size = "CDATA" (optional) color = "color" (optional) face = "CDATA" (optional)
EXAMPLE	<BASEFONT face = "Helvetica" color = "silver" size="4">
TIP	You can change the font locally using the FONT element.

Using an External Style Sheet

If you are creating an entire site that will have many pages sharing the same, overall design, consider placing your style sheet in its own, separate document. You can then place a link to this document in each of the documents in your site.

The external style sheet advantage lies in their power to affect many documents simultaneously. By making just one small change to the master style sheet, you can instantly make changes to every HTML document that links to this style sheet.

Here's how to do this. First, create a plain (ASCII) text document that contains the STYLE definitions that you want to use. Save this file using the extension .css (for example, style.css), and place this document in the same directory that contains the documents you would like to format with this style sheet.

Next, place the following LINK element within the HEAD element of each document that you want to format:

```
<LINK href="style.css"  rel="stylesheet">
```
If you would prefer, you can write this link using an absolute URL, such as the one in the following example:

```
<LINK href="http://www.myserver.org/stylesheets/
style.css" rel = "stylesheet">
```

That's all you have to do! Now you have one, central style sheet, which you can tweak until you get it just right. And every HTML page that contains this LINK statement will automatically reflect the changes you've made.

By the way, just because you have created an external style sheet doesn't rule out adding STYLE definitions within a document. And here, there is an important precedence rule: Embedded STYLE definitions (the ones placed within a document) take precedence over definitions in an externally-linked stylesheet. For example, suppose your external style sheet formats the base font using sans-serif type. You want to use all the other styles in that style sheet, but you want to change the base font. You can do so by linking to the external style sheet using the LINK element, as just explained, and by placing a very simple STYLE definition within your document:

```
<STYLE type = "text/css">
      BODY {font-family: serif}
</STYLE>
```

When embedded in your document, this STYLE definition overrides the one in the external style sheet. Since it's the only defined element, though, it does not affect all the other styles defined in the external style sheet. Incidentally, this is (partly) what the "cascading" means in Cascading Style Sheets; there are rules of precedence, which indicate the priority of style sheet documents in a "cascade" of documents.

Summary

To define document-wide presentation styles for your document, define the BODY element using the CSS background and font properties introduced in this chapter. (You can use these properties for other elements, too.) If you would like to create a version of your page that looks right when viewed with browsers that cannot display CSS, you can use the deprecated BODY element attributes and the BASEFONT element.

Now that you have defined your document's overall presentation styles, build the body of your document by using block elements. You learn how in the next chapter. Do you want to add hyperlinks? You'll find a full exploration in Chapter 10. If you would like to add graphics into your document, find out how in Chapter 16.

7

Developing Your Document's BODY

In this chapter, you will learn the following skills:

- Understanding inheritance at the block element level
- Assigning classes and ids to block elements
- Using styles to format block elements
- Inserting extended quotations
- Inserting horizontal lines
- Placing rules (borders) around block elements
- Grouping block elements for formatting purposes with DIV

This chapter is dedicated to developing your BODY. No, we're not talking about spending an hour on an exercise machine. What is covered in this chapter is a quick survey of the elements and attributes you'll use most frequently as you create a layout for the BODY of your document. Along the way, you will learn some classy things about CSS style sheet formatting, and further your training in the HTML 4 way.

If you've worked with previous versions of HTML, this chapter should be something of an eye-opener. It is completely different from similar chapters in other HTML books—at least, the ones that don't use the HTML 4.0 way. In place of the jungle of elements thrown together to the point that they can mimic presentation formatting, this chapter shows you how to write elegant, clean HTML 4.0 code within the body of your document. This code, free from extraneous clutter, can be easily read by speech synthesizers, text-only browsers, and programs designed for the use of the visually impaired. Instead of trying to format with HTML, you will learn how to use style-sheet formatting to control the presentation of your document.

If this sounds like some kind of punishment, you're missing the point. With Cascading Style Sheets, you can achieve a degree of formatting control in the body of your document that is just totally unprecedented in HTML. In this chapter, I'll show you how you can come very close to the document layout control that is characteristic of the best desktop publishing programs. Read on, and have fun!

The Stylish Approach

In Chapter 3, you learned the basics of formatting with style sheets. You included a STYLE element within the HEAD of your document (or, as you learned in the last chapter, a separate file). Also, you learned that you can specify formatting throughout your entire document by assigning properties to a specific element, such as H1 (first-level heading). For example, you learned how to define H1 so that, whenever you use it in your document, it appears with a distinctive color and font.

Inheritance at the Block Element Level

The previous chapter introduced the concept of *inheritance*, and pointed out that the styles you define in the BODY element are passed down to elements contained within BODY. Let's look more closely at how inheritance works.

There is a pecking order here: Some elements are inherently "bigger" than others. Block elements, for example, can contain inline elements. For example, P can contain B (bold) and I (italics). The BODY element is a large container. It contains all the elements, inline and block, that you can use in the BODY of the document. If you assign a property to the BODY element (such as font-family), it affects all the elements that are contained within the BODY (unless you specifically and deliberately redefine the properties of these elements.) In the previous chapter, you chose a color scheme for your document by defining STYLE properties for the BODY element.

So what's the big deal with this? Simple: A bigger element passes its properties down to the elements it contains. In other words, contained elements inherit their container's properties (unless you redefine the contained elements). This works at the block element level, too. A containing element passes all its properties to the elements contained therein.

An Example of Inheritance at the Block Level

Here's an example to clarify how this works. Suppose you have created a STYLE element that defines the P element in the following way:

```
<STYLE type="text/css">
     P {color: purple}
</STYLE>
```

This STYLE definition tells the browser to display all the P elements (text paragraphs) with the color purple. Now suppose, in your document, you include an inline element within a P element, as in the following example:

```
<P>This is a paragraph of text. <B>Here's some bold-
face text within the paragraph of text.</B> And
here's more text. And now, for the stunning climax
of this paragraph!</P>
```

In the above example, does the text within the B (bold) element lose the color purple? No, it does not. That's because the B element inherits the properties of its container element (which is P).

And now for an example of where inheritance doesn't work: suppose you have defined P to display using the color purple, but you include a different block element (Q) in your document, as in the following example:

```
<Q>You haven't learned about this element yet, but
it's used for creating an indented quotation. Any-
way, it's a block-level element.</Q>
```

This element doesn't appear in purple. Because there's no STYLE definition for this element, the browser uses the implied (default) color, black. (If you defined a font color for the BODY element, which contains both Q and P, then the Q text would inherit the BODY element's text color properties. See?)

Is there an easy-to-remember general rule here? There certainly is a rule. Block elements can contain inline elements. Block elements cannot contain other block elements. As you will see later in this chapter, though, there's a way to create a special container—a really big cereal box—that is enormous enough to contain two or more block elements. You do this using the DIV element, but we'll get back to that.

Go to the Head of the CLASS

When you assign properties to an element in a style sheet, you tell the browser how you want the element to appear throughout your document. That's great, but it's a little constraining. For example, what if you want to use more than one paragraph style? In a lot of books, for example, the first paragraph under a heading doesn't have a first-line indent, but subsequent paragraphs do. Can you do that with style sheets? You can, and as this section explains, it is really easy.

The key lies in the class attribute, which you can assign to just about every HTML element. The class attribute enables you to differentiate between two or more different versions of the same element, and to give each of them separate properties.

Here's an example. Suppose you want two kinds of text paragraphs:

- **Non-indented paragraph** This paragraph is used to begin a section, right after an H element (heading). It doesn't have a first-line indent.
- **Indented paragraph** This paragraph comes after the non-indented paragraph, and it's used for all the subsequent paragraphs in the section. It has a first-line indent.

When you create your STYLE definition, you use the class attribute to name the two different versions of your text paragraphs, as illustrated in the following example:

```
<STYLE type="text/css">
     P.no-indent {text-align: justify)
     P.indent    {text-align: justify; text-indent:
                  0.5in}
</STYLE>
```

Note the two different classes of the P element: P.no-indent and P.indent. (To define a class, you type the element name, followed by a period, and a class name. Don't use spaces and make sure the class name is all one word.)

In your document, you can now use these special versions of the P element, as in the following example:

```
<P class="no-indent">This paragraph doesn't have a
first line indent.</P>

<P class="indent">This paragraph does have a first-
line indent.</P>
```

What happens if you use the P tag without specifying the class attribute? You don't get either style. If you are using classes and your document doesn't look the way you expected, check to see whether you included the class attribute everywhere you used the element in question.

Please Show Your ID

What if you want to format just one oddball paragraph a certain way? You can use the id attribute. This attribute enables you to give a distinctive name to a particular instance of an element. Here's an example of an element that has been given a distinctive ID:

```
<P id="weird">This  text will appear with a really
ugly font and a really loud color.</P>
```

And here's the STYLE definition:

```
<STYLE type="text/css">
      P.weird {text-color: fuschia; font-family:
      Gothic; font-size: 44pt}
</STYLE>
```

Getting Control of Block Element Layout

Armed with the STYLE element and what you've learned so far, you know that you can have a lot of control over any block element's appearance. The following sections introduce the most useful properties for controlling the appearance of any block element, including the P element.

Text Alignment

To align text (left, center, right, or justified), use the text-align attribute. Here's the property definition:

PROPERTY	text-align
PURPOSE	Controls horizontal alignment of text.
INHERITED	Yes
VALUES	Left, center, right, or justify
DEFAULT	Left
USED IN	Block-level elements
SUPPORT	MSIE 3.0/Win95: Yes
	MSIE 4.0/Win95: Yes
	NN4.0/Win95: Yes
	MSIE 3.0/Mac OS: Yes
	MSIE 4.0/Mac OS: Yes
	NN4.0/Mac OS: Yes
EXAMPLE	P { text-align: justify }
TIP	This property is well supported.

Text Color

To color all the characters within an element, define the element using the color property. The property definition follows:

PROPERTY	color
PURPOSE	Specifies the foreground color of an element.
INHERITED	Yes
VALUES	Color code or mnemonic

DEFAULT	Defined by browser
USED IN	All elements
SUPPORT	MSIE 3.0/Win95: Yes
	MSIE 4.0/Win95: Yes
	NN4.0/Win95: Yes
	MSIE 3.0/Mac OS: Yes
	MSIE 4.0/Mac OS: Yes
	NN4.0/Mac OS: Yes
EXAMPLE	{ color: #C0C0C0 } or { color: red }
TIP	You can specify values using color codes or color mnemonics

Text Indentation (First Line)

Document designers sometimes like to indent the first line of each paragraph of text. With CSS, you can do this, too. You use the text-indent property.

Here is the property definition:

PROPERTY	text-indent
PURPOSE	Indents the first line of text.
INHERITED	Yes
VALUES	Any valid length or a percentage of the element's width
DEFAULT	0
USED IN	Block-level elements
SUPPORT	MSIE 3.0/Win95: Yes
	MSIE 4.0/Win95: Yes
	NN4.0/Win95: Yes
	MSIE 3.0/Mac OS: Yes
	MSIE 4.0/Mac OS: Yes
	NN4.0/Mac OS: Yes
EXAMPLE	P.indent { text-indent: 0.5in }
TIP	This property is well supported.

Line Spacing

To control line spacing, use the line height property, defined as follows:

PROPERTY	line-height
PURPOSE	Specifies the height (the distance between the baselines) of each line of text in an element.
INHERITED	No
VALUES	Specify a number to multiply with the current font height, a length, or a percentage of the current font size, or auto (same as font size).
DEFAULT	Auto
USED IN	Replaced and block-level elements
SUPPORT	MSIE 3.0/Win95: Yes MSIE 4.0/Win95: Yes NN4.0/Win95: Yes MSIE 3.0/Mac OS: Yes MSIE 4.0/Mac OS: Yes NN4.0/Mac OS: Yes
EXAMPLE	P { line-height: 24pt } or P { line-height: 2 }
TIP	If the height is set to auto, the height is determined by the intrinsic height of the element. If you specify a number, you are specifying the number of times to multiply the current line size set by the height of the font (for a 12pt font, "2" gives you 24pt line heights, or double line spacing).

Remember that you can use all of the font styles introduced in the last chapter, including font-family and font-size for any block element. They are not just for the BODY.

Examples of Block Element Formatting

Look at an example of how these properties can be used to format paragraphs. See if you can figure out what this code does.

```
<STYLE type="text/css">
      P {color: blue;
      font-family: Arial, Helvetica, sans-serif;
      font-size: 14pt;
      line-height: 28pt;
      text-indent: 0.5in;
      text-align: justify
      }
</STYLE>
```

The above STYLE definition creates a justified body text paragraph with a blue sans-serif font, double spacing (14-point type with a 28-pt line height), and a half-inch first-line indent.

Here's another one:

```
<STYLE type="text/css">
P       {text-indent: 0.5in;
         text-align: justify}
</STYLE>
```

The above creates a justified body text paragraph with single line spacing. All the lines (not just the first) are indented 0.5" from the left margin.

A Quote By Any Other Name Is Still a QUOTE

HTML 4.0 gives you two elements for quoting text: BLOCKQUOTE and the new Q element. In brief, BLOCKQUOTE is a block element, while Q is an inline element. I'll discuss BLOCKQUOTE here, and get to Q later, when inline elements are presented. Here is the BLOCKQUOTE element definition:

ELEMENT	BLOCKQUOTE
PURPOSE	Indents an extended quotation.
TYPE	Block
NESTED WITHIN	BODY element
START TAG	Required
END TAG	Required
CONTENT	Text
ATTRIBUTES	core attributes (id, class, style, title)

	language attributes (lang, dir) cite = "url" (optional)
EXAMPLE	<BLOCKQUOTE>Here's a long quotation.</BLOCK- QUOTE>
TIP	You can use the Q element for inline quotations.

Besides the standard id, class, style, title, lang, and dir attributes, which you will find in just about every element, there's only one that is of special interest here: cite. You can use this to include the url of the source document, if you wish. But browsers don't do anything with this information—yet.

Don't Use BLOCKQUOTE to Indent Ordinary Text, Please

Most browsers display BLOCKQUOTE text by indenting all of the lines about a half-inch from the left margin. For this reason, many Web authors use the BLOCKQUOTE element for indenting text for any reason, not just quoting text.

But this is deprecated in HTML 4.0. If you want to create a block element in which all the lines are indented from the left margin (or the right margin), create a STYLE definition, and use the margin-left or margin-right properties (you'll learn more about these elements in Chapter 13), as in the following example:

```
<STYLE type="text/css">
      P {margin-left: 1in; margin-right: 1in}
</STYLE>
```

The above STYLE definition creates a paragraph that is indented one inch from both the left and the right margins.

The BLOCKQUOTE element's cite attribute can be used to specify the source URL of the document being quoted, but no browser that I know of does anything with this.

What About Quotation Marks?

Note that the BLOCKQUOTE element does not automatically insert quotation marks—which is a good thing, actually, since most English style books recommend that quotation marks should be omitted from lengthy, indented quotations. The indentation serves the same purpose as the quotation marks, so they are not necessary.

Making and Breaking Rules (Horizontal Lines)

You can add rules to your document using the HR element. As with many HTML block elements, this one accumulated more than its share of extensions, including attributes that enabled Web authors to specify the width, length, and alignment of the rule. That's all deprecated in HTML 4.0; if you really want to dress up your rule, you do so by defining the HR element's properties in your stylesheet.

Here is the HR element definition:

ELEMENT	HR
PURPOSE	Inserts a horizontal rule.
TYPE	Inline
NESTED WITHIN	Any block element
START TAG	Required
END TAG	Required
CONTENT	Text and inline elements (no block elements permitted)
ATTRIBUTES	**Strict DTD:** core attributes (id, class, style, title) language attributes (lang, dir) **Transitional DTD (deprecated):** align = "(left, center, right)" noshade size = "pixels" width = "pixels"
EXAMPLE	\<P>A paragraph\</P> \<HR> \<P>Another paragraph\</P>
TIP	Use style sheets to assign presentation attributes to rules.

Adding Rules with Style Sheets

A much better way to add rules (lines) to your document involves the several border properties defined by CSS. A great feature of CSS borders is that you can independently place rules on any side of the element: top, right, bottom, and left. You can also independently adjust the size and color of each border.

If you like, you could have a great big thick red rule on top, a little thin black one on the bottom, and nothing on the sides.

To create borders, you can define the border properties independently using separate properties for the top, right, bottom, and left sides. These properties include color and width. You can also define border styles (including dotted and dashed lines).

The easiest way to define borders, though, is to use the border shorthand property, which enables you to specify all the borders at once. You can also use the shorthand property to determine which borders are added, either all four or any combination of individual borders. Begin by examining the properties for individual borders; you will learn how to use the border shorthand property at the end of this section.

Note that Netscape Navigator Version 4 cannot handle individually-defined borders. You have to use the same border color, width, and style for all four borders.

Border Colors

To define the color of borders around an element, you can use the following properties: border-top-color, border-right-color, border-bottom-color, and border-left-color.

The following property definition sums up all four of these.

PROPERTY	border-top-color, border-right-color, border-bottom-color, and border-left-color
PURPOSE	Specifies one of the four border colors individually.
INHERITED	Yes

VALUES	Specify a color code or mnemonic.
DEFAULT	Value of the color property for the current element
USED IN	Replaced and block-level elements
SUPPORT	MSIE 3.0/Win95: No MSIE 4.0/Win95: Yes NN4.0/Win95: No MSIE 3.0/Mac OS: No MSIE 4.0/Mac OS: Yes NN4.0/Mac OS: No
EXAMPLE	{ border-bottom-color: silver }
TIP	You cannot define borders individually with Netscape Navigator 4.

Instead of defining all these border color properties independently, you will find it convenient to use the border-color shorthand property, defined as follows:

PROPERTY	border-color
PURPOSE	Provides a shorthand means of specifying color settings for all borders.
INHERITED	Yes
VALUES	Specify colors for the top, right, bottom, and left borders, in that order. If you specify only one value, it applies to all four sides. If you specify two values, you define the top and bottom. If you specify three values, you define the top, bottom, and sides (left and right), respectively.
DEFAULT	Not defined
USED IN	Replaced and block-level elements
SUPPORT	MSIE 3.0/Win95: Yes MSIE 4.0/Win95: Yes NN4.0/Win95: Yes MSIE 3.0/Mac OS: Yes MSIE 4.0/Mac OS: Yes NN4.0/Mac OS: Yes
EXAMPLE	{ border-color: red }
TIP	If you specify just one value, it applies to all four margins.

In the border-color style, as in other shorthand border styles, you can specify from one to four borders, but you will need to learn how. Table 7.1 sums up the technique used to specify borders, depending on the number of values you type. For example, if you type "border-color: navy white," you've typed two values.

Table 7.1 Specifying borders in border shorthand styles

Number of values	Borders are placed
one	The value applies to all four sides
two	The first value defines the top, while the second value defines the bottom.
three	The first value defines the top, while the second value defines the left and right. The third value defines the bottom.
four	The values apply to the top, right, bottom, and left, respectively.

Border Widths

Just as you can define colors for the four borders independently, so too can you define widths. As with colors, there are separate properties for the width of all four borders, and there is a shorthand border-width property. Let's look at the separate properties first. Here's the element definition for border-top-width, border-right-width, border-bottom-width, and border-left-width.

PROPERTY	border-top-width, border-right-width, border-bottom-width, and border-left-width
PURPOSE	Specifies the width of a specific border.
INHERITED	Yes
VALUES	Specify thin, medium, or thick; or type a length.
DEFAULT	0
USED IN	Replaced and block-level elements
SUPPORT	MSIE 3.0/Win95: No MSIE 4.0/Win95: Yes NN4.0/Win95: No MSIE 3.0/Mac OS: **No**

	MSIE 4.0/Mac OS: Yes
	NN4.0/Mac OS: No
EXAMPLE	{ border-left-width: 0.5in }
TIP	You can use the border-width property to define widths for all four sides at once. This property is not supported by Netscape Navigator 4; you must use the same properties for all four borders.

Here's the property definition for the border-width style, which gives you a shorthand way of defining border widths for all four sides:

PROPERTY	border-width
PURPOSE	Provides a shorthand means of specifying width settings for all borders.
INHERITED	Yes
VALUES	Specify lengths for the top, right, bottom, and left borders, in that order. If you specify only one value, it applies to all four sides. If you specify two values, you define the top and bottom. If you specify three values, you define the top, bottom, and sides (left and right), respectively.
DEFAULT	Not defined
USED IN	Replaced and block-level elements
SUPPORT	MSIE 3.0/Win95: Yes
	MSIE 4.0/Win95: Yes
	NN4.0/Win95: No
	MSIE 3.0/Mac OS: Yes
	MSIE 4.0/Mac OS: Yes
	NN4.0/Mac OS: Yes
EXAMPLE	{ border-width: 1pt }
TIP	If you specify just one value, it applies to all four sides.

Border Styles

In addition to border colors and widths, you can also choose border styles (dotted, dashed, solid, double, groove, ridge, inset, outset). Not all of these styles are supported, even by ostensibly CSS-capable browsers, so use styles other than solid with caution.

As with colors and widths, there are separate styles for the individual borders and a shorthand property that enables you to define them all. Here is the property definition for the border-style-top, border-style-right, border-style-bottom, and border-style-right properties:

PROPERTY	border-style-top, border-style-right, border-style-bottom, and border-style-right
PURPOSE	Specifies the color of the box's bottom border.
INHERITED	Yes
VALUES	none, dotted, dashed, solid, double, groove, ridge, inset, outset
DEFAULT	Value of the color property for the current element
USED IN	Replaced and block-level elements
SUPPORT	MSIE 3.0/Win95: No MSIE 4.0/Win95: Yes NN4.0/Win95: Yes MSIE 3.0/Mac OS: No MSIE 4.0/Mac OS: Yes NN4.0/Mac OS: Yes
EXAMPLE	{ border-bottom-style: dashed }
TIP	You can use the border property to set the border properties for all four sides at once. This property is not supported by Netscape Navigator 4; you must use the same properties for all four borders. Note that neither Netscape Navigator nor Microsoft Internet Explorer support dashed or dotted border styles.

Here's the property definition for the border-style shorthand property:

PROPERTY	border-style
PURPOSE	Provides a shorthand means of specifying color settings for all borders.
INHERITED	Yes
VALUES	Specify styles for the top, right, bottom, and left borders, in that order. If you specify only one value, it applies to all four sides. You can choose from none, dotted, dashed, solid, double, groove, ridge, inset, outset.
DEFAULT	Not defined
USED IN	Replaced and block-level elements
SUPPORT	MSIE 3.0/Win95: Yes MSIE 4.0/Win95: Yes NN4.0/Win95: Yes MSIE 3.0/Mac OS: Yes MSIE 4.0/Mac OS: Yes NN4.0/Mac OS: Yes
EXAMPLE	{ border-style: double}
TIP	If you specify just one value, it applies to all four margins.

Summing It All Up: The Border Shorthand Property

Do you have to write a zillion style specifications to add borders to your elements? Nope. You can use the border shorthand property. Here is the definition.

PROPERTY	border
PURPOSE	Provides a shorthand means of specifying all types of properties for all borders.
INHERITED	Yes
VALUES	Specify any value used in the border color, border style, or border width properties.
DEFAULT	0
USED IN	Replaced and block-level elements
SUPPORT	MSIE 3.0/Win95: No

MSIE 4.0/Win95: Yes
NN4.0/Win95: Yes
MSIE 3.0/Mac OS: No
MSIE 4.0/Mac OS: Yes
NN4.0/Mac OS: Yes

EXAMPLE	{ border: 1pt blue } This places a 1pt blue border around all four sides of the element.
TIP	If you type just one measurement, it applies to all four borders.

If you need to add some padding between your borders and the text they contain, you can. Learn how in Chapter 13.

DIVvying Up Your Document

In this chapter, you have learned about containers and inheritance. The BODY element is a really big container that holds every element you can insert within the body of your document. Block elements such as P or UL contain all the inline elements you can use within them.

You may have noticed, though, that there's a big jump down from the size of the BODY container to the size of the block element containers. For example, the P element cannot contain one of the list elements described in the next chapter (OL or UL or DL). Is there a way to group a bunch of block-level containers, and make a medium-sized container? Yes. That's the function of the DIV element: The DIV element enables you to group a whole bunch of HTML code and set it aside so that it has distinctive formatting—for example, fonts, font sizes, and alignments.

The DIV Element Definition

Here is the element definition:

ELEMENT	DIV
PURPOSE	Provides a means for grouping elements and assigning attributes to the group.
TYPE	Block

NESTED WITHIN	BODY
START TAG	Required
END TAG	Required
CONTENT	Block elements
ATTRIBUTES	core attributes (id, class, style, title) language attributes (lang, dir)
EXAMPLE	<DIV> <H1>Heading</H1> <P>Paragraph 1</P> </DIV>
TIP	Use SPAN to group inline elements. Note that browsers generally place a line break before a DIV element, but impose no other presentation attributes.

This is nothing special, just the usual class, id, and language attributes. Where DIV really shines, however, is in tandem with the class attribute, as the following section explains.

Using DIV with Class

To use the DIV element, you need to create a STYLE definition for it. By itself, the DIV element doesn't add any presentation of any sort to your document; you have to define properties for it. Here, you need to use the class or id attributes to define one or more DIV styles, each with its own, distinctive class name. See the following STYLE entry that defines properties for a DIV you could use for a document's abstract:

```
<STYLE type="text/css">
      DIV.abstract {margin-left: 1in; margin-right:
      1in; text-align: justify; font-size: 10pt}
</STYLE>
```

This defines a DIV class called "abstract," in which both lines are indented one inch from the margin. In addition, this DIV has justified text and 10-point type.

Inserting the DIV Element in Your Document

In your document, use DIV to set off the elements that you would like to take on (via inheritance) the DIV element's properties:

```
<DIV class = "abstract">
      <P>This document  includes the following
      extremely cool stuff:</P>
            <UL>
                  <LI>Cool Thing #1.
                  <LI>Cool Thing #2.
                  <LI>Cool Thing #3.
            </UL>
      <P>This paragraph can be used for the author's
      name and affiliation.</P>
</DIV>
```

Remember, the DIV element contains all the block elements (and inline elements) that you place within it. So this whole block takes on the DIV element's properties, including the indents, justification, and font size.

Specifying Block Formats for Non-CSS-Capable Browsers

To create a version of your document that looks good with non-CSS-capable browsers, you need to use deprecated attributes and elements that are supported by the transitional flavor of HTML 4. You'll soon see why these elements are deprecated; they result in very complex, unreadable, messy HTML, as in the following example:

```
<CENTER><FONT face="Helvetica" size = "+3">Hello
world!</FONT></CENTER>
```

Centering Elements (CENTER)

This element can be used to center a block element or an image.

Here's the definition:

ELEMENT	CENTER
PURPOSE	Centers the text enclosed within the tags.
TYPE	Inline
NESTED WITHIN	Any block element
START TAG	Required
END TAG	Required
CONTENT	Text
ATTRIBUTES	core attributes (id, class, style, title) language attributes (lang, dir)
EXAMPLE	<CENTER>This text is centered.</CENTER>
TIP	Use DIV align = "center" instead, or style sheets.

Even for transitional flavor documents, try to avoid this tag; it is illogical and messy. In its place, you can use DIV or P with the deprecated align attribute, as explained in the following section.

Controlling Text Alignment

To specify text alignment in transitional flavor documents, it's best to use DIV or P with the deprecated align attributes. Valid values are left, center, right, and justify.

The DIV element's align attribute enables you to specify an alignment for all the block elements contained within it:

```
<DIV align="center">
     <H1>Hello World</H1>
     <P>Text of a paragraph.</P>
</DIV>
```

To align a paragraph of text, use the P element's align attribute, which takes the same values:

```
<P align= "center">Hello World</P>
```

Choosing Font Colors and Sizes

To specify font colors and sizes for block elements, you need to use the deprecated FONT element.

ELEMENT	FONT
PURPOSE	Defines presentation styles for fonts.
TYPE	Inline
NESTED WITHIN	Any block element
START TAG	Required
END TAG	Required
CONTENT	text and other inline elements
ATTRIBUTES	core attributes (id, class, style, title)
	language attributes (lang, dir)
	size = "CDATA " (optional)
	color = "color" (optional)
	face = "CDATA" (optional)
EXAMPLE	<FONT face = "Times Roman" size = "5">
TIP	Define font presentation styles with style sheets.

Use the color, size, and face attributes to specify your font choices, as in the following example:

```
<FONT size="+1" color = "silver" face =
"Arial">Here's the formatted text.</FONT>
```

To specify font sizes, you must use the relative size specifications (from the smallest [1] to the largest [7]). You can also change the current font size by adding a plus or minus sign; for example, size = "-1" means "use a font size that is one size smaller than the preceding size."

Summary

This chapter presented the block elements you can use to build your document, and further your training in the HTML 4.0 way. You learned how to specify styles for any block element. Also, you learned how to create special, named versions of block elements, called classes, to handle formatting tasks. You also learned how to use the DIV element to group block elements. By creating DIV classes, the possibilities for laying out your document are virtually endless.

8

Making a List and Checking It Twice

In this chapter, you will learn the following skills:

- Creating a numbered (ordered) list
- Creating complex nested list structures
- Selecting custom bullet types, including image bullets
- Combining bulleted and numbered lists
- Adding non-numbered explanatory text to numbered steps
- Creating a definition list

Effectively-designed documents break up the text on the page. Lists provide an easy way to do this. With HTML 4.0, you can create three types of lists:

- **Ordered (Numbered) Lists** Each item in the list is enumerated. You can choose the beginning number and the number format.

- **Unordered (Bulleted) Lists** Each item in the list is preceded by a bullet. You can choose the bullet type.
- **Definition Lists** Each item in the list is preceded by a term to be defined. The indented items contain definitions of the terms.

Remember, you can use any of the STYLE properties in the previous chapter's Table 7.1 to add visual zing to lists, including distinctive background colors, borders, varied fonts and font sizes—in fact, you can go wild, and create a monster. An HTML 4.0 master uses restraint in all things.

Previous versions of HTML included directory (DIR) and menu (MENU) lists; these are now deprecated, and for good reason. Both were designed to mimic computer directories or menus, and were to include some character formatting (such as monospace type). In practice, though, browsers didn't really support these elements and displayed them as unordered lists instead. Don't use these elements. To show a multi-column directory listing, you can create a table.

Chapter 3 introduced unordered (bulleted) lists. Here, you will learn how to create other types of lists, and how to control list styles with style sheets.

Creating an Ordered List

To create a numbered list, you use the OL element. Nested within this element, you use the LI element to define individual items within the list. You don't have to supply the numbers; the browser does this automatically. Here is how an OL element looks:

```
<OL>
      <LI>This is the first item.
      <LI>This is the second item.
      <LI>This is the third item.
</OL>
```

The browser displays the list like this:

1. This is the first item.
2. This is the second item.
3. This is the third item.

The OL Element Definition

Here's the OL element's definition:

ELEMENT	OL
PURPOSE	Creates a numbered list.
TYPE	Block
NESTED WITHIN	BODY
START TAG	Required
END TAG	Required
CONTENT	LI elements
ATTRIBUTES	**Strict DTD:** core attributes (id, class, style, title) language attributes (lang, dir) **Transitional DTD (deprecated):** type = "(disc, square, or circle)" (optional) start = "number" (optional) value = "number" (optional) compact

EXAMPLE	`<OL>`
	  `<LI>Item 1`
	  `<LI>Item 2`
	`</OL>`

TIP	Define the list style with style sheets.

Understanding Numbering Options

The default ordered list numbers your items using Arabic numbers (1, 2, 3, etc.), starting from 1. However, you can choose other numbering systems, as shown in Table 8.1.

Table 8.1 Numbering types in ordered lists

Type	Description
1	Arabic number (1, 2, 3, etc.)
a	Lowercase letters (a, b, c, etc.)

A	Uppercase letters (A, B, C, etc.)
i	Lowercase Roman numeral (i, ii, ii, etc.)
I	Uppercase Roman numeral (I, II, III, etc.)

Defining the Numbering Type

To define the numbering type in your bulleted list, use the list-style-type property as defined below:

PROPERTY	list-style-type
PURPOSE	Specifies the bullet or number style used in a list.
INHERITED	Yes
VALUES	disc, circle, square, decimal (decimal numbers), lower-roman (lower-case Roman numerals), lower-alpha (lowercase ASCII letters), upper-roman (uppercase Roman numerals), upper-alpha (upper-case ASCII letters), none (no marker)
DEFAULT	None
USED IN	OL, UL
SUPPORT	MSIE 3.0/Win95: No MSIE 4.0/Win95: Yes NN4.0/Win95: Yes MSIE 3.0/Mac OS: No MSIE 4.0/Mac OS: Yes NN4.0/Mac OS: Yes
EXAMPLE	{ list-style-type: I }
DON'T FORGET	Use the display property to set list elements to the list-item value.

To define all the numbered lists in your document with a specified numbering type, define the OL element in the HEAD, as in the following example:

```
<STYLE type="text/css">
      OL {list-style-type: A}
</STYLE>
```

This style defines all the OL lists throughout your document.

Use the class attribute to create two or more different types of ordered lists in the same document, as in the following example:

```
<STYLE type = "text/css">
      OL.arabic {list-style-type: 1}
      OL.roman {list-style-type: I}
</STYLE>
```

To use the OL classes you have defined, you need the class attribute, as shown in the following examples:

```
<OL class = "arabic">
      <LI>Item 1
      <LI>Item 2
      <LI>Item 3
</OL>

<OL class = "roman">
      <LI>Item 1
      <LI>Item 2
      <LI>Item 3
</OL>
```

To define just one instance of a non-default numbering scheme, you might wish to use an inline style, as in the following example:

```
<OL style = "list-style-type: a">
      <LI>Item 1
      <LI>Item 2
      <LI>Item 3
</OL>
```

Nesting Ordered Lists

Birds nest. Lists can, too. When you nest an ordered list, the browser automatically increases the indentation for the nested elements. Here's an example of the code used for nesting an ordered list:

```
<OL>
      <LI>This is the first item.
            <OL>
                  <LI>This is the first sub-item.
                  <LI>This is the second sub-item.
            </OL>
      <LI>This is the second item.
            <OL>
                  <LI>This is the first sub-item.
                  <LI>This is the second sub-item.
            </OL>
      <LI>This is the third item.
            <OL>
                  <LI>This is the first sub-item.
                  <LI>This is the second sub-item.
            </OL>
</OL>
```

Here's how the list looks:

1.   This is the first item.
        1. This is the first sub-item.
        2. This is the second sub-item.
2.   This is the second item.
        1. This is the first sub-item.
        2. This is the second sub-item.
3.   This is the third item.
        1. This is the first sub-item.
        2. This is the second sub-item.

Specifying Bullet Types with Styles

In the UL (bulleted list) definition (see Chapter 3), you will find a deprecated *type* attribute, which enables you to specify what type of bullet you want (disc, square, or circle). To conform to the strict flavor of HTML 4, you need to do this with the list-style-type property. Specify disc, square, or circle, as in the following:

```
<STYLE type="text/css">
     OL {list-style-type: square}
</STYLE>
```

The default is disc, which is what you'll get if you leave this style out of your style sheet.

Using an Image as a Bullet

You can use a small graphic in place of the default bullets. In previous versions of HTML, you had to insert graphic bullets by placing an IMG element at the beginning of every list item, which meant a lot of redundant coding. Thanks to the list-style-image property, you can do this just once for all the bulleted lists in your document. Here's the list-style-image property's definition:

PROPERTY	list-style-image
PURPOSE	Specifies a graphic to be used in place of a bullet in an unordered list.
INHERITED	Yes
VALUES	capitalize, uppercase, lowercase, none
DEFAULT	None
USED IN	Elements with the display property set to list-item
SUPPORT	MSIE 3.0/Win95: No
	MSIE 4.0/Win95: Yes
	NN4.0/Win95: Yes
	MSIE 3.0/Mac OS: No
	MSIE 4.0/Mac OS: Yes
	NN4.0/Mac OS: Yes
EXAMPLE	{ list-style-image: url(picture.gif) }

To add an image to every bulleted item throughout your document, define the
UL element as in this example:

```
<STYLE type="text/css">
      UL {list-style-image: url(hotbullet.gif}
</STYLE>
```

Remember that you can create classes of UL lists, each with its own, unique bullet image, as in these examples:

```
<STYLE type="text/css">
      UL.red-bullet {list-style-image:
      url(redbullet.gif)}
      UL.white-bullet {list-style image:
      url(whitebullet.gif)}
</STYLE>
```

Combining Ordered and Unordered Lists

You can combine ordered and unordered lists. Here's an example of unordered
lists nested within an ordered list:

```
<OL>
      <LI>This is the first item.
          <UL>
              <LI>This is the first sub-item.
              <LI>This is the second sub-item.
          </UL>
      <LI>This is the second item.
          <UL>
              <LI>This is the first sub-item.
              <LI>This is the second sub-item.
          </UL>
</OL>
```

Here's how the list looks with most browsers:

1. This is the first item.
    - This is the first sub-item.
    - This is the second sub-item.
2. This is the second item.
    - This is the first sub-item.
    - This is the second sub-item.

Adding Explanatory Text Within a List

If you would like to add some explanatory text within an ordered or unordered list, you can add a P element. Browsers handle this little-known capability really well; the item is indented to match the indentation of the preceding item.

```
<OL>
      <LI>This is the first item.
            <P>Here's some explanatory text.</P>
      <LI>This is the second item.
            <P>Here's some explanatory text.</P>
      <LI>This is the third item.
            <P>Here's some explanatory text.</P>
</OL>
```

The typical browser displays the list like this:

1.   This is the first item.

        Here's some explanatory text

2.   This is the second item.

        Here's some explanatory text

3.   This is the third item

        Here's some explanatory text

Note that adding the P elements does not affect the numbering.

Creating a Definition List

The last of the list elements in HTML 4.0, a definition list, enables you to type terms and definitions. Typically, the terms are shown flush to the left margin, while the definitions are indented from the left margin and set off by blank lines.

You need three elements to create a definition list: DL (the definition list element), DT (the defined term), and DD (the term's definition). They are discussed in the following sections.

The DL Element

You use the DL element to create the list. Here's the definition:

ELEMENT	DL
PURPOSE	Creates a definition list.
TYPE	Block
NESTED WITHIN	DL element
START TAG	Required
END TAG	Required
CONTENT	Text and inline elements
ATTRIBUTES	core attributes (id, class, style, title) language attributes (lang, dir)

EXAMPLE	`<DL>`
	    `<DT>term 1`
	    `<DD>definition of term 1`
	`</DL>`

TIP	Use DT within a DL list. Use DD for the definition.

The DT Element

You use the DT element to specify defined terms. The element definition follows:

ELEMENT	DT
PURPOSE	In a definition list, identifies a defined term.
TYPE	Block

NESTED WITHIN	DL element
START TAG	Required
END TAG	Optional
CONTENT	Text and inline elements
ATTRIBUTES	core attributes (id, class, style, title) language attributes (lang, dir)
EXAMPLE	<DT>antidisestablishmentarianism</DT>
TIP	Use DT within a DL list. Use DD for the definition.

The DD Element

Use DD to give the term a definition.

ELEMENT	DD
PURPOSE	In a definition list, identifies a definition
TYPE	Block
NESTED WITHIN	DL element
START TAG	Required
END TAG	Optional
CONTENT	Text and inline elements
ATTRIBUTES	core attributes (id, class, style, title) language attributes (lang, dir)
EXAMPLE	<DD>Here is the definition of the term.</DD>
TIP	Use DD within a DL list. For the term, use DT.

An Example

Here is an example of a definition list's HTML code:

```
<DL>
     <DT>This is term #1
          <DD>Here's the definition for term #1.
     <DT>This is term #2
          <DD>Here's the definition for term #2.
</DL>
```

Most browsers display this list as follows:

This is term #1

Here's the definition for term #1.

This is term #2

Here's the definition for term #2.

Controlling Your List's Presentation

As I mentioned earlier, you can use any of the formatting styles previously introduced to add formats to your lists. For example, here is a STYLE definition that formats unordered lists with justified text:

```
<STYLE type="text/css">
     UL {  text-align: justify;
            font-family: Helvetica;
     font-size: 10pt
     color: silver}
</STYLE>
```

Defining List Styles for Non-CSS-Capable Browsers

If you are creating a page using the transitional flavor of HTML 4, you can make use of several deprecated attributes. Some of them do things that style sheets cannot, such as enabling you to specify an initial number in a numbered list that is other than 1. Here's a quick look at the deprecated attributes.

Choosing the List Style

In a bulleted list, you choose the bullet style using the *type* attribute, as in the following example:

```
<UL type = "square">
```

In a numbered list, you use the *type* attribute to specify the numbering style (the default is Arabic):

```
<OL type = "a">
```

Setting the Initial Value

By default, browsers set the beginning number to 1. What happens, though, if you want to continue a numbered list that you started previously, and interrupted with some other element? The numbering is reset automatically to 1. However, you can override this by using the OL element's start attribute. This attribute enables you to specify a different beginning number.

How does this work? Suppose an earlier list got through to Step 4 of a long list of instructions, but you interrupted the list by inserting a text paragraph. To restart the list at 5, you use the start attribute as shown in the following example:

```
<OL start = "5">
    <LI>This is the fifth item.
    <LI>This is the six item.
    <LI>This is the seven item.
</OL>
```

Specifying a Value for List Items

If you would like to manually number the items in a list, you can do so by using the LI element's value attribute. This overrides automatic numbering and imposes the number that you've included as the attribute's value. For example, if you write the following LI element:

```
<LI value = "10">This  is the list item's text.
```

You get:

```
10. This is the list item's text.
```

Note that numbering doesn't necessarily follow consecutively from the number you have used in a value attribute, the way it does with the OL element's start attribute. The next LI item after the above example, for instance, would be numbered 1, unless you continued to override this manually. This is why HTML 4.0

masters say, "Once you start numbering list items manually, forever will it rule your destiny."

Changing the Numbering Scheme in List Items

When you nest an ordered list, the browser uses the default numbering scheme—Arabic numbers—to number each list item. To make the list easier to read, you may wish to change the numbering scheme that is used for the indented items. You can do this by specifying a numbering scheme with the LI element's type attribute.

Here's an example:

```
<OL>
      <LI>This is the first item.
           <OL>
                  <LI value = "a">Sub-item 1
                  <LI value = "a">Sub-item 2
           </OL>
      <LI>This is the second item.
</OL>
```

And here's how this looks:

```
1. This is the first item.
      a.   This is the first sub-item.
      b.   This is the second sub-item.
2. This is the second item.
```

Don't forget to close the nested elements. Be sure to type these lists using indentations, which make the code easier to read; if you've forgotten to type an end tag, you will be able to see this at a glance.

Summary

Bulleted and numbered lists help you break out text on the page and add white space, and add tremendously to your page's readability. Use them whenever you can list or enumerate items. With style sheets, you can give lists distinctive formats and save a great deal of coding effort.

9

Lay It on the Line (Inline Elements)

In this chapter, you will learn the following skills:

- Adding character emphases and other formats to your text
- Adding character formats for technical documents
- Increasing your document's usefulness for users with special needs
- Adding a short quotation with a URL citation
- Marking deletions and insertions in a legal or political document
- Expressing dates and times
- Using character properties in block and inline styles

In the previous two chapters, you learned how to build your document using block elements. But block elements aren't the only game in town. You can also use inline elements, which are particularly useful for overriding the properties of whatever block container they happen to be in.

For example, suppose you are writing a paragraph of text, and you want to include a couple of words in boldface. You can do so by using the <B> element, like this:

```
<B>This text appears  in bold, no matter what for-
mats you've assigned to the B element's contain-
er.</B>
```

Another way of putting this is to say that inline elements take precedence over all other styles. If you stick an inline element into your document, the browser knows you mean business, and it pays attention.

Is this still the HTML 4.0 way? After all, HTML 4.0 separates presentation from structure. But don't get carried away here. There are all sorts of valid reasons to interrupt the nice logic of style-sheet formatting to insert a specially-formatted unit of text here and there.

Elements for Character Formatting

In HTML 4.0, it is quite legitimate to introduce inline elements that format characters distinctively. You can choose from elements for character emphasis and elements for technical documents, as explained in the following sections.

If you would like to emphasize certain words or phrases in your document, you can code the text so that it shows up in bold, italics, monospace (typewriter font), a larger font size, or a smaller font size. Table 9.1 sums up your options. You can also superscript text (position it so that the characters start above the baseline) or subscript it (position it so that the characters start below the baseline).

What's the difference between I and EM? With most browsers, not much. Both are formatted with italics. But there is a conceptual difference. Elements such as EM, BIG, and STRONG are known to HTML purists as logical formatting elements. By this they don't mean that these elements can reason; rather, it's that you're leaving the exact formatting up to the browser. You can also use physical formatting elements (such as I, B, and TT) which do specify exactly what formatting is supposed to be used. HTML books are full of admonitions that you really ought to use the logical formatting elements instead of the physical ones, but frankly, very few people do this. Most Web authors want to know how emphasis is going to look, and the physical tags give you a way to do this.

Table 9.1 Elements for character formatting

Element	Description and example
B	Bold `<B>bold</B>`
BIG	Increases the current font size. `<BIG>Important!</BIG>`
EM	Emphasized (usually shown in italic type) `<EM>Important!</EM>`
I	Italics `<I>Huck Finn</I>`
SMALL	Decreases the current font size. `<SMALL>Tiny!</SMALL>`
STRONG	Stronger than bold (may have larger font size). `<STRONG>Hey!</STRONG>`
SUB	Subscript `X<SUB>1</SUB>`
SUP	Superscript `X<SUP>2</SUP>`
TT	Monospace `<TT>Type it!</TT>`

Previous versions of HTML offered two additional emphases, STRIKE (strikeout) and U (underline). Although supported by HTML 4.0, these are now deprecated. You're supposed to handle these formats with style sheets or the new INS and DEL elements, which are discussed later in this chapter.

Elements for Technical Documents

In addition to the inline elements you can use for character emphasis, you can also use a number of inline elements that are designed for technical documents. Frankly, these don't do much of anything with most browsers. They are really intended for specialized technical applications, so you can forget about them.

Table 9.2 Elements for technical documents

Element	Description and example
CITE	A bibliographic citation, usually shown in italics. `<CITE>Citation goes here</CITE>`
CODE	Used to type computer code. Generally formatted with a monotype font (not proportionally-spaced). `<CODE>Code goes here</CODE>`
DFN	Defining (generally first) instance of a term. Not distinctively formatted by most browsers. `<DFN>First instance of term</DFN>`
KBD	Used to show what you are supposed to type. Usually shown with monospace type. `Press <KBD>Ctrl + Alt + Del </KBD>`
SAMP	Used to show sample output from a program. Usually shown with monospace type. `<SAMP>Sample output goes here.</SAMP>`
VAR	Used to designate a variable. Generally formatted with italics `<VAR>x</VAR>`

Spelling Out Abbreviations and Acronyms

This section introduces a couple of new HTML 4.0 inline elements that you can use to make your document more accessible to people with special needs.

Spelling Out an Abbreviation

This element enables you to spell out an abbreviation, which might prove very useful to somebody reading your document with a speech-synthesizing browser. In supporting browsers, the spelled-out form of the abbreviation will be visible in tool tip when the user moves the mouse over the element.

ELEMENT	ABBR
PURPOSE	Indicates an abbreviation.
TYPE	Inline
NESTED WITHIN	Any block
START TAG	Required
END TAG	Required
CONTENT	Text
ATTRIBUTES	core attributes (id, class, style, title) language attributes (lang, dir)
EXAMPLE	<ABBR title = "Incorporated">Inc.</ABBR>
TIP	Use the title attribute so users can see what the spelled-out version of the abbreviation looks like.

Adding an Acronym

Acronyms give programs fits; speech synthesizers and spell checkers alike stumble over them, and most people have no idea what they mean. To remedy this situation, HTML 4.0 introduces the ACRONYM element. Here's the definition:

ELEMENT	ACRONYM
PURPOSE	Indicates an acronym.
TYPE	Inline
NESTED WITHIN	Any block
START TAG	Required

END TAG	Required
CONTENT	Text
ATTRIBUTES	core attributes (id, class, style, title) language attributes (lang, dir)
EXAMPLE	<ACRONYM title = "World Wide Web">WWW</ACRONYM>
TIP	Use the title attribute so users can see what the spelled-out version of the acronym looks like.

Future browsers might be able to show you the spelled-out version of the acronym if you click on it. That would be nice, wouldn't it? Microsoft? Netscape? Are you listening?

Adding a Short Quotation

In the previous chapter, you learned about BLOCKQUOTE, a block element that is intended to be used for an extended quotation, one that's set off from the text. However, you should use this only when the text you are citing is more than three or four lines in length. For shorter quotations, you can use the new Q element. Like BLOCKQUOTE, this element has a cite attribute, which you can use to designate the URL of the quotation's source. Unlike BLOCKQUOTE, though, Q is an inline element, so you can use it within a block element such as a P text paragraph.

Here is the element definition:

ELEMENT	Q
PURPOSE	Marks an inline quotation.
TYPE	Inline
NESTED WITHIN	Any block element
START TAG	Required
END TAG	Required
CONTENT	Text
ATTRIBUTES	core attributes (id, class, style, title) language attributes (lang, dir) cite = "url" (optional)
EXAMPLE	<Q cite = "source.html">Here's a quotation.</Q>

TIP	You can use the BLOCKQUOTE element for longer (indented) quotations. If you use Q, don't use quotation marks; they're supplied by the browser, in a way that's sensitive to the document's language code.

Browsers do not format Q distinctively; the purpose of the element is to give you a way to record the source URL of the quote. Browsers don't do anything with this, either, but at least you have recorded it in the HTML source code. Future browsers might display the source document, and enable you to access it, if you click on the cited text.

To format quoted text using the Q element, you need to add quote marks. Browsers won't do this for you:

```
A memorable quotation:  <Q cite="http://www.myserv-
er.org/quotes/money.html">"Before, I didn't  have any
money. Now, I don't have any time.</Q>
```

Is there really a point to using Q? Although it doesn't affect presentation, it does give you a way of recording where you got the quoted text. That might be useful, in case somebody asks you for the source.

Showing Insertions and Deletions

Here is a way to publish a draft document showing proposed insertions and deletions. Just how these appear is up to the browser, but they should be obvious: Insertions should be shown in a distinctive color, while deletions can be handled by using strikethrough formatting (or not showing them at all).

Here is the element definitions for INS :

ELEMENT	INS
PURPOSE	Indicates inserted text in a legal or political document.
TYPE	Inline
NESTED WITHIN	Any block element

START TAG	Required
END TAG	Required
CONTENT	Text and inline elements (no block elements permitted)
ATTRIBUTES	core attributes (id, class, style, title) language attributes (lang, dir) cite = "url" (optional) datetime = "YYYYMMDD" (optional)
EXAMPLE	We can support <DEL>10</DEL><INS>12</INS> positions.
TIP	Use DEL to show what's deleted.

And here's the element definition for DEL:

ELEMENT	DEL
PURPOSE	Indicates deleted text in a legal or political document.
TYPE	Inline
NESTED WITHIN	Any block element
START TAG	Required
END TAG	Required
CONTENT	Text and inline elements (no block elements permitted)
ATTRIBUTES	core attributes (id, class, style, title) language attributes (lang, dir) cite = "url" (optional) datetime = "YYYYMMDD"
EXAMPLE	We can support <DEL>10</DEL><INS>12</INS> positions.
TIP	Use INS to show what is inserted in place of the deleted text.

See the following example:

```
We propose raising the county tax rate by <DEL>1
percent</DEL><INS>30 percent</INS>. Please comment.
```

Note that you can use the cite attribute to specify the location of a document explaining the change, as in the following example:

```
We propose raising the county tax rate by <DEL>1
percent</DEL><INS cite="why-raise-taxes-so-
much.html">30 percent</INS>. Please comment.
```

The datetime attribute enables you to specify the date and time that the change was made. To use this attribute, you should write a date and time that conforms to the ISO 8601 format.

Styles for Character Emphases

A number of CSS properties are used to define character styles, including emphases. You can use these to define block or inline elements.

Specifying Font Styles

The font-style property enables you to choose italics. Another option is oblique (slanted) text, but this format isn't available with most browsers.

PROPERTY	font-style
PURPOSE	Defines emphasis options for text.
INHERITED	Yes
VALUES	normal, italic, or oblique
DEFAULT	normal
USED IN	All elements
SUPPORT	MSIE 3.0/Win95: Yes
	MSIE 4.0/Win95: Yes
	NN4.0/Win95: Yes
	MSIE 3.0/Mac OS: Yes
	MSIE 4.0/Mac OS: Yes
	NN4.0/Mac OS: Yes
EXAMPLE	{ font-style: italic }
TIP	Oblique is not widely supported.

Here is an example that shows how to specify italic fonts in an element:

```
<STYLE type = "text/css">
        LI.italic {font-style: italic}
</STYLE>
```

This style formats the "italic" class of LI elements with italic text.

Formatting Text with Small Caps

Although not widely implemented, the font-variant property enables you to choose small caps. Other font variants will be made available in future versions of HTML.

PROPERTY	font-variant
PURPOSE	Enables font variations such as small caps.
INHERITED	Yes
VALUES	normal or small-caps
DEFAULT	normal
USED IN	All elements
SUPPORT	MSIE 3.0/Win95: No
	MSIE 4.0/Win95: Yes
	NN4.0/Win95: No
	MSIE 3.0/Mac OS: No
	MSIE 4.0/Mac OS: No
	NN4.0/Mac OS: No
EXAMPLE	{ font-variant: small-caps }
TIP	This style is not widely supported.

See the following example that shows how to specify small caps for an H2 heading:

```
<STYLE type = "text/css">
        H2 { font-variant: small-caps }
</STYLE>
```

Determining Weight (Boldness)

With the font-weight property, you can specify the boldness of a font with more precision than HTML allows.

Here's the element definition:

PROPERTY	font-weight
PURPOSE	Determines weight (boldness) of font
INHERITED	Yes
VALUES	Normal or bold. You can also specify a numerical weight ranging from 100 (light) to 900 (dark), or relative weights (bolder or lighter).
DEFAULT	normal
USED IN	All elements
SUPPORT	MSIE 3.0/Win95: Yes MSIE 4.0/Win95: Yes NN4.0/Win95: Yes MSIE 3.0/Mac OS: Yes MSIE 4.0/Mac OS: Yes NN4.0/Mac OS: Yes
EXAMPLE	{ font-weight: bold }
TIP	Only the normal and bold values are widely supported.

The following shows how to specify bold for a class of paragraphs called "emphatic":

```
<STYLE type = "text/css">
      P.emphatic { font-weight: bold }
</STYLE>
```

Adding Space between Letters

To create special effects, you can add extra spacing between letters. Note, though, that this property is not very well supported currently.

PROPERTY	letter-spacing
PURPOSE	Adds to the default spacing between characters.
INHERITED	Yes
VALUES	Specify a length
DEFAULT	normal
USED IN	Block-level elements
SUPPORT	MSIE 3.0/Win95: No MSIE 4.0/Win95: Yes NN4.0/Win95: No MSIE 3.0/Mac OS: No MSIE 4.0/Mac OS: No NN4.0/Mac OS: No
EXAMPLE	{ letter-spacing: 1pt }
TIP	This property is not well supported.

Adding Text Decorations

With the text-decoration property, you can specify a number of special emphasis formats, including line-through (strikeover), line-over, and blinking text.

Please use blinking text sparingly! Many Web users find blinking text to be annoying, distracting, and hard to read.

PROPERTY	text-decoration
PURPOSE	Adds decorations (such as strikethrough) to text.
INHERITED	Yes
VALUES	none, underline, overline, line-through, or blink
DEFAULT	none
USED IN	Block-level elements
SUPPORT	MSIE 3.0/Win95: Yes MSIE 4.0/Win95: Yes NN4.0/Win95: Yes MSIE 3.0/Mac OS: Yes MSIE 4.0/Mac OS: Yes

	NN4.0/Mac OS: Yes
EXAMPLE	{ text-decoration: underline }
TIP	Only MSIE 4.0/Win95 supports the overline value.

Specifying Case

With the text-transform element, you can specify the case of text in an element. You can choose from first word capitalized, all uppercase, or all lowercase.

PROPERTY	text-transform
PURPOSE	Changes case
INHERITED	Yes
VALUES	capitalize, uppercase, lowercase, none
DEFAULT	none
USED IN	All elements
SUPPORT	MSIE 3.0/Win95: No
	MSIE 4.0/Win95: Yes
	NN4.0/Win95: Yes
	MSIE 3.0/Mac OS: No
	MSIE 4.0/Mac OS: Yes
	NN4.0/Mac OS: Yes
EXAMPLE	{ text-transform: capitalize }
TIP	Because this property is supported inconsistently, you will be wise to type the characters with the capitalization pattern you prefer.

Creating Inline Styles

The previous chapter briefly mentioned *inline styles,* which make use of the nearly ubiquitous *style* attribute (found in almost every HTML 4 element). This is a handy attribute when you want to make style changes on the fly. In addition to using inline styles, you can also group inline elements (and define their attributes) using the SPAN element.

Using Inline Styles

To change any aspect of character formatting, use an inline style. In the following example, a paragraph of text takes on special formats:

```
<P style = "font-weight: bold;font-family: Arial,
sans-serif;font-size: 10pt">
```
You can add an inline style to just about any element, including inline elements, as in the following examples:

```
<STRONG style = "font-family: Copperplate;font-size:
18">
```

Note that inline styles use the same CSS syntax that's found within the STYLE element; just be sure to place all the CSS within quotation marks as shown in the two examples above.

Grouping Inline Elements with SPAN

Like DIV, SPAN does not show up on the browser's screen. In fact, it won't do anything at all unless you assign a class or id name to it and write a STYLE definition that assigns properties to the class or id. Here is an example of a SPAN element within the body of the document:

```
<P><SPAN class="small-caps">This is the text I want
to format with SPAN.</SPAN> And here's more text in
the same block element.<./P>
```

Note that this element is defined using the class "small-caps." To define this class, write a STYLE definition like this:

```
<STYLE type="text/css">
     SPAN.small-caps {font-variant: small-caps}
</STYLE>
```

You could write numerous class definitions to handle all the special font formatting jobs in your document. Just remember, though, that the SPAN element can be used within block elements only. If you want to format text that encompasses two or more block elements, use DIV, as explained in Chapter 7.

Summary

Inline elements enable you to affect the presentation of text within any block element. You can enter a number of character styles and emphases directly, including bold and italics. With styles, you can add a variety of character styles and emphases to virtually any block or inline element. The SPAN element enables you to group inline elements for formatting purposes, and is every bit as handy as the DIV element introduced in an earlier chapter.

It's time to get serious about linking. Chapter 10 delves into the topic in detail.

10

The Art of the Hyperlink

In this chapter, you will learn the following skills:

- Increasing hyperlink accessibility with tab order and shortcut keys
- Specifying forward and reverse link relationships so that search engines can index your site more effectively
- Opening a page in a new window
- Linking to destination anchors within the same document
- Using the BASE element to simplify editing tasks when you need to move documents to a different directory

Links make the Web and so, it stands to reason, the more you know about links, the more Web you'll make. Already, you have learned how to create hyperlinks using the A element, and you know the difference between absolute and relative URLs. This chapter goes into the A element in more detail, and covers some new material as well, including anchors (link locations inside the same document that contains the link). Perhaps most important of all, this chapter shows you how to take advantage of the new accessibility features of HTML Version 4, including the ability to define shortcut keys for hyperlinks.

Terminology: Links and Anchors

Let's start by clarifying our terminology.

Table 10.1 Essential hyperlinking terms

Term	Definition
source	The document that contains the link.
destination	The document that appears when users activate the link.
link	The relationship that exists between the source and the destination.
anchor	The end of a link. There is a source anchor and a destination anchor.

Strictly speaking, the term "link" really shouldn't be used to describe anything but the relationship between the source anchor and the destination anchor, but that is not how people use the term. When most HTML authors say "link," they are referring to the linking element (the A element) and the specific use of it within the source document to create a source anchor. The link is the relationship; the source anchor is the highlighted, clickable text that appears within the HTML document when displayed by a browser.

You may be surprised to learn this, but the Web lacks sophisticated hyperlinking capabilities. More advanced hypertext systems offer several different types of links, including links that embed portions of the destination document within the source document, as if there were no distinction between the two. HTML is a very simple hypertext system—crude, really—that does little more than enable users to access distant documents by clicking on a source anchor. There is a lot more to a full-blown hypertext system than HTML currently offers.

Take the \<A\> Train

To create a source anchor, you use the A element. Here's the element's definition:

ELEMENT	A
PURPOSE	Inserts a hyperlink.
TYPE:	Inline
NESTED WITHIN	BODY
START TAG	Required
END TAG	Required
CONTENT	Contains inline elements and text
ATTRIBUTES	core attributes (id, class, style, title) language attributes (lang, dir) accesskey = "character" (optional) charset = "charset" (optional) href = "url" (optional) hreflang = "langcode" (optional) rel = "link-type" (optional) rev = "link-type" (optional) tabindex = "number" (optional) target = "(_blank, _self, _parent, _top, or name)" (optional)
EXAMPLE	\<A href = "http://www.yahoo.com">Yahoo!\</A>
DON'T FORGET	Make sure you have surrounded the URL with quotations.

In practice, most Web authors use only the href attribute—but, as you will see, there are some cool tricks lurking among these attributes. Table 10.2 sums up the A element's attributes; subsequent sections take a closer look at the highlights. You'll learn more about the name attribute in the section on anchors, later in this chapter. The following sections explain what you can do with the more useful of the remaining attributes. There is quite a bag of tricks to be learned by reading these sections.

Table 10.2 Attributes for A hyperlinks

Attribute	Definition
accesskey	Defines a shortcut key to launch this hyperlink. accesskey = "k"
charset	Specifies the character encoding of the linked document. `charset - "euc-jp"`
href	Specifies the link's destination. You can use an absolute or relative URL. `href = "contents.html"`
name	Specifies an anchor name for this link. `name = "link10"`
rel	Specifies the relationship of the source (current) document to the destination document. You can choose from the link types described in Table 10.3. To specify more than one link type, use commas. `rel = "contents, copyright"`
rev	Specifies the relationship of the destination document to the source (current document). You can choose from the link types described in Table 10.3. To specify more than one link type, use commas. `rev = "previous"`
tabindex	Specifies the current link's location in a sequence of tab keystrokes. `tabindex = "3"`
target	Specifies where the link should appear. To open

the link in a new window, use the _blank target name.

```
target = "_blank" (opens the link in
a new window)
```

Accesskey: Enabling Shortcut Keys for Hyperlinks

To make the Web easier to use, HTML Version 4 enables Web authors to define shortcut keys for hyperlinks (and some other feature as well, such as form fields, as discussed in Chapter 17). To define a shortcut key, you choose a letter from the visible text (case doesn't matter), and define the key using the accesskey attribute. Here's an example:

```
<A HREF = "contents.html" accesskey = "c">Table of
Contents</A>
```

Browsers are supposed to automatically detect that you are defining a shortcut key and highlight the shortcut key automatically, generally by adding an underline character under the shortcut key. Users will need to press the standard "hot key" for their systems, such as the Mac's Command key or the PC's Alt key.

One of the best things about HTML 4 lies in its authors' awareness of Web users with special needs. For example, people with repetitive stress injuries (RSI) may have difficulty using a mouse; more severely handicapped users may be browsing with speech-recognition software, which requires keyboard input. If the Web is to be more accessible to users with special needs, though, you need to remember to use these attributes consistently. Start making a habit of it! Don't write an anchor without including an accesskey attribute.

Charset: Specifying the Destination's Character Set

This might be worth doing if you are referring to a document using a character set that is not very widely known; perhaps the browser would be set up to determine whether it can handle the character set, and if not, it could display an error message. Then again, it might just download the document anyway and fill the screen with incomprehensible garbage. You can help the browser prepare in another way, too: use the hreflang attribute to specify the two-letter language code of the destination document.

Rel and Rev: Are These For Real?

With the rel and rev attributes, you can describe the specific type of relationship that exists between the two documents linked together by an A element. There is a conventional nomenclature you can use, too, as shown in Table 10.3. What are these all about?

In brief, the rel and rev attributes specify the relation between the source and the destination. Suppose your Web site has several pages, including a copyright page, a table of contents (index) page, and a home page. You can use rel and rev to describe the relationships among these pages, as follows

- **rel** This specifies the nature of the forward link, the link between the source document and the destination document. For example, suppose you're creating a link from the table of contents page back to your site's home page. If you specify *rel = "start"*, you are specifying that the link goes to the beginning page of a series of documents.
- **rev** This specifies the nature of the reverse link, the link between the destination document and the source document. Suppose the page containing the source anchor is the home page, and you are writing a link to the table of contents page. The link that goes from the contents page to the home page is *rev = "start"* (but it would be *rel = "contents"*). Get it?

Frankly, very few Web authors make use of these attributes—for the very simple reason that the browsers don't do anything with them. However, the information contained in the rel and rev attributes can be very helpful to search engines. If you're writing a source anchor to one of the document types described in Table 10.3, be sure to include the rel and rev attributes.

Table 10.3 Conventional link types

Link types	Description
alternate	The link refers to a different version of this document. `rel = "alternate"`

bookmark	The link refers to an anchor location.
	`rel = "bookmark"`
contents	The link describes a table of contents for this site.
	`rel = "contents"`
copyright	The link describes the copyright page for this site.
	`rel = "copyright"`
help	The link describes a help page for this site.
	`rel = "help"`
index	The link describes an index for this site.
	`rel = "index"`
next	The link describes the next page in a sequence of pages.
	`rel = "next"`
previous	The link describes the previous page in a sequence of pages.
	`rev = "previous"`
start	The link describes the first document in a sequence of pages.
	`rel = "previous"`
stylesheet	The link refers to a stylesheet for this document.
	`rel = "stylesheet"`

Tabindex: Specifying the Tab Order

There is another way you can increase the accessibility of your Web pages: Spend some time thinking about the tab order.

By default, most recent browsers enable users to access links by pressing the Tab key; once a link is selected, users can launch the link by pressing Enter. The default tab order is simply the order in which you placed the source anchors in your document. You may wish to override the default tab order by putting the most-likely-to-be-clicked links at the top of the queue. For example, suppose you are creating a page that enables users to branch off in two different ways. Although there are a lot of other links on the pages, these are the two most important ones, and they're the ones that users are most likely to access.

With the tabindex attribute, you can specify the order in which hyperlinks are highlighted when users press the Tab key. Here's an example:

```
<A HREF="welcome.html" tabindex = "1">Welcome</A>
<A HREF="contents.html" tabindex = "2">Contents</A>
<A HREF="copyright.html" tabindex = "3">Copyright
Statement</A>
```

Users can press Tab to go to each of these links in sequence. Pressing Enter launches the link. This is an important benefit for users whose physical limitations prevent them from using a mouse.

Target: Directing Output to a Window

The target attribute comes into play when you create framed documents (see Chapter 14) but it has uses in ordinary hyperlinks. Among the reserved values for this attribute is "_blank," which directs the browser to open a link in a new window. See the following example:

```
<A HREF = "page-1.html" target = "_blank">Page 1</A>
```

This opens "page-1.html" in a new window, leaving the source document on-screen in its original window.

Anchors Away!

In addition to linking to external documents, you can also link to named locations within the same document. To do this, you need to define anchors.

You define anchors with the A element's name attribute. Here is an example:

```
<A name = "funds">An Introduction to Mutual
Funds</A.
```

Now you can include a link in your document to this anchor. Here's how it is done:

```
<A HREF="#funds">Learn more about mutual funds</A>.
```

Anchors are easy to use. There are just a couple of things to keep in mind. First, note the pound sign (#) in the link (<A HREF="#funds">). This is needed to identify the anchor's location. Also, note that most browsers don't format the anchor text in any unusual way. Readers don't even know that the anchor is there—until they jump to it, and find that the anchor location is now positioned at the top of the page.

You can also write a link that jumps to an anchor in an external document. To do so, just append the anchor name to the document name in the referenced URL, as in the following example:

```
<A HREF="www.somewhere.org/welcome.html#contents>Con-
tents</A>
```

This link goes to the external page and displays the anchor Contents. If this is somebody else's document, you will not of course be able to place the anchor in the text, so you cannot do this unless somebody has defined the anchors already. You can't see the anchors either, but you can learn of their existence by navigating around the site a bit. Look in your browser's status line to see the URL of the links at the site—if you see an anchor, you can write a link that jumps to it.

The Mailto URL

Here's a very easy way to create user feedback: Place a mailto URL in your document, and include your e-mail address. When users click on this URL, their browser will start a mail program and display a new, blank composition window that is addressed to you. (Of course, not all browsers can do this, but almost all of them can, these days.)

To create a mailto URL, use the A element and href attribute, but write the URL with the word mailto followed by a colon and your e-mail address.

```
<A HREF="mailto:me@mymailbox.net">Write to me!</A>
```

Clicking this anchor brings up a mail window addressed to me@mymailbox.net.

For the benefit of those few individuals who are still using really ancient, non-mail-compliant browsers, you may wish to include your e-mail address as the visible text in the hyperlink, as in this example: <A HREF="mailto:me@mymailbox.net">me@mymailbox.net</A>.

Getting to First BASE

When you use relative URLs, the browser talks to the server to try to figure out what these URLs mean. From the server, the browser learns precisely where the current page is located. Using this information, the browser can infer the location of any relative URL that you use, as in the following examples:

contents.html	A document in the same directory
/images/wow.gif	An image one directory beneath the current directory
../../index.html	A document two directories up from the current directory

With relative URLs such as these, the browser correctly infers the base URL from the referring document—that is, the URL that provides the point of reference for determining the location of all those relative URLs. However, there is a way that you can override the base URL information that the browser gets from the server. You can use the BASE element, explained in the following:

ELEMENT	BASE
PURPOSE	Specifies an absolute URL to use as the basis for resolving relative URLs in your document.

TYPE	inline
NESTED WITHIN	HEAD element
START TAG	Required
END TAG	Forbidden
CONTENT	Empty
ATTRIBUTES	href = "url"
EXAMPLE	<BASE = "www.myserver.org/myhome/">
TIP	Always use relative URLs within your document and specify the base with this element.

The BASE element must be positioned within the HEAD element. Here's an example:

```
<HEAD>
        <BASE = http://www.nodomain.org/contents.html">
</HEAD>
```

This element essentially tells the browser that it should consider any relative URL in the current document to be relative to the position of the document defined in the BASE tag. In other words, suppose you create the following link with a relative URL:

```
<A HREF = "intro.html">Introduction</A>
```

The browser will then interpret the location of intro.html to be http://www.nodomain.org/intro.html. And that is true even if the source document—the one containing the relative URL—is located on a totally different computer.

When is the BASE tag useful? Suppose you have a whole long list of links, which use relative URLs, that was created for documents housed on www.example.net/stuff/docs/. You would like to copy this list, but you really don't want to go through the whole list and change all the relative URLs to absolute ones. (This is lots of work!) The simple solution would be to use the BASE element to define the base URL to be http://www.example.net/stuff/docs/.

The LINK Element

The LINK element appears within the HEAD of your page—and, as such, it does not affect your document's appearance. So why should you use it? You can define link types using the conventional link types defined in Table 10.3, and that's supposed to benefit search engines in compiling a more accurate picture of the documents at your site. But the META nomenclature discussed in Chapter 12 would seem better suited to this task, as you will see. So what's LINK for? If you are using style sheets, plenty.

The LINK element has come to life as a way of referencing external style sheets. Suppose I prefer to keep just one style sheet for my entire site, rather than placing STYLE information within the HEAD of every document. This way, I can make just one change to the style sheet, and it affects all the linked documents.

To define the external style sheet, use the LINK element, as in the following example:

```
<LINK rel="stylesheet" type = "text/css" href =
"mystyles.css">
```

Note the three attributes: rel (defines the relationship using the stylesheet link type), type (specifies the language of the style sheet), and href (specifies the style sheet's location—here, using a relative URL). Note that all three of these attributes are required.

Summary

Hyperlinks provide the soul of the Web's interactivity, but plain hyperlinks leave a lot to be desired. Make your hyperlinks more accessible to impaired users by defining the tab order and creating shortcut keys. If you are linking to any of the document types described in Table 10.3, be sure to specify link relationships with rel and rev.

Learn how to finish your page by adding a few important but often neglected touches; Chapter 11 shows you how.

11

Finishing Touches

In this chapter, you will learn the following skills:

- Making your page easier to find by search engines
- Rating your page
- Signing your page
- Creating an automatic "we've moved" page

With this chapter, you come to the end of the basic HTML for entering block and inline elements. Here, you will learn how to add some finishing touches to your page; for example, you'll write invisible tags that make your page much easier to retrieve by means of search engines.

The META Element: Coming of Age?

The META element, which lives within the HEAD, has been around since the beginning of HTML, but it hasn't been used very often, save by programmers who create pages designed to take advantage of specialized server functions. With HTML Version 4, however, that's all in the past. Now it is possible to argue that every author should include a META element and make full use of its functionality. As you'll see in the sections to follow, using the META element can greatly increase the chance that a search engine will retrieve your page.

Meta: It's About "About"

What's the META element for? It is intended to contain information about the current HTML document. The term comes from metainformation, which means information about information.

On the Web, metainformation is sorely needed. Just ponder what happens when you perform a search. Suppose you're looking for information about what it's like to have a gerbil for a pet. You will find all kinds of stuff—pages describing peoples' pet gerbils, proposals to legalize gerbils in California, information about feeding gerbils, scientific notes on the evolution of gerbils, and an adult page that includes the word "gerbil" in a huge, hidden key-word list, which is used to snooker people in to visit their page (even if they didn't start out looking for naughty pictures). And that leaves out the home page of Gerbil, Gerbil, and Gerbil, a Cucamonga, CA-based law firm, tips on navigating the Straits of Gerbila near Zanzibar, and an astronomer's page on the galaxy code named G-ERB (il-9).

This kind of unwanted document retrieval wouldn't happen if the Web had been designed from the beginning with some way of describing what type of document a given page is, and what it is about. For example, metainformation could include the document's author, a list of keywords describing the contents of the site, a PICS (Platform for Internet Content Selection) statement that warns kids away from the site if it contains adult content, and a resource type statement that specifies that the document contains practical information about gerbils rather than ads for pet stores.

Providing the Framework, Not the Specifics

Metainformation sounds great, but there's a catch. Although HTML Version 4 defines the structure of the META element, it does not specify the exact terminology with which metainformation is classified. For example, suppose you want to indicate that your site is suitable for kids. How do you do this?

HTML Version 4 does not supply an answer to this question. Instead, you're pointed to a number of independent efforts to create metainformation classification schemes. There are good reasons for leaving the terminology to others; after all, HTML's creators don't have the necessary expertise. (For example, the complex task of creating subject classification schemes is best left to professional librarians.) In the META realm, then, structure and content are decoupled (separated).

The decoupling of structure and content poses a dilemma. In the absence of any "official" nomenclature for describing a document's content, which scheme should you use? In one proposed scheme, you use the term "Author," while in another, you use "Creator." Unless search engines were programmed to look for both ways of indicating the page's author, a search for pages by a specific author may not produce all the relevant documents.

So, the META element is well on its way, but it isn't there yet. For now, there are a number of differing content description systems. Happily, the World Wide Web Consortium (W3C) is uniting all of these separate efforts in support of a Resource Description Framework (RDF), which is currently under development. It is a complex job. Among the requirements of a rich metainformation system are better searching, more effective content screening for adult material, a better method of describing the relationships among multiple documents at a site, a way to incorporate digital signatures into the metadata information, and more. Don't expect RDF anytime soon. For now, you are limited to using one or more of the existing schemes. Let's take a look at the META element first and then explore your current content description options.

Using the META Element

Take a look at the META element's definition.

ELEMENT	META
PURPOSE	Creates a client-side imagemap.
TYPE	n.a.
NESTED WITHIN	BODY
START TAG	Required

END TAG	Forbidden
CONTENT	Empty
ATTRIBUTES	core attributes (id, lang, class, style) language attributes (lang, dir) http-equiv = "text" name = "text" content = "CDATA" scheme = "CDATA"
EXAMPLE	\<META name = "keywords" content = "Chesapeake Bay, cruising, sailing, marinas">
TIP	A number of content description schemes are under development, but most browsers do not yet recognize them.

Of the META tag attributes, the ones that you will use most often are name and content. The http-equiv attribute plays a technical role that has to do with the messages sent in response to a document request; basically, you'll use this attribute for a few technical applications (such as the PICS rated scheme). The scheme attribute might be used by some content terminology schemes. It is name and content that you'll use most often, as the next section clarifies.

Telling Search Engines What's in Your Document

If you want to tell search engines some things about your document, see the example that follows. Some search engines privilege this information, if it is found; for example, they'll show the Description text to searchers if you've included it.

```
<HEAD>
    <META name = "author" content = "William
    Smith">
    <META name = "description" content = "This
    page summarizes what we've learned about Laser
    sail trim; check it out if you're interested
    in dinghy racing.">
    <META name = "keywords" content = "sails,
    trim, racing, laser, sailing">
</HEAD>
```

Where did this META terminology come from? It was pushed by a few search engine firms in an attempt to improve document retrieval. But it is neither standardized nor sufficiently elaborate to meet the needs of the Web, which is why various committees are busy at work inventing alternatives. Let's look at them.

Don't omit this META nomenclature! AltaVista and other search engines will use the "description" blurb to describe your document's contents to people searching for information. This is much better than the default content description, which is usually drawn from the first few sentences of your page. These sentences may not do a very good job of telling people why they should visit your site!

On the Road to Dublin (The Core Data Set)

Of the several attempts to develop a sophisticated terminology for metainformation, the Dublin Core Data Set is one of the best. Spearheaded by OCLC, Inc., a leader in the online database market, the Dublin Core provides a well-thought-out set of content descriptors. Like everything else connected with the META tag, though, it is neither finished nor universally accepted. Still, it makes excellent sense to fill out as many of these META descriptors as you think might be relevant to your document; doing so will force you to think of ways that people might be searching for your document, and this will enhance the retrievability of your Web publications.

Table 11.1 The Dublin Core Data Set

Name	Purpose and example
title	Specifies the document's title.
	`<META name = "title" content = "Rappahannock River Sailing Gazette">`
creator	Specifies the document's author.
	`<META name = "creator" content = "Bryan Pfaffenberger">`
subject	Specifies the overall subject of the page using a recognized subject classification scheme, such as Library of Congress subject classifications. You

can also use this to list keywords.

```
<META name = "subject" content =
"Northern Neck, Rappahannock River,
Sailing — Recreational">
```

description   Provides space for a brief informative abstract.

```
<META name = "description" content =
"News and perspectives about recre-
ational sailing on the Rappahannock
River, located off the Chesapeake
Bay near Virginia's Northern Neck."
```

publisher   Specifies the organization that is responsible for publishing the document.

```
<META name = "publisher" content =
"Rappahannock River Sailing Club">
```

contributor   Lists additional people who contributed to the current document.

```
<META name = "contributor" content =
"James Smith, Jan Andersen">
```

date   Specifies the date of publication or last updating of the document. Use an 8 digit number in the form YYYYMMDD (19980220 is February 20, 1998).

```
<META name = "date" content =
"19980220">
```

resource   Specifies the document type, using a controlled vocabulary (which isn't yet developed).

format   Specifies the MIME data type.

```
<META name = "format" content =
"text/html">
```

identifier   Specifies a unique string or number that identifies this particular document. You could use this to number all the documents in your site consecutively.

```
<META name = "identifier" content =
"23">
```

source   Specifies the source, if any, from which this document is drawn.

```
<META name = "source" content =
"Rappahannock River Sailing Gazette,
July 9, 1998">
```

language   Specifies the language in which the document is presented.

```
<META name = "language" content =
"EN">
```

rights   Specifies the location of a copyright document.

```
<META name = "rights" content =
http://www.rappahannockriver.org/co
pyright.html>
```

Keep Your PICS Clean (Using PICS Rules)

Please rate your site so that parents and kids know whether it is appropriate for children to see. This only takes a couple of minutes.

The Platform for Internet Content Selection (PICs) is an emerging set of content-description rules that enable anyone to devise content rating vocabularies, generally concerning adult content. PICs is very complex and you don't want to develop your own rating scheme. Instead, you log on to the Web server of one of the services that has developed a PICs rating scheme, and provide your document's URL. You fill out a questionnaire indicating what type of content your site has (just what is asked depends on which rating service you are accessing). The service then generates the PICs rating code, which you paste into your HTML document. You'll find a list of rating services in Table 11.2.

Table 11.2 PICS rating services

Service	Description
RSACi	Recreational Software Advisory Council on the Internet (www.rsac.org/homepage.asp). Rates language, nudity, and violence.
Safe for Kids	www.weburbia.com/safe/classify.htm. A very simple rating system (safe for kids, parental guidance, adults only).
SafeSurf	www.safesurf.com/classify/index.html. Rates age range and adult themes.

Once you paste the generated META element into your document's HEAD, you will have provided all the information needed for PICs-enabled browsers (such as Microsoft Internet Explorer) as well as PICs-aware content filtering programs (such as SurfWatch) to open your site to kids, or block it from them, depending on your site's content. Please do this before publishing your page.

What's Your ADDRESS? Signing Your Page

The ADDRESS element, an inline element, provides a way to include your name and address. It is distinctively formatted by browsers, generally in italics, and, by convention, appears at the end of documents. Be sure to include contact information so that people can get in touch with you. Here is the element definition, which is pretty simple, since there aren't any attributes peculiar to this element:

ELEMENT	ADDRESS
PURPOSE	Provides information about the author.
TYPE	Inline
NESTED WITHIN	Any block element
START TAG	Required
END TAG	Required
CONTENT	Text
ATTRIBUTES	core attributes (id, class, style, title) language attributes (lang, dir)

EXAMPLE	<ADDRESS>John Doe (<A HREF= "mailto:arwen@rivendell.org> arwen @rivendell.org </A>) </ADDRESS>
TIP	Place this element at the bottom of your page to indicate who is responsible for its maintenance. Use a mailto URL (as shown) to incorporate a clickable e-mail link. Usually rendered in italics.

See the following example:

```
<ADDRESS>This page created by Thomas Smith
(tps3x@rappahannock.org) on February 20,
1998.</ADDRESS>
```

To enable readers to get in touch with you, include your e-mail address using the mailto URL, as in the following example: <A HREF=mailto:tps3x@rappahannock.org>tps3x@rappahannock.org</A>. By echoing the e-mail address within the visible text, you enable users with mail-challenged browsers to see your address.

Creating a "We've Moved!" Page

If you need to move your Web page to a new location, be sure to leave a notice in the previous page's location. With this trick, you can take viewers to the new page automatically. This works with most recent browsers, including Netscape Navigator, Netscape Communicator, and Microsoft Internet Explorer.

To pull off this trick, create your "we've moved" page. In this page, insert a link to the new page's location, and also tell users that, if they are using a recent browser, they will be taken to the new page automatically. Users of older or text-only browsers should be told to click the link to go to the new page's location.

To set up automatic forwarding, add the following META element (in place of "url," be sure to type the URL of the new page's location):

```
<META http-equiv="refresh" content="45; url =url">
```

This META element instructs the browser to access the URL given in the URL attribute after a delay of 45 seconds.

Summary

With the completion of this this chapter, you've reached the end of the basic HTML structural markup for Web documents. In Part Three, you move to considerations of element positioning on the page, beginning with the awesome new capabilities of next-generation CSS positioning properties. You will also learn how to position content with tables and frames.

Part Three explores document layout with style sheets, tables, and frames. Move your Web publishing skills to the next level!

Part Three

Lay It Out With STYLE

12

Creating Magazine-Quality Layouts

In this chapter, you will learn the following skills:

- Understanding and using the CSS box formatting model
- Adding margins and padding to elements
- Fixing elements in absolute positions on the page
- Superimposing text over graphics
- Creating a two-column newspaper layout

You have been adding HTML elements like crazy and formatting them with CSS.1 style sheets, but you haven't done much about document layout—the overall arrangement of elements on the viewed or printed page. In fact, you haven't been able to do much more than merely list the elements in the order you want them to appear. From there, the browser takes over and places them according to its default settings, which, I'm sure you'll agree, are not very exciting. There is really nothing in your pages, yet, that looks like the visually

219

appealing layout you'd find in any reasonably-well-designed magazine or newspaper. What gives?

Until recently, HTML just did not provide any intended means to lay out elements on the page with any degree of precision. But Web authors quickly discovered that one could use an unintended means, tables (to be introduced in the next chapter). Virtually all of the tables you will find in Web documents are really being used to present tabular data. People use them to create magazine and newspaper layout effects, such as multiple columns and graphics positioning. But that's a bad thing. Tables weren't intended for this use, and what's worse, transform the underlying source code into an unreadable mishmash.

The HTML Version 4 way provides an alternative worth considering. The CSS Level 2 style sheet model enables you to position elements on the page in absolute, fixed positions. Such elements can include virtually anything you can put into an HTML page, including (of course) graphics, but also including text elements, such as paragraphs and lists. To be sure, these extensions are not widely supported yet. But we will discuss them here, thanks to the fact that they are fully supported by Microsoft Internet Explorer Version 4.

This chapter presents the impressive new capabilities of the CSS positioning properties. Once you figure out how they work, you have document layout in the bag.

If you would rather not tie your site down to Microsoft Internet Explorer Version 4, you'll have to learn how to do document layout with tables, as described in the following chapter.

Box It Up

Before getting into absolute positioning, let's take a closer look at the existing CSS.1 layout model. It is important to understand how this works. You will get the maximum effect from absolute positioning if you learn how to blend the existing CSS.1 layout properties with the nifty new positioning ones.

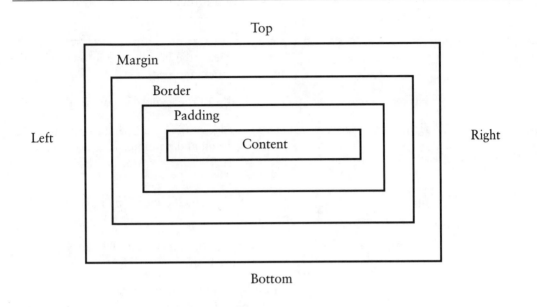

Figure 12.1 The CSS box formatting model

Put It in This Box, Please

The CSS Level 1 style sheet specification envisions a box formatting model, in which each element resides in a rectangular box. A box can fit within a box, like Chinese boxes.

In Figure 12.1, you see how the various boxes fit together, using three separately-defined properties.

All of the box properties listed below are optional:

- **Margins** Transparent space indented from the document window.
- **Borders** Rules in a variety of styles.
- **Padding** Space that is placed between the borders and the object.

Table 12.1 introduces some useful terminology for talking about the box formatting model.

Table 12.1 Some useful terms for box formatting

Term	Definition
left outer edge	The left edge of the box, taking into account the margin, border, and padding.
left inner edge	The left edge of the enclosed content.
right outer edge	The right edge of the box, taking into account the margin, border, and padding.
right inner edge	The right edge of the enclosed content.
top	Top of the box, including the margin, border, and padding.
bottom	Bottom of the box, including the margin, border, and padding.
width	Width of the enclosed content. If you box a replacable element (such as an image), the default width is the width of the replaced element. (If you specify a different width, the browser resizes the element.) If you box a block-line element, the default value of the width is "auto," which means that the browser calculates the element's width so that the seven horizontal elements (left and right margin, border, and padding, plus the content itself) equals the width of the parent element.
height	Height of the enclosed content. If you box a replacable element (such as an image), the height is the height of the replaced element. (If you specify a different height, the browser resizes the element.) If you box a block element, the default height is calculated by the current line height settings (which depends on the font size you choose).

What Can You Put in the Box?

Within a CSS.1 formatting box, you can put either of the following:

- Any block–level element, including DIV.
- A *replacable element*, including IMG. A replaceable element is one that's replaced with an object, such as an image or movie.

So How Do You Do This?

You can add box formatting properties to any replaceable or block element in two ways:

- By defining the element's properties in a style sheet.
- By adding style information in-line.

Here are examples of both types. The first defines P elements in a style sheet:

```
<HEAD>
     <STYLE type = "text/css">
     P {margin-left: 1in}
     </STYLE>
</HEAD>
```

And here is the in-line version:

```
<P style = "margin-left: 1in">Enclosed content</P>
```

Marginal Utility Explained

Margins enable you to indent items from the top, right, bottom, left, or any combination of these. You may ask, "indented from what?" The parent element. But what is the parent element?

If there is no other box defined, the parent element is the BODY. Suppose you have indented the BODY by a half inch left and right. Then you create a box with another half-inch left and right indentation. The box will be indented a total of one inch from the left and right window border.

Remember that although margins, borders, and padding aren't inherited, their effects are cumulative, as the previous example demonstrated. If the parent element has a one inch left and right margin and you insert a box with a two inch left and right margin, the total indentation is three inches.

Among the great things you can do with margins is something absolutely unthinkable in previous versions of HTML: You can outdent a left margin by using a negative left margin. This is a style you often see in print media layouts. Note: So that the left margin is fully visible, give the entire BODY a positive left margin. For example, if you define H1 with a left margin of negative one (–1) inch, give the BODY a left margin of positive one (+1) inch.

CSS Box Properties: Margins

To create margins, you use the CSS margin properties.

As with borders (discussed in Chapter 7), you can define margins independently by using the individual properties (here, margin-left, margin-right, margin-bottom, and margin-top), or you can use the shorthand property (margin) to define them all at once.

You'll find the shorthand property much easier to use than the individual margin properties; it enables you to set all the margins at once.

Defining Margins Individually

Here are the properties you can use to define margins individually.

PROPERTY	margin-left, margin-right, margin-bottom, and margin-top
PURPOSE	Specifies the width of the box's bottom margin.
INHERITED	Yes
VALUES	Specify a length or a percentage of the containing block.
DEFAULT	0
USED IN	Replaced and block-level elements
SUPPORT	MSIE 3.0/Win95: Yes

	MSIE 4.0/Win95: Yes
	NN4.0/Win95: No
	MSIE 3.0/Mac OS: Yes
	MSIE 4.0/Mac OS: Yes
	NN4.0/Mac OS: Yes
EXAMPLE	{ margin-bottom: 0.5in }
TIP	You can use the margin property to set the margin for all four sides at once.

Using the Margin Shorthand Property

You can define all four margins at once with the margin shorthand property. Like other shorthand properties that you'll learn in this chapter, it's vastly preferable to typing out separate definitions of the left, right, bottom, and top margins.

Following is the definition for the margin shorthand property.

PROPERTY	margin
PURPOSE	Provides a shorthand means of specifying settings for all margins.
INHERITED	Yes
VALUES	Specify lengths for the top, right, bottom, and left borders, in that order. If you specify only one value, it applies to all four sides. If you specify two values, you have defined the top and bottom. If you specify three values, you define the top, bottom, and sides (left and right), respectively.
DEFAULT	Not defined
USED IN	Replaced and block-level elements
EXAMPLE	{ margin: 0.5in }
TIP	If you specify just one value, it applies to all four margins.

CSS Box Properties: Padding

Padding is inserted between the element and the borders. As with margins and borders, you can add padding all around, or to each of the sides independently. You can specify the size of the padding.

Defining Padding for Individual Padding Zones

The following properties enable you to add padding zones individually to the top, right, bottom, or left sides of an element. The padding appears between the element and the border.

PROPERTY	padding-top, padding-right, padding-bottom, and padding-left
PURPOSE	Provides a means of specifying settings for individual padding zones.
INHERITED	Yes
VALUES	Specify a length or percentage of the enclosing element.
DEFAULT	Not defined
USED IN	Replaced and block-level elements
EXAMPLE	{ padding - left: 0.25in }
TIP	Padding is inserted between the enclosed element and the border, if any.

Using the Padding Shorthand Property

Here is a shorthand property that enables you to define all padding zones at once.

PROPERTY	padding
PURPOSE	Provides a shorthand means of specifying settings for all padding zones.
INHERITED	Yes
VALUES	Specify lengths for the top, right, bottom, and left padding zones, in that order. If you specify only one value, it applies to all four sides. If you specify

two values, you have defined the top and bottom. If you specify three values, you define the top, bottom, and sides (left and right), respectively.

DEFAULT	Not defined
USED IN	Replaced and block-level elements
EXAMPLE	{ padding: 0.25in }
TIP	If you specify just one value, it applies to all four paddings.

CSS Box Properties: Controlling Element Size

By default, the boxed element's width and height are set to auto, which means the following:

- **Width** The browser sizes the element's height based on the size of the original replacable element or the line height of text.
- **Height** The browser sizes the element's width based on the size of the original replacable element. For text blocks, the auto setting sizes the width dynamically based on the available space after margins, borders, and padding are taken into account.

You can override these settings by using the width or height properties, or both.

Using the Height Property

Here's the definition for the height property:

PROPERTY	height
PURPOSE	Specifies the height of an element.
INHERITED	No
VALUES	Specify a length or a percentage of the containing block, or auto
DEFAULT	auto
USED IN	Replaced and block-level elements
SUPPORT	MSIE 3.0/Win95: Yes
	MSIE 4.0/Win95: Yes
	NN4.0/Win95: Yes

	MSIE 3.0/Mac OS: Yes
	MSIE 4.0/Mac OS: Yes
	NN4.0/Mac OS: Yes
EXAMPLE	{ width: 50%}
TIP	If the height is set to auto, the height is determined by the intrinsic height of the element.

Using the Width Property

Here is the definition for the width property:

PROPERTY	width
PURPOSE	Specifies the width of an element.
INHERITED	No
VALUES	Specify a length or a percentage of the containing block, or auto
DEFAULT	auto
USED IN	Replaced and block-level elements
SUPPORT	MSIE 3.0/Win95: Yes
	MSIE 4.0/Win95: Yes
	NN4.0/Win95: Yes
	MSIE 3.0/Mac OS: Yes
	MSIE 4.0/Mac OS: Yes
	NN4.0/Mac OS: Yes
EXAMPLE	{ width: 50%}
TIP	If the width is set to auto, the width is determined by the intrinsic width of the element.

It All Adds Up

If you are getting strange results with margins and padding, bear in mind that a containing element's margins and padding are added to the margins and padding you specify for a contained element. For example, the BODY element contains the P element, and the P element can contain the IMG element. If you specify one inch margins for the all three, the IMG element will have a three inch margin.

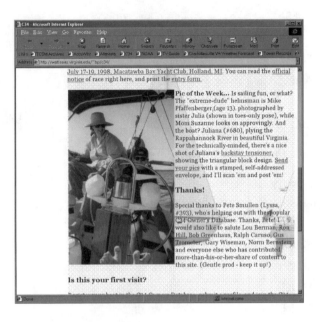

Figure 12.2 A graphic floated to the left of the page

Let Me Float This By You

In addition to positioning images with margins, borders, and padding, you can specify float properties—specifically, you can float an image to the right or to the left, with text "wrapping" around the images. You can float replaceable elements, such as images. You can also float elements grouped with DIV. Without a float, the element just appears where you have placed it within the text.

Figure 12.2 shows how floated graphics appear. This graphic has been floated to the left, with text flowing to the right. To float elements, you use the float and clear properties. The float property creates the float; the clear property controls where the floating element allows other elements to flow around it (right, left, or none). Here is the float property definition:

PROPERTY	float
PURPOSE	Floats an element to the left or right, so that text flows around it.

INHERITED	No
VALUES	left, right, or none
DEFAULT	none
USED IN	All elements
EXAMPLE	{ float: left }
TIP	You can float replaceable elements, such as images, or text elements grouped with DIV.

Following is the clear property's definition:

PROPERTY	clear
PURPOSE	Determines whether an element will allow floating elements on its left side, its right side, or both sides.
INHERITED	No
VALUES	left, right, both, or none
DEFAULT	both
USED IN	All elements
EXAMPLE	{ clear: left }
TIP	You don't need to use this property unless you want to prevent other elements from flowing around the floated element.

Please Get into Position—Absolutely!

In this section, you will learn how you can position anything you want on your page with a degree of precision that was only dreamed of just a few months before this book was written. It's called *absolute positioning*. Not well supported (only Microsoft Internet Explorer currently recognizes the absolute positioning properties), absolute positioning is nevertheless destined to become *the* way Web page designers create page layouts.

Why Is Absolute Positioning Needed?

Although it is very nice to be able to float graphics to the left or right and have text flow around the graphic, this capability isn't sufficient. If you look at the typical commercial Web page, you'll see a lot of little graphics positioned here

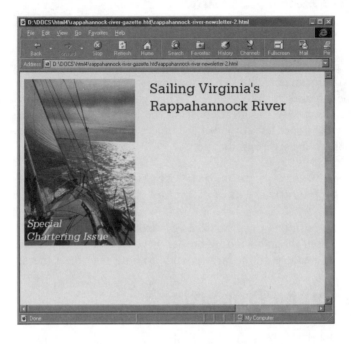

Figure 12.3 Text superimposed on graphic

and there. Web authors typically do this by means of complex tables, which make the underlying source code very difficult to read and edit. Thanks to proposed extensions to the CSS style sheet standard, you can now position graphics (and other objects) in absolute locations on the page—that is, by means of x and y coordinate specifications, which tell the browser precisely where the object is supposed to be located. As a measure of how much this capability is needed, it's already supported by Microsoft Internet Explorer 4.0. This section shows you how to position graphics in fixed locations.

If this sounds complicated, read on. These new capabilities are enormously helpful and useful. For example, you can superimpose text over a graphic! Yes, that's right, we're talking about three dimensions here, not just two. In Figure 12.3, for example, you see white text positioned over an inline image. You can assign an absolute position to anything contained in a replaceable element (such as images) or a DIV or SPAN element. This means, in effect, that you can position any group of elements anywhere you want.

What Do You Mean, Absolute?

So how does positioning work? To understand this, you need to learn the term *current positioning context*. Absolute positioning always works within the current positioning context. By default, the current positioning context is the HTML document itself. The coordinates of the upper left corner are 0, 0 (flush to the left and flush to the top). When you specify an absolute positioning context, you specify the location using the left and top properties, which identify where the upper left corner of the object begins. For example, consider the following in-line style specification:

```
<IMG src ="icon.gif" style="position: absolute;
top: 24pt; left: 12pt">
```

This tag positions the graphic 24 pts from the top of the HTML page, and 12 points from the left window border. If you don't specify a width or height, the browser creates a frame large enough to hold the object (here, a graphic).

CSS Positioning Properties

To create the positioned element, you use the position property. You use the offset properties (top, right, bottom, left) to specify the offset from the default HTML "page."

Using the Position Property

This element sets up the absolute positioning. Here is the definition:

PROPERTY	position
PURPOSE	Determines whether an element flows with the text (static), occupies a fixed position (absolute), or flows in relation to an absolutely-positioned element (relative).
INHERITED	No
VALUES	absolute, relative, or static
DEFAULT	normal
USED IN	All elements
EXAMPLE	{ position: absolute }

TIP	Positioning properties are supported only by Microsoft Internet Explorer Version 4.

Specifying the Offsets

To specify the offset from the HTML "page," you use the top, right, bottom, and left elements. If you specify the top but not the bottom offset, or the left and not the right offset, the element's size is determined by its intrinsic width or height. (You can specify these, if you wish, by using the width and height properties, discussed earlier in this chapter.) Here is the definition for the offset elements:

PROPERTY	top, right, bottom, and left
PURPOSE	Specifies an offset from the top, right, bottom, or left of a positioned-element's reference box.
INHERITED	No
VALUES	Specify a length or percentage of the reference box's width.
DEFAULT	0
USED IN	All elements
EXAMPLE	{ top: 2.5in; left: 0.5in }
TIP	If you don't specify a width for an absolutely-positioned element (using the width property), the width is determined by the element's intrinsic size.

Using Relative Positioning

You may be wondering why there's a relative as well as static value for the position element. Here's why: The static value is the default for all objects; it permits no positioning other than those you can achieve with other CSS.1 properties, such as floating (discussed above).

The relative value does something special and really great. It establishes a new positioning context within which you can absolutely position child elements (elements included within the surrounding element's tags). The relative element flows with the rest of the elements on the page.

An element positioned relatively flows just like any static element—it doesn't stay put. So why should you use it?

Why Is Relative Positioning Needed?

A relatively positioned element resets the current positioning context. Unless you nest positioned elements, the coordinates you are using are those of the entire BODY of the document, conceptualized as a box with four corners. At the upper left is coordinate 0,0 (flush to the left and flush to the top). Once you're away from the top of the page, it's a real bear to figure out exactly where to position elements vertically. Relative positioning really helps simplify subsequent absolute positioning by, in effect, giving you a new "top of the page."

Using Relative and Absolute Positioning Together

Here is an example of using relative positioning to start a new "top of the page" and then specifying subsequent absolute element positions with ease. Check out the line with the double top border and single bottom border, below the graphic (see Figure 12.4).

Take a look at the HTML that adds the place and date of publication. You put this at the end of the BODY, after everything else we've discussed.

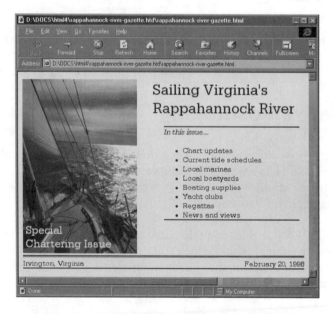

Figure 12.4 Relative positioning starts a new positioning context

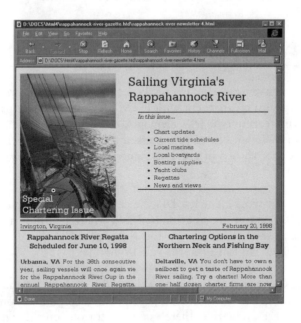

Figure 12.5 New positioning context started below graphic

```
<DIV style = "position: relative; border-top: dou-
ble; ">
        <SPAN style = "text-align: left; position:
        absolute; top=5pt">Irvington, Virginia</SPAN>
        <SPAN style = "text-align: right; position:
        absolute; top=5pt; border-bottom: thin
        solid">February 20, 1998</SPAN>
</DIV>
```

Here is how this works: The DIV element defines a new positioning context. However, the element, and everything it contains, flows in-line with the rest of the content. Since it comes last in the BODY, that's where it appears in the document when viewed by the browser (see Figure 12.5). But this relatively-positioned DIV element establishes a new "top of the page" for the absolutely-positioned SPAN elements to follow. The first one determines the place of publication to be five points below the top of the new positioning context, allowing room for the border, and it formats the text flush left. The second one places the date of publication in the same vertical position, but formats it flush right.

Creating Newspaper Columns

CSS doesn't have properties expressly designed to create newspaper columns, but it is very easy to create them with HTML 4 and CSS float properties. The trick here lies in creating two DIV elements, one with the class name "left" and the other with the class name, you guessed it, "right." Figure 12.5 shows how the Web newsletter shown in previous figures can be spiffed up with a two-column text layout.

How does this work? The left DIV element is given a width of 50% of the available window space, and it is floated left. There is a 0.25 inch padding on the right, and a thin solid rule on the right, as well, which serves to divide the columns. (You can leave out the rule if you like.)

The right DIV element is also given a width of 50% of the available window space, and it is floated right. There is a 0.25 inch padding on the left. Since the left border inserts the rule, there's no need for one on the right.

Here's the style sheet that sets up these DIV elements:

```
<HEAD>
<STYLE type = "text/css">
    DIV.left { width: 50%;
            text-align: Justify;
            clear: none;
            float: left;
            padding-right: 0.25in;
            border-right: solid thin;
    }
    DIV.right {
            width: 50%;
            text-align: Justify;
            clear: none;
            float: right;
            padding-left: 0.25in;
    }
</STYLE>
</HEAD>
```

See below for the classes as they are inserted in your document:

```
<DIV class = "left">
     <P>Here's a paragraph for the left column.</P>
     <P>And here's another paragraph for the left
     column.</P>
</DIV>

<DIV class = "right">
     <P>Here's a paragraph for the right
     column.</P>
     <P>And here's another paragraph for the right
     column.</P>
</DIV>
```

You could set up three columns by defining the DIV classes with fixed widths, but I wouldn't recommend it. The two-column layout ensures that just about anyone will be able to read your document, even if they are using a notebook computer with low resolution. What's more, using percentage widths ensures that the columns still look nice after users resize the screen.

Summary

This chapter showed you how to position elements on the page with style sheets and that's the way to go. If you are intending to create a version of your site for people using non-CSS-capable browsers, though, you'll have to use tables and frames to lay out your document. Find out how in the next couple of chapters.

Chapter 13 shows you how to use tables. You are supposed to use these only for putting information in tabular form, but the reality is that they are still indispensable for layout purposes if you're creating documents for non-CSS-capable browsers.

Chapter 14 shows you how to create framed documents, which—even though they are not very popular with users—are part of the transitional flavor of HTML 4.

13

Using (and Slightly Abusing) Tables

In this chapter, you will learn the following skills:

- Understanding the basics of HTML tables
- Choosing table formatting options
- Adding data to your tables
- Creating headers and captions
- Grouping data by rows and columns
- Using styles to format tables

Using tables, you can group data into rows and columns, which form rectangular cells. Within each cell, you can add as much text as you want; the browser automatically sizes the cell so that there is enough room. Here, I'm not just talking about numerical "data"—a table cell can contain anything you can put into an HTML document, including paragraphs of text, graphics, videos, and even nested tables. With tables, it is possible to create very complex structures for grouping your material.

This chapter shows you how to create tables with HTML, going over the basics and highlighting new HTML Version 4 capabilities for grouping columns and rows. As you will learn in this chapter, HTML purists, including the HTML Version 4 specification team, would prefer that tables are used only for tabular data, but not for layout and presentation purposes. If you're creating a page for non-CSS-capable browsers, you will probably wind up using tables to specify document layout, unless you are willing to create frames (discussed in the next chapter). In the strict flavor of HTML 4, the use of tables for layout is forbidden, but it is tolerated in the transitional flavor. Whether you use tables for tabular data or for layout purposes, the elements are the same. In this chapter, you will learn how to use them.

Are Tables Worth Doing Manually?

Let's begin with a reality check. The HTML table tags are a bear to use and even harder to read. But there is a reason for this; they were not meant to be worked with. The design of these tags is optimized so that editor programs can automate the table-creation process. For example, Microsoft FrontPage enables you to

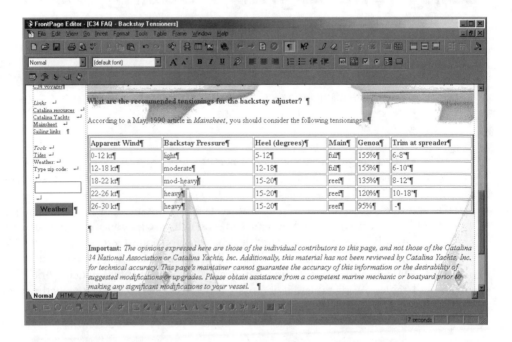

Figure 1.1 Hypertext enables readers to choose their own way

create tables just as you would with a word processing program; in a "what-you-see-is-what-you-get" (WYSIWYG) environment, you can lay out the table by inserting and modifying the matrix of rows and columns. Adding text or graphics is easy; you just click within a cell, and add content. In Figure 13.1, you see a Microsoft FrontPage table under construction in a WYSIWYG environment.

Frankly, I would advise you to create your tables with a WYSIWYG editor such as FrontPage. That is by far the easiest way to get your table going. As you will quickly learn, though, WYSIWYG table editors do not implement all the things you can do with tables. Even with a tool as useful as FrontPage, I often find myself having to "tweak" tables by dealing with the table code. You'll almost certainly find yourself going into the table tags and doing some hand editing.

So what's to gain by reading this chapter? Plenty. Unless you understand the table elements, you will be completely lost when you try to edit the tags. This does not mean you have to memorize all the tags down cold; it just means that you should work through this chapter so that you understand how tables work. Later, when you're trying to "tweak" a table to get it to look right, you will know just what to look for within the wilderness of table tags.

Putting Your Cards on the TABLE (Table Basics)

Let's jump right in and take a look at a simple table's structure. First, you need to understand the relationship between the TABLE element and the elements that it contains. Next, you can look at a simple example. From this, you'll see how basic tables work.

The TABLE Element as a Container

As you have learned, it is useful to think of some elements as containers that contain something. Don't let your eyes glaze over; this is a simple concept.

An HTML table begins and ends with TABLE tags. The TABLE element can contain the following:

- **A caption** You create captions with the CAPTION element.
- **Rows** Every table must have at least one row. You create rows with the <TR> element.
- **Columns** Every table must have at least one column. You create columns by specifying a cols attribute when you define the table with the TABLE element. (If you don't define the number of columns, the

browser infers the number of columns by counting the table data elements. As as you'll see, it is better to define the number of columns from the outset.)

- **Table Data** At each intersection of a table and row, there is a cell. Within the cell, there is an HTML container for the table data, defined by the TD element. As you will see later, cells can span rows or columns, but let's stick to a simple table for now.

Let's put off the element definitions for a bit, and see how this all works.

A Simple Table

Here is a very simple table. Try to figure out how many rows and columns it contains:

```
<TABLE>
     <TR>
             <TD>This is cell 1.
             <TD>This is cell 2.
             <TD>This is cell 3.

     <TR>
             <TD>This is cell 4.
             <TD>This is cell 5.
             <TD>This is cell 6.

</TABLE>
```

Did you guess three columns and two rows? If so, you are right. Here's how this table looks:

```
cell 1        cell 2        cell 3
cell 4        cell 5        cell 6
```

Note the following true facts about tables:

- You start and end the table with the TABLE element.
- Within the TABLE element, you next define rows using TR.
- Within the rows, you create columns by adding TD elements.
- The table data goes in the TD elements.

Looking at this example, you can see that it is important to indent the various tags so that the table's structure is immediately apparent. This is even more important when you nest tables, as discussed later in this chapter.

Another Example

Here's another example.

```
<TABLE>

    <TR>
            <TD>This is cell 1.
            <TD>This is cell 2.
</TABLE>
```

This table consists of only one row, and two columns. Believe it or not, that is precisely the structure underlying a very high proportion of professionally-designed Web pages.

```
cell 1        cell 2
```
Sized appropriately, you get a wonderful layout for navigation aids, as in the following example:

Welcome   Welcome to my site! Here, you'll
Contents   find the new, the hot, the cool,
New   and if that's not enough, a whole
Hot   bunch of links.
Cool
Links

The only problem with this layout is that, when the user scrolls down to read the text in cell 2, the navigation aids (cell 1) scroll out of sight. This is the principal justification for using frames, which enable you to define independently-scrollable rectangular areas within your frame (but to my mind, it is the only justification). You learn about frames in the next chapter.

A Look Ahead at Cell Spanning

A previous section mentioned that you can make cells span rows or columns. You will learn how to do this later. For now, look at what spanning can do.

Here is a somewhat more elaborate example of the layout just shown:

My Totally Cool Site

Welcome   Welcome to my site! Here, you'll
Contents   find the new, the hot, the cool,
New   and if that's not enough, a whole
Hot   bunch of links.
Cool
Links

Note that the first row spans two columns. You can also create a cell that spans two or more rows, as you'll see later.

Those are the basics! Now take a closer look at the various tags, their element definitions, and the many attributes you can use to control table layout.

Defining Your Table's Appearance

The TABLE element enables you to choose options for your entire table, including a number of presentation aspects.

Here is the TABLE element definition; note that some of the defaults may vary depending on the browser you are using:

ELEMENT	TABLE
PURPOSE	Creates a table.
TYPE	Inline
NESTED WITHIN	COLGROUP element
START TAG	Required
END TAG	Required
CONTENT	Table tags and text
ATTRIBUTES	**Strict DTD:** core attributes (id, class, style, title) language attributes (lang, dir) summary = "text" (optional) width = "length" (optional)

border = "pixels" (optional)
frame = "(void, above, below, hsides,lhs, rhs,vsides, box, border)" (optional)
rules = "(none, groups, rows, cols, all)" (optional)

Transitional DTD (deprecated):
align = "(left, center, right)"
bgcolor = "color"

EXAMPLE

```
<TABLE>
      <TR>
            <TD>Cell 1
            <TD>Cell 2
      </TR>
</TABLE>
```

TIP

Use the summary attribute to specify a brief summary of the table for people using non-graphical browsers.

The following sections look at these attributes in order of importance, with the more essential ones first. Table 13.1 sums them the TABLE element's attributes for handy reference purposes.

Table 13.1 TABLE element attributes

Attribute	Use and example
align	Aligns the whole table (deprecated; for use only in the transitional flavor of HTML 4). `<TABLE align = "center">`
bgcolor	Chooses a background color for the whole table (deprecated; for use only in the transitional flavor of HTML 4). `<TABLE bgcolor ="yellow">`
border	Specifies the border width, in pixels. If you specify a border width, this automatically sets frame to "border" (all sides shown) and rules to "all." `<TABLE border = "2">`

cellspacing

This controls spacing between the table cells. With most browsers, the default is 1 pixel; you can increase this if you wish.

`<TABLE cellspacing = "3">`

cellpadding

This controls the extra space inserted within cells.

`<TABLE cellpadding = "1">`

cols

Specifies the number of columns so that the browser can immediately proceed to lay out the table structure; speeds table display.

`<TABLE cols = "5">`

frame

Specifies which sides will be visible. Choose from void (no sides are visible; this is the default value), above (top border only), below (bottom border only), hsides (top and bottom borders), vsides (left and right borders), lhs (left-hand-side only), rhs (right-hand-side only), box (all four sides), border (all four sides).

`<TABLE frame = "top">`

rules

Specifies which internal rules should be visible. You can choose from none (the default value), groups (rules appear between column and row groups only, as defined by the COL, COL-GROUP, THEAD, TBODY, and TFOOT elements); rows (rules appear between rows only); cols (rules appear between columns only); all (rules are drawn around every cell).

`<TABLE = rules = "all">`

width

Specifies the table width. The default is 100% of window width.

`<TABLE width = 75%>`

Defining the Number of Columns

All the TABLE element's attributes are optional, as you can see from the element definition. And as you have already learned, the browser can figure out the number of columns by counting the number of TD elements in a row.

So why define the number of columns? Simple: This enables the browser to "predict" the table's structure, enabling it to start displaying the structure even before it has finished reading all the data. The result is faster display.

If you set up a table with 3 columns, use the cols attribute to define the number of columns, as in the following example:

```
<TABLE cols="3">
```

Aligning the Table

To align the table relative to the window borders, you can use the align attribute. (This is a deprecated element, which you should use only in the transitional flavor of HTML 4.) You can choose from left (the default), center, or right.

Here is how to center your table:

```
<TABLE align = "center">
```

If you're adhering to the strict flavor of HTML 4, you can align your table with DIV, as in the following example:

```
<DIV align = "center">
     <TABLE>
     [ ... ]
     </TABLE>
</DIV>
```

Specifying the Table's Width

By default, your table will span all the available space in the window (in other words, the width attribute is implicitly 100%).

You can change this by specifying any valid length, as in the following examples:

```
<TABLE width = "75%">
<TABLE width = "225">
```

In the first example, the table spans 75% of the available window space. In the second example, you see an absolute width specification: Here, 225 pixels.

Be very careful about specifying absolute table widths. It is difficult to predict the type of display people are going to be using. If you use absolute widths, the table might not be completely visible. Some text-only browsers display a maximum of 80 columns of text. Many laptop users have displays that can show only 640 pixels horizontally and 480 pixels vertically (640 x 480).

Specifying the Table's Border

Just how table borders appear depends on the browser. Most display a 1 pixel border by default on all four sides of the frame (top, right, bottom, left), as well as drawing rules around all cells. In previous versions of HTML, if you wanted to make sure borders were hidden, you used the following:

```
<TABLE border = "0">
```

This still works in HTML Version 4, and you will be wise to use it, to ensure backwards compatibility with previous browsers. However, the correct means of hiding borders is the following:

```
<TABLE border = "1" frame = "void" rules = "none">
```

New to HTML Version 4, the frame and rules attributes enable you to specify just where borders and rules appear. The various options are listed in Table 13.1.

Here are some examples so you can see how the frame and rules attributes work:

```
<TABLE border = "5" frame = "hsides" rules = "cols">
```

In the above example, the frame attribute tells the browser to add 5-pixel (thick) borders to the top and bottom of the table, as well as between table columns. Here's how this looks:

```
Cell 1      Cell 2      Cell 3
Cell 4      Cell 5      Cell 6
Cell 7      Cell 8      Cell 9
```

See the following for another example:

```
<TABLE border = "3" frame = "lhs" rules = "rows">
```

This places a border on the left side of the table, and rules between rows, as shown here:

```
Cell 1      Cell 2      Cell 3
Cell 4      Cell 5      Cell 6
Cell 7      Cell 8      Cell 9
```

HTML Version 4 enables you to do some great things with borders and rules around group columns and rows; you will learn about this in a bit, after grouping has been introduced.

Creating a Row

To create a row, you use the TR element.

You may have noticed that there is no rows attribute in the TABLE element's definition. That's because you specify the number of rows by adding TR elements. If you forget to include these, or forget to close them, some or all of your data will not appear.

Here's the TR element definition:

ELEMENT	TR
PURPOSE	Creates a table row.
TYPE	Inline

NESTED WITHIN	TR element
START TAG	Required
END TAG	Optional
CONTENT	Table tags and text
ATTRIBUTES	core attributes (id, class, style, title) language attributes (lang, dir) align = "(left, center, right,justify,char)" char = "character" charoff = "length" valign = "(top, middle, bottom, baseline)"

EXAMPLE	`<TR>`
	    `<TD>Cell 1`
	    `<TD>Cell 2`
	`</TR>`

TIP	You can omit the end tag.

This element has many attributes, as usual, but you're already familiar with them; Table 13.1 defines them, and the following sections discuss the high points. Note that the TR element doesn't have to have an end tag. You can make your HTML more readable by omitting it.

Remember that the attributes you choose will be inherited by all the elements contained within TR—that is, the TD elements (data cells). It is a lot easier to specify alignment attributes at the row level rather than defining them for each cell individually. Define alignment at the cell (TD) level only when you want to change the alignment in a particular cell.

Controlling Vertical and Horizontal Alignment

If you define alignment using TR, the alignment you specify affects all the cells (TD elements) within the row. That is efficient, so here's a good place to choose alignment options.

Using the align and valign attributes, you can control the alignment of cell data in a variety of ways. In this example, the data within the row appears vertically and horizontally centered:

```
<TR align = "center" valign = "middle">
        <TD>Cell 1
        <TD>Cell 2
        <TD>Cell 3
```

Aligning Table Data by Character

New to HTML Version 4 is the ability to align by a character. By this I do not mean that you're going to get Ace Ventura to clean up your table. This is most often used to align numerical data by the decimal point, as in the following example:

```
<TR align = "char" char = ".">
        <TD>1,211,597.35
<TR align = "char" char = ".">
        <TD>23.0077894
<TR align = "char" char = ".">
        <TD>125
```

Here is how this looks:

```
1,211,597.35
        23.0077894
   125.0
```

Take a look at character-aligned data with your browser to see how it looks. If the data looks like it is being pinched on the left or right side of a cell, you can use the charoff attribute to specify how far the specified character should be indented from the cell's left border.

Locking Up Data In Their Cells

Now you are ready, finally, to type some actual data. Remember that all the data in your table lives in TD elements, which are enclosed within rows. That is why we say, "With HTML, the data come marching in row-by-row."

Here is the element definition:

ELEMENT	TD
PURPOSE	Creates a table cell.
TYPE	Inline
NESTED WITHIN	TR element
START TAG	Required
END TAG	Optional
CONTENT	Table tags and text
ATTRIBUTES	**Strict DTD:**
	core attributes (id, class, style, title)
	language attributes (lang, dir)
	dir = (rtl, ltr) (optional)
	axis = "text" (optional)
	headers = "ID list" (optional)
	scope = "(row, col, rowgroup, colgroup)"
	rowspan = "number" (optional)
	colspan = "number" (optional)
	align = "(left, center, right, justify, char)"
	char = "character"
	charoff = "length"
	valign = "(top, middle, bottom, baseline)"
	Transitional DTD (deprecated):
	nowrap (optional)
	width = "length" (optional)
	height = "length"
EXAMPLE	`<TR>`
	`        <TD>Cell 1`
	`        <TD>Cell 2`
	`</TR>`
TIP	You can omit the end tag.

Note that the TD element's end tag is optional. Don't use it; the table element syntax is confusing enough. It's like the LI element. You don't really need the end tag since the next TD element (or the close of a row) signifies the end of the data.

Aligning Cell Data

You definitely do not want to handle alignment by typing alignment attributes in every cell; that's a job for the containing elements, and the bigger, the better.

In the previous section, you learned that the TR element's alignment affects all the cells in the row, unless you specify otherwise; similarly, you'll learn later that the THEAD, TBODY, and TFOOT elements enable you to specify alignments for groups of rows. That is even more efficient.

So when do you specify alignment in a TD element? Simple; when you want to change the alignment for one cell, and one cell only.

If you specify left alignment in a TR element, you will get left alignment in all the cells in the row, except for those for which you've inserted an align attribute with a different value. In this way, you could have a row that is centered, except for one cell, which is formatted with right alignment.

Spanning Rows and Columns

The colspan and rowspan attributes enable you to create cells that span more than one column or row. This is needed to produce effects such as the following:

```
       This cell spans three columns
This cell           Cell 3      Cell 4
spans two rows      Cell 5      Cell 6
```

Here's the HTML that produces this table:

```
<TABLE border = "1" cols = "3">
     <TR>
          <TD colspan = "3">This cell spans three
          columns
     <TR>
          <TD rowspan = "2">This cell spans two
          rows
          <TD>Cell 3
          <TD>Cell 4
     <TR>
          <TD>Cell 5
          <TD>Cell 6
</TABLE>
```

Table Header Cells (TH)

The TH (table header) element enables you to create cells that get extra emphasis from browsers, such as boldface type. For example, you could use TH instead of TD in the first row to produce the following table:

```
                    Chapter 14  Chapter 15
Mountain Dew        12          9
Jolt Cola           26          13
```

Here is the HTML that produces this table:

```
<TABLE border = "1" cols = "3">
    <TR>
        <TH>
        <TH>Required for Chapter 14
        <TH>Required for Chapter 15
    <TR>
        <TH>Mountain Dew
        <TD>12
        <TD>9
    <TR>
        <TH>Jolt Cola
        <TD>26
        <TD>13
</TABLE>
```

Note that you don't need to boldface or otherwise emphasize the TH text. That's done automatically by the browser.

How About a Caption?

If you are creating an honest-to-goodness table (rather than using tables to fake desktop publishing effects), you may wish to give your table a caption. You can do this with, you guessed it, the CAPTION element, which must live within the TABLE element.

Here's the CAPTION element's definition:

ELEMENT	CAPTION
PURPOSE	Creates a caption for a table.
TYPE	Inline

NESTED WITHIN	TABLE element
START TAG	Required
END TAG	Required
CONTENT	Text
ATTRIBUTES	**Strict DTD:** core attributes (id, class, style, title) language attributes (lang, dir) **Transitional DTD:** align = "(top,bottom,left, right)"
EXAMPLE	\<CAPTION\>Table 19.3 Expected vs. Actual Values\</CAPTION\>
TIP	You must use this immediately after the TABLE element's start tag. You can specify only one caption per table.

The only new attribute here is the align attribute, which specifies where the caption is located. By default, it is located at the top of the table; most browsers center it, too. This attribute is deprecated in the strict flavor of HTML 4; you can achieve the same effect by using the following STYLE coding:

```
<STYLE type = "text/css">
     CAPTION { text-align: center }
</STYLE>
```

To add a caption, place it after the TABLE start tag but before the first row, as shown:

```
<TABLE>
     <CAPTION>Number of colas required</CAPTION>
        <TR>
             [and so on...]
```

Grouping Rows and Columns

A new and very much needed capability of HTML Version 4 is row and column grouping, which enable you to group a number of rows or columns so that they share the same attributes. This is great not only for formatting purposes (with the row-grouping elements, for instance, you can assign the same attributes to a bunch of rows at once) but also for the new browser capabilities that they will enable. For example, by grouping rows, you will be able to define a table header and footer group that stays put and remains visible in the window, even if the user scrolls down in the table. Column grouping is even more convenient, but let's look at row grouping first.

Grouping Rows: THEAD, TBODY, TFOOT

These three elements enable you to group one or more rows, and define them as table header rows (THEAD), table body rows (TBODY), or table footer rows (TFOOT). In the following example, there are three groups: a table header, a table body, and a table foot. The three groups can be seen (logically, at least) in the following:

```
Caffeine Source    Chapter 14  Chapter 15
Mountain Dew       12          9
Jolt Cola          26          13
TOTAL              38          22
```

What's the point of grouping the data if you are not interested in quick-and-easy formatting? HTML 4-capable browsers will keep the header and footer in view even if there is more table body data than the window can accommodate. This will increase the usefulness of tables when there's a lot of table body data involved. Here's the HTML that groups the data in this table:

```
<TABLE border = "3" frame = "border" rules = "group"
cols = "3">
      <THEAD align = "left">
            <TR>
                  <TH>Caffeine Source
                  <TH>Required for Chapter 14
                  <TH>Required for Chapter 15
      <TFOOT align = "left">
            <TR>
                  <TH>TOTAL
                  <TH>38
                  <TH>22
      <TBODY align = "left">
            <TR>
                  <TH>Mountain Dew
                  <TD>12
                  <TD>9
            <TR>
                  <TH>Jolt Cola
                  <TD>26
                  <TD>13
      </TABLE>
```

I am sure you noticed that the TFOOT element comes before the TBODY part. No, this is not a typo: This is necessary to ensure that the browser can display the foot before the possibly very long list of TBODY data.

If you're going to use THEAD or TFOOT, then you must use the TBODY element; otherwise, it is optional. Each element (THEAD, TBODY, TFOOT) must contain at least one TR element.

Here are the definitions of these three elements:

ELEMENT	THEAD, TBODY, and TFOOT
PURPOSE	THEAD creates a fixed table header; TBODY creates a scrolling table body, and TFOOT creates a fixed table footer.
TYPE	Inline
NESTED WITHIN	TABLE element
START TAG	Optional
END TAG	Optional
CONTENT	Table tags and text
ATTRIBUTES	core attributes (id, class, style, title) language attributes (lang, dir) align = "(left, center, right,justify,char)" char = "character" charoff = "length" valign = "(top, middle, bottom, baseline)"
EXAMPLE	

```
<THEAD>
    <TR>
        <TH>Header 1
        <TH>Header 2
    </TR>
</THEAD>
<TBODY>
    <TR>
        <TD>Item 1
        <TD>Item 2
    </TR>
</TBODY>
```

Why Column Grouping is Needed

It is nice to be able to use THEAD, TBODY, and TFOOT to group rows; you can save some time by assigning alignments to entire groups of rows. But that still doesn't solve a big problem: How do you format columns? In most real-world tables, it is the *columns*, not the rows, that have distinctive formats. One column might list dollar amounts, requiring alignment by decimal, while another might include explanatory text.

Please see the following simple example:

```
            Amount        Explanation
Monday      $3.89         Potato chips
Tuesday     $7.41         Chocolate
```

In the second column, you find dollar amounts aligned by their decimal point.

To format this data with TD, you will have to do a lot of tedious work, like this, because you cannot define the default alignment with TR:

```
<TABLE cols = "3" border = "1">
      <TR>
              <TH>
              <TH>Amount
              <TH>Explanation
      <TR>    <TD>Monday
              <TD align = "char">$3.89
              <TD align = "center">Potato chips
      <TR>
              <TD>Tuesday
              <TD align = "char">$7.41
              <TD align = "center">Chocolate
</TABLE>
```

As you can see, you have to specify alignments for each cell, unless, that is, you know how to use the COLGROUP and COL elements.

Using COLGROUP and COL

With the COLGROUP and COL elements, you can define default attributes for entire columns of data. Both of these elements come before the first TR element in your table. They enable you to define groups of columns, if you wish, and then to specify attributes for each individual column in your table. Let's keep it simple for now by defining just one column group for the table. Take a look at this example:

```
<TABLE cols = "3" border = "1">
    <COLGROUP span = "3">
            <COL align = "left">
            <COL align = "char">
            <COL>align = "center">
    <TR>
            <TH>
            <TH>Amount
            <TH>Explanation
    <TR>    <TD>Monday
            <TD align = "char">$3.89
            <TD align = "center">Potato chips
    <TR>
            <TD>Tuesday
            <TD align = "char">$7.41
            <TD align = "center">Chocolate
</TABLE>
```

The COLGROUP element groups columns (going from left to right); the element's span attribute specifies how many columns you are talking about (here, it is 3, which equals the total number of columns in the table).

Did you see that there is just one column group in this table? Following the COLGROUP element, you see COL elements, which define the columns, again going from left to right. The first column aligns text left. The second column aligns text by character (for English, the default is the decimal point, so this is perfect for the Amount column). The third column centers the text.

Defining More Than One Column Group

What's the use of defining more than one column group? Well, remember the rules attribute in the TABLE element? This attribute's group value automatically inserts rules between groups, which enables you to create some nice-looking tables. In the following example, there are two column groups; the first has just one column, while the second has two. Also, there is a table header that's set off from the table body:

```
              Amount       Explanation
Monday        $3.89        Potato chips
Tuesday       $7.41        Chocolate
```

Here is the HTML:

```
<TABLE cols = "3" border = "3" frame = "border"
rules = "group">
      <COLGROUP span = "1">
            <COL align = "left">
      <COLGROUP span = "2">
            <COL align = "char">
            <COL>align = "center">
      <THEAD>
            <TR>
                  <TH>
                  <TH>Amount
                  <TH>Explanation
      <TBODY>
            <TR>  <TD>Monday
                  <TD align = "char">$3.89
                  <TD align = "center">Potato chips
            <TR>
                  <TD>Tuesday
                  <TD align = "char">$7.41
                  <TD align = "center">Chocolate
</TABLE>
```

Looking at the COLGROUP Element Definition

Let's take a closer look at the capabilities of COLGROUP by examining the element definition.

ELEMENT	COLGROUP
PURPOSE	Groups columns and sets default alignments.
TYPE	Inline
NESTED WITHIN	TABLE element
START TAG	Required

END TAG	Forbidden
CONTENT	Empty
ATTRIBUTES	core attributes (id, class, style, title)
	language attributes (lang, dir)
	span = "number" (optional)
	width = "lengths" (optional)
	align = "(left, center, right,justify,char)"
	char = "character"
	charoff = "length"
	valign = "(top, middle, bottom, baseline)"
EXAMPLE	<COL width= 20 span=3>
TIP	This is an empty element that contains attributes only. To create columns, specify TD elements within a TR element. To define the attributes of individual columns and override COLGROUP, use COL.

You have met most of these attributes before, but the new ones are span and width. Span enables you to define how many columns are in the group, going from left to right. The width attribute is the real star of the show here, because it enables you to specify a default width for an entire column.

In addition to the usual pixel and percentage length, the width attribute can also have a special value: 0* (this specifies that the column width should be the minimum necessary to keep all the data in the column displayed).

Here's an example of span and width in action:

```
<COLGROUP span = "2" width = "0*">
```

This COLGROUP element groups two columns, and tells the browser to keep them wide enough so that all the data in the columns can be seen.

Looking at the COL Element Definition

And now for COL:

ELEMENT	COL
PURPOSE	Identifies individual columns so that you can assign attributes to them.
TYPE	Block
NESTED WITHIN	COLGROUP element
START TAG	Required
END TAG	Forbidden
CONTENT	Empty
ATTRIBUTES	core attributes (id, class, style, title) language attributes (lang, dir)) dir = (rtl, ltr) (optional) span = "number" (optional) width = "lengths" (optional)
EXAMPLE	<COL width= 20 span=3>
TIP	This is an empty element that contains attributes only. To create columns, specify TD elements within a TR element.

The COL element takes exactly the same attributes as the COLGROUP element does, which means that you can define all these attributes for individual columns.

Doing Tables with STYLE

As this chapter earlier indicated, the Level 1 style sheet specification just doesn't do a very good job of dealing with the special characteristics of tables. That is why HTML Version 4 includes a lot of presentation attributes amidst the various table elements, as you've seen, and you should not hesitate to use them. (The recently-announced CSS Level 2 specification provides much better support for tables, but it isn't supported by current browsers.)

You can still use style sheets, though, to define those aspects of table elements that style sheets handle well, such as fonts.

Here's an example:

```
<STYLE type="text/css">
     TABLE {background-color: white}
     TH {font-family: Helvetica, sans-serif}
     TD {font-family: Courier}
</STYLE>
```

The CSS Level 2 specification includes some very interesting new styles for tables, including collapsing rows and columns. Just announced as this book was going to press, these new styles aren't yet supported by browsers, so they're not covered in this edition. For more information, go to www.w3.org, and follow the links to CSS.

Summary

It's difficult to create tables by hand. It is much easier to use a WYSIWYG editor to create the initial table. However, you will probably find you have to get into the table code and "tweak" it in order to get everything to look right. This chapter's explanation of how tables work, and its detailed examination of all the table tags, should give you all the knowledge you need to make your table look just the way you want.

Another layout option involves frames. Learn their mysteries and maladies in Chapter 14.

14

It's a FRAME-Up

In this chapter, you will learn the following skills:

- Setting up your frame document
- Inserting documents within the frames
- Making use of options such as scrolling, movable borders, and targets
- Opening a document in an inline frame

With frames, you can lay out a page that contains two or more independently-scrollable areas. To some people, that's the greatest thing since sliced bread. To others, it's a horrifying abomination that ought to be stamped out, before the disease spreads.

Where is the truth? HTML Version 4 lends a great deal of legitimacy to frames by including the frames elements in the Frameset version of HTML 4. But it's not exactly an enthusiastic endorsement. The draft specification points out that HTML needs to recognize that there are a lot of sites out there using these darned tags, and so they're included in the specification—but with obvious reluctance. I wouldn't term this "deprecation," exactly; "denigration" is likewise too strong. Perhaps "aspersion" would do it. Take a look for yourself.

Mixed Feelings about Frames?

You've run into framed documents on the Web, I'm sure, and you've seen what they can do. The browser's screen divides into a number of scrollable panels, which might be completely independent; for instance, you might see navigation icons in one frame, a banner in another, and the site's various pages in a third. Although many Web authors use tables to achieve these effects, frames are far superior in one respect; in a framed document, you can scroll down in one frame while another stays put.

Be aware, though, that many people have mixed feelings about frames. Users don't like them, because they make navigation more confusing—it's anyone's guess what's going to happen when you click the Back button. Also, I find the frame borders very ugly (there's a way to hide them now, thank goodness). Worst of all, unscrupulous Web authors have figured out how to use frames to "trap" users, so that your attempts to escape from a site fail; every new page you see occurs within one of the trapping site's frames, as if the entire Web were somehow owned by the trapper. To get out, you must use your browser's "open this frame in a new window" command, if there is one. Moreover, there are browsers out there that don't recognize frame tags, although these browsers are not widely used.

Should you use frames? Users dislike them. I believe that tables are superior to frames for document layout. More browsers support tables; users don't feel trapped in documents containing tables. And if you're writing with CSS, you can use absolute positioning to create far nicer layouts than frames will give you.

Introducing Frames

To implement frames, you need more than one document. The master document contains the frame layout, which determines just what users see when they access your framed presentation. There isn't any content within the master document—instead, it contains one or more FRAMESET elements that define the frame layout, and FRAME elements that specify just which documents are supposed to be loaded into which frames. The actual documents are separate, individual Web pages.

The weird thing about the master document is this: It doesn't contain a <BODY> element (unless you want to provide some content for people using frameless browsers, as I'll explain later in this chapter). Instead, it contains a HEAD and a FRAMESET element. The FRAMESET element, as you'll learn in the next section, specifies the overall layout of the framed document.

Don't forget that the master document isn't supposed to have a BODY element right after the head. If you develop your master document using a template, as I've suggested in previous chapters, your template may enter a BODY element. If this comes before the FRAMESET element, your framed document won't work. Keep this in mind if you can't get the frames to appear when you test them with your browser!

Ready, SET, FRAME!

Like a table, a framed document consists of rows and columns, which enable you to create various kinds of rectangular spaces. But you define the rows and columns in a way that completely differs from the TABLE element's syntax. For the moment, then, forget everything you learned in the last chapter—sorry—and get ready for a new experience.

Introducing the FRAMESET Element

To define frames, you use the FRAMESET element. Here's the element definition:

ELEMENT	FRAMESET
PURPOSE	Defines frame sizes and positions in a framed document.
TYPE	n.a.
NESTED WITHIN	HTML
START TAG	Required
END TAG	Required
CONTENT	FRAME elements
ATTRIBUTES	core attributes (id, class, style, title) language attributes (lang, dir)

rows = "comma-separated list of lengths" (optional)
cols = "comma-separated list of lengths" (optional)

EXAMPLE

```
<FRAMESET cols = "15%, *">
        <FRAME src = "navaids.htm">
        <FRAME src = "page1.htm">
</FRAMESET>
```

TIP

Don't use a BODY element on a page containing frame elements, or the frames won't work.

What's the "comma-separated list of lengths" business all about in the rows and cols attributes? Essentially, this value enables you to specify the number of rows and columns, and to determine the size of each. If you want to define more than one row or column, you separate the lengths by commas, as in the following example:

```
<FRAMESET rows = "35%, 50%, 15%">
```

Figure 14.1 Frame rows (35%, 50%, and 15%)

Browsers read this tag top to bottom, so the frames look like Figure 14.1 (the 35% row is on top, the 50% row is in the middle, and the 15% row is on the bottom).

Table 14.1 Specifying length lists in the FRAMESET element

Value	Meaning
percentage (%)	Percentage of available window space.
pixels	Absolute number of screen pixels.
number and asterisk	Adjust the size of the specified column (1, 2, 3, and so on) to take the remaining space.

Columns work the same way, except that the browser reads the list from left to right. Look at this element:

```
<FRAMESET cols="35%, 50%, 15%>
```

Figure 14.2 shows what this does.

Figure 14.2 Frame columns (35%, 50%, and 15%)

Note that the 35% column is on the left; the 50% column is in the middle, and the little 15% one is on the right.

In the element definition, you may have noticed that the cols and rows attributes are optional. If you don't specify a cols attribute, the browser doesn't divide the screen horizontally, but you can still have rows; these will span the whole window. If you don't specify a rows attribute, the browser doesn't divide the screen vertically; your columns go all the way down to the end of the document. If you don't specify either attribute, you don't get columns or rows—there's just one, big, undifferentiated window.

More Ways to Specify Frame Length

As Table 14.1 indicates, you can specify frame widths or heights (lengths) in percentages or pixels. If you specify the length in percentages, which is the best way, the browser dynamically sizes the rows or columns depending on the current window width. However, you may wish to specify the width of a particular row or column in pixels, if you wish to accommodate an object of fixed size (such as a graphic).

OK, that's easy enough. But what's this business with a number and an asterisk? The number is used to specify which row or column you're talking about (going top to bottom or left to right). And the asterisk says, "Just give this whatever space is left."

Here's an example:

```
<FRAMESET cols = "290, 2*">
```

This says, "Give the first column a width of 290 pixels and give the second column whatever is left." What if you've used two or more asterisks? The browser divides the remaining space equally among them.

Creating a Grid

The examples you've looked at so far specify columns or rows, but not both. However, you can specify both at the same time, creating a grid.

Here's an example:

```
<FRAMESET cols="50%, 50%" rows = "50%, 50%">
```

Figure 14.3 Two columns (50%, 50%) and two rows (50%, 50%)

This creates a two-by-two grid, like the following:

For now, note that when you use both attributes, rows and cols, the frames are numbered by going left to right on the first row, and then left to right on the second row, and so on. So here is how the above frames would be numbered:

```
Frame 1        Frame 2
Frame 3        Frame 4
```

This is important, as you will see in a minute.

Creating Nested Frame Structures

On the Web, very few of the framed sites you see have a grid-like structure like the one just shown. Usually, they look something more like Figure 14.4.

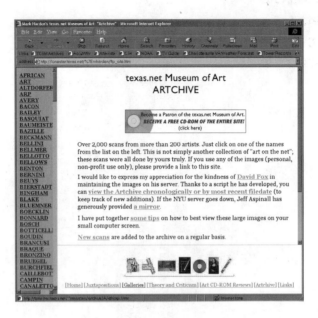

Figure 14.4 This site uses frames to enhance navigation

How's this done? It is accomplished by nesting FRAMESET elements. Before you learn how to do this, though, you need to learn the FRAME element.

Hanging Pictures on the Wall with FRAME

You can define rows and columns all you want, but nothing shows up in them without the FRAME element. The FRAME element enables you to specify just what appears within each of the rectangular spaces you've defined.

Looking at the FRAME Element Definition

Here's the FRAME element definition:

ELEMENT	FRAME
PURPOSE	Specifies the document to be loaded into a frame.
TYPE	Inline
NESTED WITHIN	FRAMESET

START TAG	Required
END TAG	Forbidden
CONTENT	Empty
ATTRIBUTES	core attributes (id, class, style, title)
	language attributes (lang, dir)
	src = "url" (optional)
	longdesc = "url" (optional)
	name = "CDATA" (optional)
	frameborder = "(1, 0)" (optional)
	marginwidth = "pixels" (optional)
	marginheight = "pixels" (optional)
	noresize (optional)
	scrolling = "(yes, no, auto)" (optional)
	target = "(_blank, _self, _parent, _top, or name)" (optional)
EXAMPLE	\<FRAMESET cols = "15%, *"\>
	\<FRAME src = "navaids.htm"\>
	\<FRAME src = "page1.htm"\>
	\</FRAMESET\>
TIP	Don't use a BODY element on a page containing frame elements or the frames won't work.

Table 14.2 explains what the various attributes do. They're all optional, but you certainly don't want to omit src, which enables you to specify the HTML document that you want inserted into the frame. Without this attribute, the frame will be blank.

You can specify the frame's source document by using a relative or an absolute URL, as in the following examples:

```
<FRAME = "contents.html">
<FRAME = "http://www.nodomain.org/lusers/~bp/
contents.html">
```

Table 14.2 Quick guide to the FRAME attributes

Attribute	Use and example
name	Enables you to name a frame so that it can function as the target for a link.
	\<FRAME name = "contents"\>

src	Specifies the Web page that you want inserted into this frame. `<FRAME src ="contents.html">`
frameborder	Specifies whether or not the frame has a border. You can choose 1 (yes) or 0 (no). The default is 1. `<FRAME frameborder ="0">`
marginwidth	Adds a left and right margin to the frame. You must specify this in pixels. The value must be greater than 1 (the default). `<FRAME marginwidth = "10">`
marginheight	Adds a top and bottom margin to the frame. You must specify this in pixels. The value must be greater than 1 (the default). `<FRAME marginheight ="10">`
noresize	Fixes the frame so that it cannot be resized. `<FRAME noresize = "noresize">`
scrolling	Selects scrolling options. You can choose from auto (the default setting; displays scroll bars only when the window is not large enough to accommodate the frame), yes (always displays scroll bars), no (never displays scroll bars). `<FRAME scrolling = "no">`

Fun with FRAME

The FRAME element's attributes (Table 14.2) enable you to do a couple of sneaky and cool things.

- **Fix the frame size** (<FRAME noresize="noresize">) By default, the user can change the size of frames by dragging the frame borders. User resizing is rarely a good idea, unless you're worried that a right-most column won't appear on an especially narrow window. Noresize enables you to prevent the user from hiding important material.

- **Hide the borders** (<FRAME frameborder="0">) If you're planning to use noresize, consider using this attribute. Your page will look like you've laid it out with a table, but the user gets all the benefits of having one frame stay put while the other scrolls. Figure 14.4 shows the very nice effect achieved by hiding the borders.

Putting FRAME in Its Place

OK, now you've learned the basics of the FRAME element. So where does it go? It belongs within the FRAMESET element, obviously, but in the correct order. And what's the correct order? You have to list the FRAMES in the order that they're read by the browser.

Here's an example. In the preceding discussion of the FRAMESET element, you learned that each frame gets its own number. If you define only columns, the frames are numbered left to right. If you define only rows, the frames are numbered top to bottom. If you define both rows and columns, the frames are numbered by going left to right, moving down a column, going left to right, and so on.

If you define two rows and two columns, you need four FRAME tags, and they must be in the correct order if you want them to appear in the right place.

Here's an example:

```
<FRAMESET cols="50%, 50%" rows = "50%, 50%">
      <FRAME src = "frame1.html">
      <FRAME src = "frame2.html">
      <FRAME src = "frame3.html">
      <FRAME src = "frame4.html">
</FRAMESET>
```

See the following for how these frames would be laid out:

```
frame1.html                    frame2.html
frame3.html                    frame4.html
```

Nesting Frames

Now that you've got the basics of frame layout down, it is time to investigate nesting. .Nesting enables you to create complex screen designs, with frames positioned within frames.

Basically, here's how nesting works with frames. When you nest a FRAMESET element, you can further divide the current frame. Here's a simple example:

```
<FRAMESET cols = "150, 2*">
    <FRAME src = "frame1.html">
    <FRAMESET rows = "150, 2*">
        <FRAME = "frame2.html">
        <FRAME = "frame3.html">
    </FRAMESET>
</FRAMESET>
```

Looking at what I just typed, I think I realize another reason there are so few framed sites on the Web—this is confusing. But here's how to deal with this.

First, look at the FRAME elements. They're numbered in order, as you've already learned: frame 1, frame 2, and frame 3. Now let's look at the FRAME-SET elements.

The first FRAMESET element defines a document with two columns. The first column is 150 pixels wide; the second takes up the remaining space. The first FRAME element defines a column 150 pixels wide; this goes on the left.

Before the poor browser gets to the second FRAME element, though, a nested FRAMESET element intrudes; it says, essentially, "Whoa, divide the next frame as instructed." This would have been a nice, big column on the right. But what does this nested FRAMESET element do? It divides this big frame into two rows, one 150 pixels high and another sized with whatever is left of the window space.

Here's how this looks:

```
                    Frame 2
    Frame 1
                    Frame 3
```

This Isn't a Bad Design, Actually

The frame design just illustrated is not a bad layout for a lot of documents. Think of the possibilities: In frame 1, you put your navigation aids, while in frame 2, you show your site's title. Frame 3 gets the content.

Let's flesh this out a bit with some attributes:

```
<FRAMESET cols = "150, 2*">
    <FRAME src = "frame1.html" noresize="noresize"
    frameborder="0" scrolling = "no">
    <FRAMESET rows = "150, 2*">
        <FRAME = "frame2.html" noresize=
        "noresize" frameborder="0" scrolling =
        "no" >
        <FRAME = "frame3.html" frameborder="0">
    </FRAMESET>
</FRAMESET>
```

Users can't resize or scroll frames 1 or 2, but that's OK—you want these frames to stay put because they contain your navigation aids (frame 1) and your site's title (frame 2). Only frame 3 is scrollable.

Sounds great, huh? Don't rush off to your text editor just yet. You need to learn how to define targets so that the links in your navigation aid panel will display documents within frame 3, instead of leaving the frames entirely and opening a totally separate document.

Hitting the Target (Targeted Frames)

If you put a link in a framed document, it works just like any other hyperlink. It takes the user out of the current document on a one-way trip to another Web document. In other words, bye-bye frames.

In order to make a linked document appear within one of the frames you've defined, you need to do two things:

1. Give a name to the frame in which you want documents to appear. You can call this frame anything you like, for example, "Alice." Only, the name must begin—as Alice does—with alphabetical characters (uppercase or lowercase). You name the frame with the name attribute (as in FRAME name = "Alice").
2. When you write a hyperlink to a document that you want to appear in this frame, use the target attribute and name the frame, as in the following example: <A HREF = "document.html" target = "Alice">.

If you are going to define a number of hyperlinks and want them all to appear in a particular frame (such as "Alice"), name the frame and include a BASE element within your document's HEAD, as in the following example: <BASE target = "Alice">. After doing this, you don't need to worry about defining a target frame for any of the hyperlinks you define in the document.

You can make use of a few special tricks by using reserved target names, as Table 14.3 explains.

Table 14.3 Reserved target names

Target name	What it does
_blank	Opens the linked document in a new window.
_self	Loads the linked document into the very same frame that contains the link.
_parent	Loads the linked document into the next frame up in the frame list.
_top	Loads the document into the full window, cancelling all frame effects.

We Do *Not* Like Frames

Some people just don't like frames. Other people don't have frames-capable browsers. Still others don't know what they want, but like to explore options. And even still others have absolutely no idea what they are doing. How do you deal with this?

Simple: Give people an alternative. If you are going to use frames, you ought to develop a non-frames version of your site. It's a lot of work. Still, you want to reach a wide audience, don't you? Are you convinced?

To make sure that people with non-frames browsers are able to see something when they access your framed page, include a BODY element after the FRAME-SET elements, and include a link to the welcome page of the non-frames version of your site.

This example shows how to deal with non-frame-capable browsers:

```
<BODY>
        For a non-framed version of this site, please
        access <A HREF="noframes.html">
</BODY>
```

Just make sure this comes after all the FRAMESET elements.

Adding an Inline Frame

Here's a great way to add a frame (containing another document) in any ordinary HTML page. It's called an *inline frame* and you add it with the IFRAME element. Here's the element definition:

ELEMENT	IFRAME
PURPOSE	Creates an inline subwindow in which you can insert another document.
TYPE	Inline
NESTED WITHIN	Any block element
START TAG	Required
END TAG	Required
CONTENT	Text and inline elements (no block elements permitted)
ATTRIBUTES	core attributes (id, class, style, title) lang attributes (lang, dir) longdesc = "url" (optional) name = "CDATA" (optional) src = "url" (optional) frameborder = "(1,0)" (optional) marginwidth = "pixels" (optional) marginheight = "pixels" (optional) scrolling = "(yes, no, auto)" (optional) align= "(top, middle, bottom, left, right)" (optional)
EXAMPLE	<IFRAME src = "insert.html" width = 200 height = 300 scrolling = "yes" frameborder = "0">Your browser doesn't support frames. However, you can visit the <A href = "insert.html"> document </A> that would have been shown here.

TIP	Place text to be viewed by non-frame browsers between the tags.

You can insert an inline frame anywhere in any HTML document by using the IFRAME element. Here's an example:

```
<IFRAME src = "essay.html" width = "200" height =
"200" scrolling = "yes" frameborder = "1">Your
browser doesn't support frames. But you can access
the document at <A HREF = "essay.html">this loca-
tion</A>. </IFRAME>
```

This element sets up an inline frame inside a 200 x 200 square, with scrolling enabled and a one-pixel border. If the user's browser doesn't support frames, the text within the IFRAME tags appears.

Summary

Frames are easy to implement. In the master document, use FRAMESET to set up the frame structure, and use FRAME to specify which documents will be loaded into which frames. Just make sure to omit the BODY element, or the frames will not show up. Give some thought to the various options, such as hiding borders.

Are you wondering how to set up a site with lots of pages? You will find out how in the next chapter.

15

Making a Really Big Site with Lots of Pages

In this chapter, you will learn the following skills:

- Deciding when one page is enough
- Understanding and applying the various multi-page site organization options
- Giving your site structure while at the same time promoting freedom of exploration

Up until now, we have been talking about creating a Web page. But serious Web publishing generally involves creating more than one page. What's involved?

In brief, you will need to think through some fairly serious issues about site structure. Above all else, you need to think about user convenience, and what you are trying to accomplish with your material. As you read through the multi-page structural options in this chapter, you'll get some great ideas for organizing your pages in a way that's right for your content, right for your readers, and right for you.

When One Page IS Enough

Before you delve more deeply into this chapter, let's talk about situations where one page really is just fine.

- **Don't hack up your content into tiny, one-paragraph pages just so you can show off your hyperlinking skills.** This is irritating, maddening, and unprintable. No, I don't mean that I'm criticizing these people; I'm talking about the impossibility of printing the content of such a site. Such sites are deservedly ignored.
- **Even if your content is really, really lengthy, it belongs in one page if you think that your readers need to print it.** The HTML Version 4 specification is a case in point. It is a huge document—hundreds of pages. It is tedious to read on-screen, so I printed it and put it in a big three-ring binder. If you can't make up your mind whether to divide ("chunk") your content or create one huge file, why not do both? By creating alternative versions of your site, you give people the power to choose the presentation format they prefer. It's a bit more work, admittedly, but the people who access your site will appreciate your thoughtfulness.

In short: If they need to print it, make it available in a single file, however lengthy.

The Semantic Cloud

Close your eyes. Zen time. Imagine egoless floating through space. OK, got it? Now you're ready.

The semantic cloud (Figure 15.1) is a pure expression of the hypertext principle (see Chapter 1). Basically, you present an unstructured "cloud" of information. You don't try to compel people to go through it in one way or another. In fact, you make no attempt to provide any specific way of navigating through the many pages you publish. You provide plenty of navigation options, to be sure, but you don't structure them.

To create a semantic cloud, your basic aim lies in creating as many possible potential synergies among concepts as you can. You do not try to force concept pairings on people by means of your site's structure; in contrast, you facilitate all possible pairings, even those you think might be absurd. Surely, somebody interested in sailing would not be interested in kayaking. Well, don't be too sure. On the way back to my "office" (a Catalina 34), I passed a really nice sailboat with two one-person kayaks lashed to either side of the mast. I'll bet there's a page out there about sailing and kayaking; a quick search will probably produce quite a few cool pages to link to.

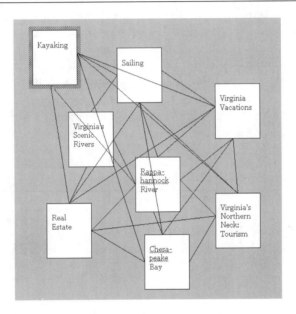

Figure 15.1 A semantic cloud (unstructured site with multiple links)

Figure 15.1 represents a semantic cloud, but it omits all the potential links out of the site. In a true semantic cloud, there's no center at all. The focus is totally relative to where you happen to be at the moment. The Chesapeake Bay page, for instance, has links going off in all directions, including out of the site. If you were to make this page the center, the cloud would shift its focus; ideally, though, there wouldn't be any reduction in the number or utility of links to allied concepts. Obviously, this requires letting go of the compulsion to keep people within your site, and not give them the tools to link out. It takes a lot of humility to create a true semantic cloud.

The Forced March

Let's move to the exact opposite of the semantic cloud. I call it the forced march. In this way of organizing a multi-page site, the author has not let go of authorial control. Rather, you see a rigid sequence of pages, such as those shown in Figure 15-2.

Suppose that I want to develop my site about Virginia's Northern Neck, but I'm really a real estate agent, and I want to sell you a house or lot. I'm going to get you interested in the wonders of this area and then hit you with a pitch. In a forced march, there's no way you can escape.

In the forced march, you don't see a lot of side linking. Of course not; the author wants to keep readers marching along in sequence, leading to the desired goal.

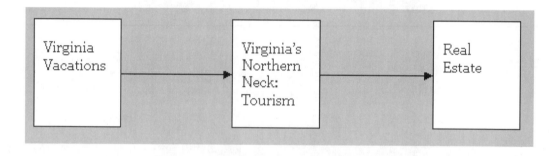

Figure 15.2 A forced march structure gives the reader no choice

Although the forced march is the polar opposite of everything the Web stands for, it is not evil, although it's almost always at least slightly unpleasant. (I personally hate being given only one navigation option, "Next."). Still, I might put up with it if there's a payoff. For example, suppose I want to learn how to bargain for the best price on a used car. I'm willing to go through a sequence of information to learn this, because I believe it will pay off for me. To create a successful forced march, you need to make this clear up-front.

The Guided Cloud

A guided cloud provides more structure than a pure semantic cloud, but does not force the user into a specific sequence of pages. This is by far the most widely-used organizational principle for multi-page sites on the Web, and for good reason.

In a guided cloud, you publish a series of pages, and each of them contains a structured table of contents, such as the one in Figure 15.3. The site begins with a welcome page that contains an explanation of the purpose and scope of the site, and also suggests—but does not require—specific navigation pathways. Because exactly the same navigation aids appear on every page of the site, it is easy for users to choose their own path through the material. If they need help, they can get it by going to the welcome, about, or info pages.

In a guided cloud, there's only one level. On every page, you see a complete list of every page that's available. Figure 15.4 shows how all the pages in a guided cloud have exactly the same menu of options.

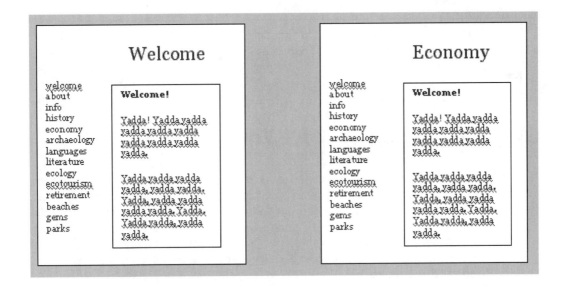

Figure 15.3 A guided cloud provides both structure and freedom

Figure 15.4 In a guided cloud, all the pages have the same navigation aids

Multi-Level Guided Clouds

In the previous section, you learned about the guided cloud. If you develop a guided cloud, though, you will find that various sub-topics pop up that really deserve treatment, even though they are not important enough to appear on the top-level menu.

In Figure 15.3, for example, you may wish to further develop the Economy page by adding subpages for industrial relocation programs, finance and banking, the local stock market, and currency exchange. A multi-level guided cloud looks like Figure 15.5.

In principle, you could add further levels to a multi-level guided cloud, but adding too many levels could confuse users. To prevent this, be sure to use exactly the same navigation aids on every page of your site, even the ones in subordinate levels. These aids keep your site's top-level options clearly in view and prevent confusion.

Creating a Style Sheet for Your Entire Site

To cut down on site maintenance tasks, do not forget to create a single, master style sheet for every page in your site. As far as possible, refrain from defining any presentation elements within the individual documents you create. Instead, define them in your style sheet. What is the rationale for this? You won't believe how much work and sweat you'll save. With a single, master style sheet for your entire site, you make just one little change, and suddenly every page in your site reflects this change.

Figure 15.5 Multi-level guided cloud with navigation aids on every page

You can create your master style sheet as a simple text file, saved with the extension css (for example style.css). The file should contain nothing but style information, enclosed within STYLE elements. You do not need (and should not include) the HTML and HEAD elements.

Summary

If you plan to create a multi-page site, you need to think about your structural options. The semantic cloud conforms most purely to the hypertext ideal, but it's difficult to navigate and leads users off to other sites. The forced march locks readers into a rigid sequence of information, but you'll need to sell them on why this is desirable. Most well-designed multi-page sites use a guided cloud or a multi-level guided cloud structure. These options give the user a fixed, unchanging panel of navigation aids (a table of contents) that appears on every page of the site. You can use the IFRAME element to create a master navigation aids list that is automatically inserted into each of your site's pages. This will save you tons of time when you add more items to your navigation aids.

Part Four

Adding Visual Excitement and Interactivity

16

Getting Your IMG into Focus

In this chapter, you will learn the following skills:

- Understanding and selecting graphics formats
- Reducing color depth and creating transparent graphics
- Creating animated GIFs
- Positioning graphics with style sheets
- Positioning graphics for non-CSS-capable browsers
- Creating client-side imagemaps

The typical Web page consists of HTML, a few links, and a few in-line images, or pictures, placed amidst the text. But the IMG element—the element that is used to insert and align images—provides very little control over the graphic's position. (You learned to use the IMG element way back in Chapter 3.) To be sure, the IMG element in previous versions of HTML did have certain presentation elements, but they did not work very well. To position graphics, authors had to resort to all kinds of devious tricks, such as placing graphics within tables. If you take a look at the source HTML in virtually any lavishly-illustrated Web page, you'll find that the authors have used tables to position the graphics. I'm sure you are ready for what is coming next: In the strict flavor of HTML Version 4, the use of tricky means to position graphics has been deprecated. Instead of using table tricks to position graphics, you should use the new positioning capabilities of CSS Level 1 style sheets, discussed in Chapter 12.

This chapter introduces graphics in general, providing an overview of graphics file formats and the IMG element. You'll also learn how to take advantage of a number of very important graphics tricks, including creating transparent GIFs, animated GIFs, and progressive JPEGs. All of these can add visual excitement to your Web page, transforming it into something people will notice. You'll also learn how to position graphics when you are writing for non-CSS-capable browsers.

Picture This!

Web pages without pictures are like…well, how about TV without sound? Burgers without fries? Tahiti without beaches? It is one thing to insist that your page ought to have graphics, but it's quite another to figure out where to get them and where to put them. Let's start by examining the larger issues connected with Web graphics, and then move on to the specifics of incorporating graphics on your pages.

Bad Things about Graphics

Although most well-designed Web pages include graphics, it is important to remember some of their limitations:

- **Some people turn graphics off, or use non-graphical browsers.** Many people switch off automatic graphics displays to speed downloading (and avoid advertising). Also, an estimated five percent of Web users are still using text-only browsers. If you make graphics part of your message, they will miss it.
- **Search engines cannot index graphics.** They can't tell whether your graphic shows a picture of a house, Hunan province, or Attilla the Hun.
- **Colors that look good on your monitor may look just terrible on somebody else's.** There's no way of standardizing color displays, yet.
- **Images with thousands or millions of colors may look terrible when displayed on monitors capable of displaying only 256 or 16 colors.** There are still a lot of people out there with 1 MB video cards, which means

that they're restricted to these limited color palettes if they want to use their cards' maximum resolution.

- **Big graphics take forever to download.** Users with 28.8Kbps modem connections may not appreciate your efforts to add visual spice to your page.

Ways to Counteract the Bad Things about Graphics

You can't exactly wave a magic wand and make all those negatives go away, but you can reduce their sting. Here's how:

- **Provide alternate text** This is text that is displayed when somebody can't see your graphics. Also, this tells search engines more about your page's contents.
- **Test your page on a variety of computers and displays** See what your images look like when you reduce your display's color depth to 256 or 16 colors. If an image looks terrible, you may wish to use a graphics program to reduce the color depth in a way that preserves the image's quality. (You will learn how to do this later in this chapter.)
- **Use small graphics files** Use several small graphics rather than one large one. Reduce the color depth (as described later in this chapter) to cut down file size. Use the same graphics on additional pages; if you do this, browsers will retain the graphic in memory and subsequent pages will appear to download much faster.

Ways to Get Graphics for Your Web Page

You've decided to use graphics. Fine. Now how do you get them?

If I Had a Scanner...

You'd scan it in the morning, and you'd scan it in the evening. The question is, is it legal? People do it all the time, but that doesn't make it right (see the section, "A Not-So-Small Matter of Copyright," in this chapter).

Assuming you can copy graphic images legally, a flatbed scanner is a wonderful aid to Web publishing. Bear in mind, though, that older scanners come with non-Internet-savvy scanning software, which cannot save images in the file formats preferred for Web use. (You'll learn about these file formats subsequently.) This is not a fatal problem because you can use graphics programs (such as Paint Shop Pro or the Windows 98 version of Windows Paint) to open scanned graphics files and save them in the correct formats for Internet use.

Everyone Say "Cheese"!

The latest and perhaps the best method for acquiring graphics is the new generation of digital cameras, such as Epson's PhotoPC. These cameras save digitized images, which you can then download to your computer and re-save in Web-enabled graphics formats. The possibilities here are fantastic. For example, real estate agents can photograph and publish pictures of properties they are listing, and companies can create employee databases with pictures of employees.

If you want to publish pictures of people, bear in mind that you need to have a model release. Otherwise, you could be liable for damages. Don't publish pictures of people you don't know.

Obtaining Graphics from the Web

It's all too easy. You just access a site, move the mouse pointer to a graphic, click the right mouse button, and choose the Save Image option from the pop-up menu. And then, it is yours. Or is it?

Just because it's so easy to copy graphics doesn't make it right! If you'd like to use a graphic from somebody else's Web site, ask permission. You can do this via e-mail. It doesn't hurt to ask, and many Web authors will respond positively. They may ask that you give them credit.

Make sure that the people who give you permission to copy a graphic actually have the right to do so. Did they copy the picture from somewhere else, illegally? I once asked a Web author for permission to copy a graphic, and he wrote back and said "Sure." I got another message about a week later that said, "By the way, I copied the pictures from some other site, actually, so I suppose you'd better ask them too."

Clip Art

You can buy CD-ROMs chock full of clip art, and there is quite a lot of clip art available on the Web. But the same cautions apply. You'd be surprised at how many commercial clip art libraries are copyrighted; the accompanying documentation states that the art can be used for personal purposes but not for commercial ones. So what are we paying for when we buy these things? Much of the clip art on the Web is actually copyrighted as well, and it is impossible to tell just who created the images. Don't buy a clip art library unless it expressly states that the images are in the public domain.

A Not-So-Small Matter of Copyright

Some Internet users are under the impression that the Internet is such a profound revolution that it renders antiquated notions, such as copyright, obsolete. Copyright holders may see things quite differently, however. The same goes for judges and juries. To put it plainly, you are taking a risk if you publish copyrighted graphics on your Web page. (Please note: The following should not be taken as expert legal advice. I'm not an attorney. You should speak with an attorney about any of these matters if you want to make sure you are up on the latest law.)

Just how much risk are you taking by using copyrighted graphics on your site? More than a few Web authors have received "cease and desist" letters from attorneys representing copyright holders. Others have wound up in court, facing possible financial ruin. If a copyright holder can prove lost revenue due to your appropriation of an image, you could be liable for this lost revenue and punitive damages.

What about "fan sites"? Aren't you giving the copyright holder free advertising? Yes, but content providers want to control who is doing their advertising and how they do it. If you create a fan site with lots of copyrighted images for which you haven't asked permission, you may get a "cease and desist" letter—or worse.

What about "fair use"? Copyright law enables authors to reproduce small amounts of text (generally less than five percent of the source document) for purposes of commentary, analysis, or review, including satire. But this doesn't apply to poetry, and it most emphatically does not apply to graphic images.

Because the U.S. is a signatory to international copyright conventions, artists no longer have to include a copyright notice, or even obtain a copyright certificate, to put forward a valid claim to their creative work. The lack of a copyright notice on a Web page does not mean that you can freely copy anything you find.

Understanding Graphics File Formats

A graphics file format defines the way a graphic image is stored on a computer. Some kind of format (data storage technique) is needed because the eye (and camera) sees continuous gradations of color. However, computer displays require some kind of digitization of the image, in which continuous gradations are replaced by tiny points (picture elements, or pixels for short), each of which displays a single color. The result is a *bitmap*, in which a picture is represented by what amounts to a mosaic image.

In a bitmapped graphic, each pixel on the screen is independently given a color. As long as the pixels are too small to be seen by the eye, the picture looks OK (see Figure 16.1). If you enlarge a bitmap to the point that the individual picture elements (pixels) become visible, the realism collapses, and the picture looks terrible (see Figure 16.2).

Figure 16.1 Bitmapped picture at 100% size (photograph by the author)

Figure 16.2 Overenlarged bitmapped graphic with "jaggy" distortion

To solve this problem, you could create a file that contains zillions of pixels—but then the difficulty of file size rears its ugly head. The file gets too big. So that's the tradeoff. Big files look good, but they are too big. To deal with this, there are a couple of tricks. You can reduce the color depth (the number of colors the image contains) and you can use compression to reduce the size of the file. The following sections look at these tricks. Next, you will learn how the most popular graphics file formats—GIF and JPEG—implement these tricks. You'll also learn which file format to choose for a given type of graphic.

Color Depth

Graphics file formats vary in their color depth (the number of distinct colors that the format can represent). The number of bits used to store colors dictates the number of possible colors. For example, a graphics file format that uses a two-bit color storage technique can represent only four colors. The more bits, the more colors. A four-bit format can represent 16 colors, while a 24-bit format can store a whopping 16.7 million colors. The size/quality tradeoff applies: The more colors, the bigger the file. Table 16.1 sums up the relationship between the number of bits stored per pixel and color depth.

Table 16.1 Color depth in bitmapped graphics

Bits stored per pixel	Color depth
1	2 colors
4	16 colors
8	256 colors
15	32K colors
16	64K colors
24	16.7M colors

In general, you are asking for trouble if you assume people can display more than 256 colors. If you load up your site with graphics having more colors, they look terrible on a monitor that's configured to display only 256. If your graphic has too many colors, you can use a graphics program to reduce the color depth. There is an additional payoff: the graphic will download much more quickly and will consume less storage space.

Resolution

Resolution refers to the sharpness of an image, as determined by the number of pixels that can be crammed into a given space. This is determined by the display capabilities of the monitors people use to display graphics.

The resolution of a bitmapped graphic is usually described as the graphic's size in pixels, measured in the number of pixels across the screen and the number of vertical lines. A graphic that is described as 152 by 68 (152 x 68), for example, occupies a rectangular space 152 pixels horizontally by 68 vertical lines. But this tells you nothing about its sharpness; on a 640 by 480 monitor, for example, this graphic will look fairly big and the underlying graininess may show; it will look much smaller and sharper on a 1280 by 1024 monitor.

How big should you make your graphic? This question really boils down to another question: How wide are your users' screens? It would be nice if the whole world were using 1024 by 768 monitors (SuperVGA), but many people browse the Web using notebook computers capable of only 800 by 600 resolution. Still others are using antiquated VGA monitors (640 by 480). If you want to assure the widest possible audience, you shouldn't use graphics wider than 640 pixels or taller than 480—and you will need to leave room for text, too.

Compression

To cope with the huge size of graphics files, compression comes into play. You will find two kinds of compression techniques in common use: lossless and lossy. In lossless compression, information is removed from the file to reduce its size, but it is restored when the file is decompressed for display. In lossy compression, the file's size is reduced by removing some information permanently. This results in a degraded image, but it's possible to remove some information in a way that is not obvious to the human eye.

The Big Three : GIF, JPEG, and PNG

Now that you've learned how to understand graphics file formats, take a closer look at the three most important graphics formats for Internet use: GIF (pronounced "jiff"), JPEG (pronounced "jay-peg"), and PNG (pronounced "ping").

Do It in a GIF

Developed by the online service CompuServe, the Graphics Interchange Format (GIF) is very widely used on the Web. But there is a problem. In 1994, Unisys announced that the company would zealously pursue its patent rights concerning the compression scheme used to create GIF graphics. For a month or two, there was utter hysteria; some predicted that Unisys would go after anyone who ever put a GIF on their Web page, asking for substantial back fees for the use of GIF graphics. But it was not to be. Unisys decided to levy fees only on the companies that published programs capable of creating or processing GIF graphics. In something of a huff, the Internet community has decided to take its ball and go play somewhere else; that's the reason, as you'll see, for the development of the patent-free PNG standard. Still, nearly four years down the road from the Unisys imbroglio, GIF is still the most widely-used graphic format on the Web.

There is good reason for GIF's popularity. GIF graphics combine a reasonably good lossless compression technique (called LZW compression) with a compact color depth (a maximum of 256 colors).

In the latest version of the GIF specification (GIF 89a), the format includes some extremely useful goodies:

- **Transparency** You can set one of the graphic's 256 colors to be a transparent color, which means that it automatically takes on the color of the background. This explains why you see so many great looking graphics that seem to "float" on a colored background (for an example, see Figure 16.3).
- **Animation** A single GIF graphic can contain multiple images, along with instructions about how they should be displayed. This enables graphic artists to create simple animations that can be played back without requiring users to download huge plug-in programs. GIF animations are in very widespread use on the Web.
- **Interlacing** An interlaced GIF is drawn by skipping lines, so that a low-focus version of the image appears almost immediately. This is useful because the person browsing your page can get a quick idea of what the image contains. Unlike a non-interlaced GIF, which starts appearing at the top of the graphic and gradually appears line-by-line, an interlaced GIF image appears almost instantly as a rectangle, and gradually takes on more definition until it is sharp.

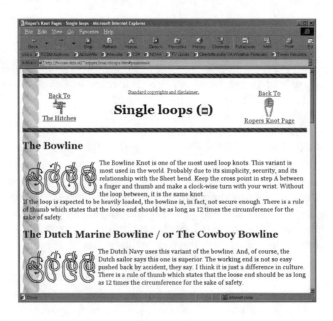

Figure 16.3 This page uses transparent GIFs effectively

> *The GIF compression format codes redundant data, so it works best for graphics with regions of solid color. GIF is the format of choice if you're using graphics that have solid color regions. However, it is not a good choice for graphics that have more than 256 colors, unless you want to reduce the color depth. In general, the JPEG format is much better for complex graphics such as photographs that do not have regions of solid color.*

The JPEG Alternative

If you would like to include a digitized photograph or artwork on your page, JPEG is probably the best choice. (JPEG is short for the Joint Photographics Experts Group, an organization affiliated with the International Organization for Standardization.) Unlike GIF, which uses a lossless compression scheme, JPEG uses a very clever lossy scheme that eliminates information that the eye doesn't see. A compressed JPEG graphic may be up to ten times smaller than the original, but the human eye cannot really tell the difference. What's great about JPEG is that it gives you a huge color depth—up to 16.7 million colors—and compact files, thanks to its super compression technique. Still, GIF is a better choice for images that contain 256 colors (or fewer), and especially for images that contain large regions of solid color.

Unlike the GIF 89a format, JPEG doesn't include some of the tricks that make GIFs so popular: animations and transparency. But the format does enable a progressive display of the image, which resembles GIF interlacing.

On the Internet, the JPEG file format of choice is the *JPEG File Interchange Format (JFIF)*, which doesn't include anything that's patented—or so many believe. But you never know when somebody is going to crawl out of the woodwork and claim that he or she invented the mouse pointer or something, and everyone has to shell out millions.

Going Patent-Free: The PNG Format

Short for Portable Network Graphics, the PNG format provides a patent-free alternative to GIFs. The question is, will anyone use it?

Like GIFs, PNGs use a lossless compression technique, but it is superior—you get from 10 to 30 percent better compression. Also like GIFs, PNGs can have transparent colors—but it is not an on-off, either-or thing. A PNG's transparent color can have up to 256 degrees of transparency, ranging from totally transparent to totally opaque. Unlike GIF, PNG supports truecolor formats with color depths of up to 48 bits. It is a single-image format, and doesn't support animations. Another feature is gamma correction, which refers to brightness. With PNG, authors can specify a brightness level for their graphic, which helps ensure that the graphic will look right (not too dark or too light) on a given monitor.

So why aren't PNG graphics more widely used? They ought to be. It's just that graphics programs have been slow to support PNG, and the major browser publishers are just getting around to including PNG (see Table 16.2). The support just is not there quite yet.

Still, PNG graphics are impressive. Once the two major browsers fully support PNG graphics, they are sure to become more widely used. For now, you should use PNG graphics only if you supply JPEG or GIF equivalents; you'll learn how to do this later in this chapter.

Table 16.2 Support for PNG Graphics

Browser and version	PNG graphic support
Netscape Navigator 2.0 and 3.0	via plug-in
Netscape Communicator 4.0	via plug-in
Microsoft Internet Explorer 3.0	None
Microsoft Internet Explorer 4.0	Native (full support)

Choosing the Right Graphics Format

The following table provides a handy guide to choosing the right graphics format. I have not included PNG since this format is not very widely supported as yet.

Table 16.3 Choosing the right graphic format

Graphic format	Use when any of these apply:
JPEG	You don't care so much about edge sharpness, as in a photograph.
	Your graphic is complex, such as a photograph, with lots of gradations of color.

GIF	You don't want to lose any of the edge sharpness in the image.
	You want a transparent background, so that the image seems to "float" over the background color of your Web page.
	Your graphic has large areas of solid color

Graphics Processing for Non-Artists

To publish graphics effectively, you will have to learn a few graphics-processing tricks. No, I'm not asking you to become an artist. The following is fairly simple to learn.

Although this chapter is not the place for a lengthy treatise on graphics processing, it makes sense to at least point you in the right direction. In the sections to follow, you will learn some essential graphics tricks, including reducing color depth, creating interlaced GIFs or progressive JPEGs, and creating transparent GIFs.

There are lots of programs you can use to pull off the graphics tricks discussed in this chapter. But my personal favorite is Paint Shop Pro, a shareware program created by Jasc, Inc., and quite readily available (for Windows 95, 98, and NT) from your local neighborhood FTP site, or Jasc's Web site (http://www.jasc.com).

Reducing Color Depth

The fewer colors your graphic has, the smaller its size, the faster the download, the happier the audience, the greater your reputation as a Webmaster, the less the wear on your server's hard drive, etc. Well, you get the idea. You can go too far, of course. If you reduce the color depth to 1 bit, you get nothing but black and white.

To find out how many colors your graphic has, you can use Paint Shop Pro's Count Colors Used command (found in the Colors menu). My picture of sailboat Juliana plying the Rappahannock has 32K colors, and looks pretty good. But, it also uses 52K of disk space. That means it will take up to a minute to download on a really slow modem line.

After using the Decrease Color Depth command, also in the Color menu, Juliana's picture takes up only 25K. Take a look at Figure 16.4, and see if you can tell the difference. On the left is a version of the photograph with 32K colors, and on the right is the 256-color version that takes up half the disk space (and downloads twice as fast). The smaller version of the file looks good, except that it's not as contrasty—and here, that's not really a defect.

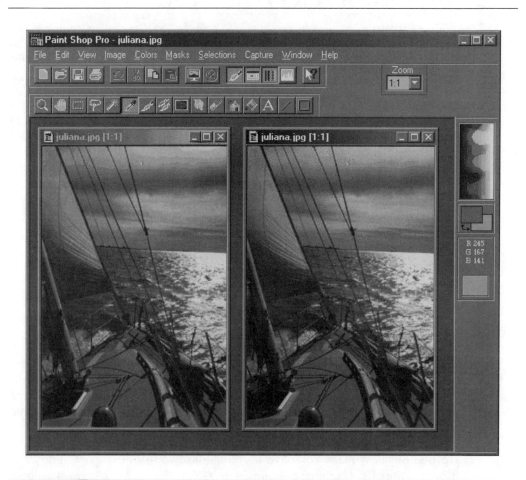

Figure 16.4 Reducing color depth (left: 16.7M; right, 256)

Creating Interlaced GIFs and Progressive JPGs

Creating interlaced GIFs and progressive JPGs couldn't be easier. You just choose Save As from the File menu, and pick the Interlaced option (GIFs) or the Progressive option (JPEGs).

Creating Transparent GIFs

You can make a transparent GIF out of any image that has a solid-color background. To make the GIF transparent, you need to figure out which color the background is.

With Paint Shop Pro, you can do this by clicking the Dropper tool on the background image, and then choosing Edit Palette from the Colors menu. The bottom of this dialog box, shown in Figure 16.5, gives the color number. Then, open the File menu, choose Preferences, choose File Preferences, and click the GIF tab. In the dialog box that appears, set the transparency value to the graphic's background color number, and click OK. When you open the graphic in a browser, the background blends with whatever color you have chosen for the Web page's background.

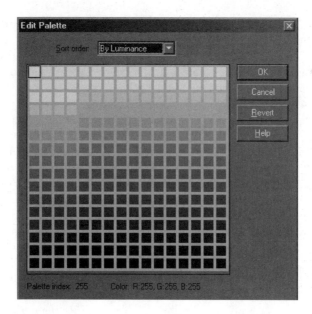

Figure 16.5 Determining the background color number

Animated GIFs

It is amazingly easy to create an animation for your Web site. You don't need an expensive multimedia production program. All you need is software that enables you to edit the control information that is embedded in a GIF 89a file, and that's made possible by a number of shareware programs. My favorite is GIF Construction Set (Alchemy Mindworks, accessible on the Web at www.mindworkshop.com). I will not go into all the details of how you create an animated GIF with a program such as GIF Construction Set; this is just an overview so you can see how easy it is.

The key to making an animated GIF lies in realizing that a single GIF 89a file can contain dozens of separate graphics, along with control information that specifies the order in which these files should be displayed. To create an animated GIF, you create a series of separate GIF files, in which each of the images has been slightly altered. For example, you could create ten GIF files showing a ball. By adjusting the position of the ball within each GIF slightly, you can make a series of graphics so that, when played back rapidly, the ball appears to bounce up and down. If you loop the sequence, it seems as if the action is continuous. There is nothing fancy here; this is just a computerized version of those flip books you used to play with when you were a kid.

In Figure 16.6, you see how GIF Construction Set displays the control information. It begins with a header, followed by a LOOP command, which tells the program to repeat the sequence of images endlessly. After each CONTROL statement is a reference to an image. When you select one of these images, you see the image in the preview area.

Many animated GIFs are created by taking an image, such as the simple one shown in Figure 16.6, and rotating it slightly. By creating a whole series of duplicates of the image, each one slightly rotated from the previous, you can create the illusion of animated motion when the images are played back rapidly. In Figure 16.7, notice how the next image in the sequence has been rotated slightly. This isn't rocket science. For example, you could take an arrow and make a number of copies, each of which positions the arrow a few tenths of an inch to the right; the effect would resemble an arrow shooting across the screen.

Positioning Images with STYLE

In style sheet terminology, graphics are *replaceable elements*; that is, the browser replaces the tag that inserts them (IMG) with the graphic itself. By default, the

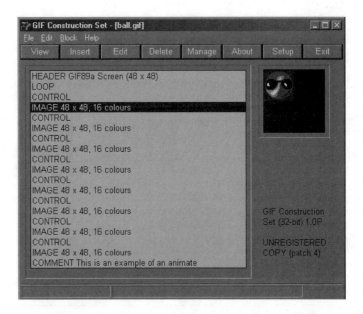

Figure 16.6 GIF Construction Set displays the animated GIFs control info

displayed element's size is the image's intrinsic size, determined by the file itself. Within the CSS box formatting model (see Chapter 12), you can do any of the things you would do to any other element, including the following:

- Adding a margin offset with the margin properties
- Adding a border offset with the border properties
- Adding padding with the padding properties
- Floating an image left or right with the float property
- Positioning an image in an absolute position on the page

To apply presentation formats to images, you can create a single IMG style definition, such as the following:

```
<STYLE type = "text/css">
     IMG { margin: 0.5in;
           border: thin solid;
           float: left }
</STYLE>
```

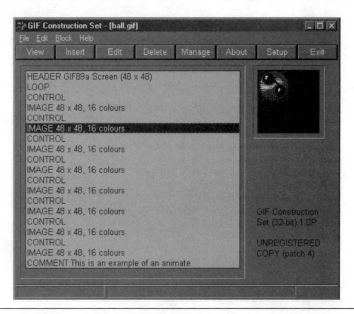

Figure 16.7 The next image in the sequence has been rotated slightly

You can use the class attribute to define two or more IMG styles. Here, you see the style definitions for two basic IMG formats. One floats the graphic to the left, while the other floats the graphic to the right.

```
<STYLE type = "text/css">
     IMG.left {  margin: 0.5in;
                 border: thin solid;
                 float: left }
     IMG.right { margin: 0.5in;
                 border: thin solid;
                 float: right }
</STYLE>
```

You can format individual images by using the id attribute. Alternatively, you can use the IMG element's style attribute, and format the image with an inline style, as in the following example:

```
<IMG src = "picture.jpg" style = "margin: 0.5in;
float: right">
```

Formatting Images for Non-CSS-Capable Browsers

If you are using the transitional flavor of HTML and writing for non-CSS-capable browsers, you will need to use the IMG element's deprecated attributes in order to control image formats. Table 16.4 lists these attributes and illustrates their use.

Table 16.4 Deprecated image presentation attributes

Attribute	Use and example
align	Specifies the image's alignment. Valid values are bottom, middle, top, left, and right. `<IMG align = "right">`
borders	Creates a border around the graphic. Specify the border width in pixels. To display the image with no border, specify 0. `<IMG border = "1">`
height	Overrides the physical size of the image and specifies the height to which the user's browser should size the image. `<IMG src = "sailboat.gif" height = "150">`
hspace	Inserts a horizontal offset (top and bottom), defined in pixels. `<IMG hspace = "3">`
vspace	Inserts a vertical offset (left and right), defined in pixels. `<IMG space = "5">`
width	Overrides the physical size of the image and specifies the width to which the user's browser should size the image. `<IMG src = "icon.gif" width = 52">`

Here's what the alignment options do:

- **align = top** Aligns adjacent text with the top of the image.
- **align = middle** Aligns adjacent text with the middle of the image.
- **align = bottom** Aligns adjacent text with the bottom of the image. You can also float the graphic to the left or right of the page, so that surrounding text flows around it.
- **align = left** Floats the image to the left and flows text around the right of the image.
- **align = right** Floats the image to the right and flows text around the left of the image.

Positioning Graphics with Tables

CSS provides much better control over image placement—so much so, in fact, that Web authors frequently use tables to position graphics when they are writing for non-CSS-capable browsers. To position a graphic left of some text, for example, create a two-cell table; put the graphic in the left cell, and the text in the right one. If you hide the table borders, you'll achieve a neat-looking effect that's not obviously a table. For information on tables, see Chapter 13.

Creating an Imagemap

An imagemap (also called a clickable map) is a graphic that contains two or more hyperlinks, each tied to a particular region of the image. I'm sure you've seen lots of these on the Web. In this section, you will learn how to create client-side imagemaps, which don't require any fancy fussing with your Web server. As you will see, it is easy to create imagemaps, but you'll need some special software.

How does an imagemap work? It's an ordinary graphic, but it has been marked in such a way that the mouse pointer's position is linked with a URL. When you have put the mouse over Illinois in an imagemap of the U.S., and then click the mouse button, you see the Illinois page.

This section fills you in concerning imagemaps, beginning with an explanation of the two different kinds of imagemaps (very hard and very easy). I think you will prefer very easy, so this chapter concentrates on them.

How Do Imagemaps Work?

You can create imagemaps in two ways:

- **Server-side imagemaps** Formerly, this was the only kind of imagemap you could create. You had to make a special data file, as well as a CGI script. Unless you knew something about servers and could configure the server to work with your file, you could not use imagemaps.
- **Client-side imagemaps** This type of imagemap is a lot easier to make. It doesn't require any fussing with the server. However, client-side imagemaps require a relatively recent browser—version 3.0 or later of the two market leaders (Internet Explorer and Netscape Navigator).

Although HTML provides elements (including MAP and AREA) for imagemaps, very few Web authors use these elements directly. These elements require you to specify the exact coordinates (in pixels) where the various clickable shapes exist within the graphic, and to link each shape with a URL. It is very tedious work to determine the map coordinates manually. Instead, just about everyone uses imagemap editors, which automatically determine the coordinates and generate the HTML code; you then paste this code into your document.

Thanks to client-side imagemaps, any reader of this book can include imagemaps. Just remember that you will be excluding a small proportion of viewers who are using older browsers, as well as people who have switched graphics off. Prepare an alternative menu of text-only navigation links, or consider offering a text-only version of your site.

Choosing an Appropriate Graphic

With client-side imagemaps, you cannot get very fancy in terms of image geometry: you're limited to rectangles, circles, and polygons. For this reason, you will be very wise to choose a graphic that's full of plain geometric shapes (such as the one shown in Figure 16.8). Stick to geometric shapes (circles, squares, rectangles, and polygons).

Editing Your Imagemap

To make your imagemap, you need an imagemap editor. That's a program (or a utility within a bigger program) that enables you to select the rectangle, circle, or

polygon that you want, and then assign a URL to it. The program then generates the necessary HTML code, and inserts it into your Web page. What could
be easier?

There are a number of image map editors available, but this chapter focuses on
one that I find particularly easy to use: MapEdit (www.boutell.com/ mapedit).
This site offers lots of information concerning MapEdit, including online registration using a secure server. You can use the evaluation version of the program
for free for 30 days; subsequently, registration is $25.

Getting Started with MapEdit

To create an imagemap for your Web page, you need to begin with a draft of the
HTML page that includes the graphic. Remember that your graphic should contain regular shapes so that the user can see what should be clicked (see Figure
16.8).

Once you have created a draft of your page with a graphic, it is time to start the
imagemap editor and tell the program which file you're using. With MapEdit,

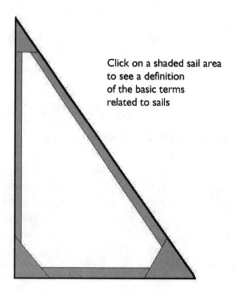

Click on a shaded sail area
to see a definition
of the basic terms
related to sails

Figure 16.8 This figure is OK for an imagemap

you see the dialog box shown in Figure 16.9. Here, you specify the location of the file and the name of the graphic that you want to use as an imagemap. Since you are creating a client-side imagemap, it does not matter whether you choose NCSA or CERN.

Planning the Links

Before you spend a lot of time marking up your imagemap, take a moment to think about how you want to organize the various files on your server. If they are all in one directory (this is the easiest way), or in a directory beneath the one in which the imagemap document is stored, you can use relative URLs (URLs that include nothing but the filename, such as "sail.html"). Otherwise, you will be wise to use absolute URLs. This is particularly true if you think you will some-day move the imagemap document to a different directory location, without also moving the linked files.

I recommend that you simply keep all your files in one directory. This is much less confusing, unless you're planning to create a really huge site. Another plus: You can create and test all the necessary files on your local system, without even being connected to the Internet. Just place the imagemap file, the graphics, and all the linked files in one directory.

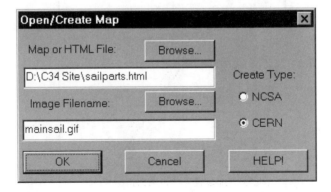

Figure 16.9 Opening the file with MapEdit

Once you've decided how you're going to organize your files on the server, make a list of the exact file names of the all the URLs you want to include in the imagemap. You'll need to type these precisely.

Marking the Shapes and Linking to URLs

After you've identified the files you want to use, you will see your graphic in the map editor's window (see Figure. 16.10). Most map editors, such as the one shown, give you a variety of tools to work with. MapEdit includes tools for rectangles, polygons, and circles.

To mark a shape, select the tool you want to use, and drag over it. When you are finished dragging, click the button again. You'll see a dialog box asking you to identify the URL you want to use. Type the URL. Be sure to include alternate text for the benefit of people who are not browsing with graphics turned on.

Continue adding shapes and URLs until you have linked to all the files you want to include, and save your work. MapEdit automatically adds the needed HTML elements to your draft Web page.

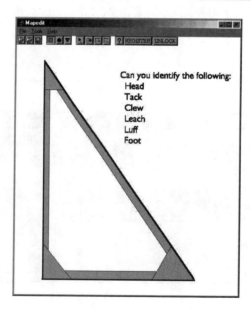

Figure 16.10 Displaying the image in the MapEdit window

Testing Your Work

Switch to your browser, open the imagemap document, and test the links you have created.

When you view your imagemap document with your browser, you will find that there's a big (probably blue) border around it. This looks ugly, doesn't it? This is automatically supplied by your browser, which has detected hyperlinks within the graphic. To get rid of the border, edit the underlying HTML, and add a BOR-DER= "O" tag to the <IMG> tag that references your imagemap.

Editing the Imagemap

Should you discover an error in a URL you have assigned to a shape, switch back to your imagemap editor. Generally, there is a way you can edit the URL. In MapEdit, choose Test + Edit from the Tools menu, and double-click the region that contains the erroneous URL.

Summary

It's easy to add graphics to your page. Without the slightest artistic talent, you can process graphics so that they download more quickly and keep users happy. You can quickly and easily position graphics by using the CSS box positioning properties (Chapter 12). If you are writing for non-CSS-capable browsers, you will need to use the IMG element's deprecated presentation attributes, such as align. Client-side imagemaps are really easy to create, but you will need an imagemap editor.

Make your pages more interactive with forms. You'll learn how to create forms in Chapter 17.

17

True to FORM

In this chapter, you will learn the following skills.

- Receiving form output as e-mail and decoding the output
- Creating text boxes, list boxes, check boxes, and radio buttons
- Creating scrollable text input boxes
- Making your forms easier for users with special needs
- Grouping form areas for more logical data entry and processing

Forms are the key to Web interactivity. I'm sure you've filled out a few; you've typed stuff, chosen something from a list box, placed your check in the check box, and hit the Submit button.

By themselves, forms don't do anything unless their output is routed to an interpreting program, located on a server, or an e-mail address. Chances are good that your Internet service provider has already installed programs that can accept, decode, and save form output. Alternatively, you can create forms that send electronic mail to your account. A variety of shareware programs enable you to decode and process the e-mailed data.

This chapter examines the component of forms that's relevant to HTML Version 4—the tags and their orderly deployment in a way that's consonant with the HTML Version 4 way. If you've used previous versions of HTML, there's plenty of news here. Forms were singled out for special attention by great minds at the World Wide Web Organization, and the result is good news indeed. New features include keyboard access to form fields, an important gain for users who can't use a mouse; the ability to select a form item just by clicking its name; provisions to create scripts to check for valid user input; and much more.

Whether you have ever created a form before or not, this chapter shows you everything you need to know. Don't let forms scare you off; they can transform your relatively ordinary Web page into something into a much more interesting experience. For one thing, consider the value of soliciting content from users. You would be surprised by the number of people willing to contribute to a Web publishing enterprise; it's a great way to build a site.

What Is a Form?

A form enables a Web user to make responses to a number of input fields, called controls, and to send these responses somewhere. The "somewhere" might be nothing fancier than your mailbox, or it might be a program, which intercepts and processes the submitted data. Either way, a form provides users with a chance to talk back. To define your form, you need to decide from the outset what sort of information you need, and then ask for it. Figure 17.1 shows an example.

The key to forms is the FORM element, as you might have guessed. FORM demarcates a special part of an ordinary HTML document that is designed to enable user input, which is then collected into what amounts to a really long character string. This string is then sent to a mailbox or program. As for the controls, they're the same ones you're used to from any GUI (graphical user interface): text boxes, list boxes, check boxes, and radio buttons.

What does form output look like? It's a mess, loaded with extraneous characters. By default, HTML's form tags create a long character string in which all the data is there, together with the names of all the controls, but unfortunately it's all one long string! In order to make this meaningful you must run a program to *parse* it, which means getting rid of the garbage and making it meaningful.

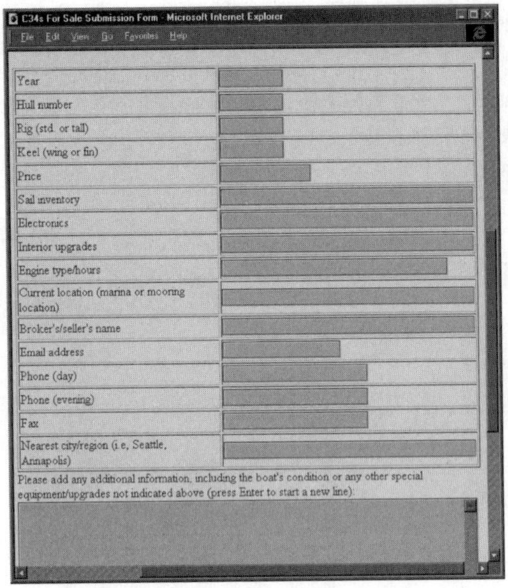

Figure 17.1 Think through what type of information you want to ask for

There are loads of programs that can parse form output, and some of them are very easy to use. Of these, one of the best is FormPost, a shareware program created by CT Software (4510 E. Muriel Dr., Phoenix, AZ 85032, 800-617-7740). Figure 17.3 shows the output after FormPost decodes it. Essentially, this program strips the extraneous characters out, inserts line breaks, and presents the submitted data in a human-readable way. The resulting file could be easily imported to a database program.

Is creating a form difficult? Actually, it is not. There's the usual welter of attributes, but we'll cope with them by putting most of them in this chapter's tables, and concentrating on the highlights. Most form authors use only a few of the many possibilities available.

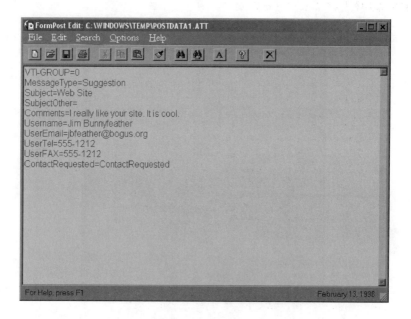

Figure 17.2 Form output after decoding by FormPost

The FORM Element

Most HTML documents that contain forms also contain additional HTML. In fact, they are just ordinary pages. What gives them those special, cool form characteristics—the radio buttons, check boxes, and all the rest—is the FORM element.

The FORM element is a container for everything that's in a form. What's more, it is also a data submission unit. When the user clicks the Submit button, all the responses within the FORM container are collected together and launched forth, all at once.

A Really Simple Example

Don't drown in the complexities of forms—start modestly. The following shows a simple example.

```
<FORM action = "mailto:me@mymailbox.net"
method="post">
<P>What's your first name? <INPUT type= "text" name
= "first-name" size  = "15">
<P>What's your favorite color?
        <SELECT name = "favorite-color">
              <OPTION selected>Cerulean blue
              <OPTION>Mahagony
              <OPTION>Ultramarine
              <OPTION>Tangerine
        </SELECT>
<P><INPUT type = "submit" value = "Send">
<P><INPUT type = "reset">
</FORM>
```

Actually, about 90% of the forms you will find on the Web aren't much more complex than this example. Here's what it does:

- The FORM element sets up the form. It is a container for all the other form tags.
- The FORM element's action attribute tells the browser what to do. Here, it's submitted as a mailto URL to your mailbox. (Try substituting your own e-mail address for "me@mymailbox.net.") Be sure to use the method = "post" attribute. I'll explain why later.
- The INPUT element enables you to define a control—here, a text input box that is 15 characters wide.
- The SELECT element enables you to create a drop-down list box. By default, Cerulean blue is selected.
- More INPUT elements enable you to display the Submit and Reset buttons.
- Note that forms can contain ordinary HTML text and elements in addition to the form-specific elements. In fact, you can arrange the various controls in a table, if you wish.

It's really easy. Everything else is icing on the cake (well, sort of). But you can do it. Trust me.

Looking at the FORM Element Definition

You're ready for all the details. The form element definition is:

ELEMENT	FORM
PURPOSE	Creates a form for user input.
TYPE	Block
NESTED WITHIN	BODY
START TAG	Required
END TAG	Required
CONTENT	INPUT and SELECT elements; text
ATTRIBUTES	core attributes (id, class, style, title) language attributes (lang, dir) action = "url" (required) method = "(get, post)" enctype = "MIME type" (optional)
EXAMPLE	<FORM method= "post" action = "script.cgi"> <INPUT type = "text" size = "60" > </FORM>
TIP	To direct the output of a form to your e-mail address, use method= "get" and action = "mailto:youraddress@yourserver"

The two important attributes here are action and method, which are discussed in the following sections.

Using the Action Attribute

In brief, the action attribute tells the browser where to send the form output, while the method attribute tells how to send it. Both are easy to use. For the action attribute, you just specify the URL of the program that is going to process your form's output (or a mailto URL, if you'd like to route the form output to a mailbox for later processing).

Using the Method Attribute

For the method attribute, you have only two choices, get and post. Almost always, you will choose post. In fact, the other one, get, is officially deprecated in HTML Version 4.

What's the difference between the get and post methods? Both send the form's data by means of name/value pairs (each named response field is paired with a user-selected value). In the simple example given above, the name/value pairs could be the following:

```
first-name/Harvey
favorite-color/tangerine
```

The post method sends the name/value pairs independently of the URL, while the get method appends the name/value pairs to the URL. The difference between them is of interest only to programmers; you just need to find out which method is required by the program to which you're sending the data. Ask. And while you're at it, make sure you have got the URL right. If you're experimenting with sending form data to your mailbox via the mailto method, use post.

Get Control! (Creating Controls with INPUT)

Within your form, you can use the following controls: text boxes, password text boxes, check boxes, radio buttons, text entry boxes, and list boxes. In addition, you can insert buttons for submitting data or resetting the form. In the following sections, you will learn how to create all these controls.

Most of the controls discussed in this section use the INPUT element; you select the control using the type attribute. You can define 10 different types of controls with INPUT, and only some of the attributes are relevant to each of the types. For this reason, the following section spreads the discussion of the INPUT element's attributes around, discussing them where they are relevant. But here's the element definition, for starters:

ELEMENT	INPUT
PURPOSE	Accepts user input within a form.
TYPE	Inline
NESTED WITHIN	FORM
START TAG	Required

END TAG	Forbidden
CONTENT	Empty
ATTRIBUTES	core attributes (id, class, style, title)
	language attributes (lang, dir)
	type = "(text, password, checkbox, radio, submit, reset, file, hidden, image, button)" (required)
	name = "CDATA" (optional)
	value = "CDATA" (optional)
	checked (optional)
	disabled (optional)
	readonly (optional)
	size = "CDATA" (optional)
	maxlength = "number" (optional)
	src = "url" (optional)
	alt = "CDATA" (optional)
	usemap = "url" (optional)
	tabindex = "number" (optional)
	accesskey = "character" (optional)
EXAMPLE	<INPUT type = "text" size = "60" >
TIP	Many of the attributes have specific meanings for a given input type; for example, in a text input box, the size attribute governs the length of the box that's displayed on-screen.

As you can see, the INPUT element is empty; it doesn't take any content. What is its purpose? To create a control. Although none of the attributes other than type are required, the program processing your form requires that you define the name attribute so that the supplied value can be paired with a name.

Although there are a lot of attributes in the INPUT element, don't let this scare you; most of them are used for specific controls, as you will see in the following pages.

Single-Line Text Boxes

To create a single-line text box, you use the INPUT element with the type = "text" attribute. Relevant attributes include a name (a unique string of characters that gives a name to the value supplied by the user), the text box's size in characters, and the maximum input length (again, in characters). See Table 17.1 for a list of relevant attributes for text boxes.

Here's an example of a text input box:

```
<INPUT type = "text" name = "hull-number" size = "4"
maxlength = "4">
```

In the above example, the maxlength specification acts as a limiter, of sorts, on the data supplied by the user. The field asks for a number that actually cannot be any more than four characters in length; if the user tries to type more, the browser will not permit it.

Table 17.1 Attributes for INPUT text boxes

Attribute	Use and example
maxlength	Maximum number of characters for text input field.
	`maxlength = "80"`
name	Names the control.
	`name = "first-name"`
readonly	Prevents the user from making any changes to the text.
	`readonly`
size	Specifies the width of the text box in characters.
	`size = "45"`
tabindex	Specifies the tabbing order for accessing this field with the tab key.
	`tabindex = "2"`
type	Creates the control.
	`type = "text"`

Consider using a drop-down menu or list box if you want users to pick from a finite list of options. The problem with text boxes is typos; if you ask people to type their state, for example, you'll get a lot of spelling mistakes. It is much better to have users choose their state from a list box. That way, the correct value is always uploaded. This makes it much easier to group data subsequently.

Password Text Boxes

A password text box is exactly like an ordinary text input text box, except that it displays the user's input using asterisks. This is intended to prevent "shoulder surfing," a means of learning other people's passwords by observing them while they're typed. See Table 17.2 for a list of relevant attributes for text boxes. Here is an example of a password input box:

```
<INPUT type = "password" name = "pass-phrase" size =
"12" maxlength = "12">
```

You would use this if you were setting up a site with password-based authentication. To make this work, you need to consult with your service provider to configure the server correctly.

Check Boxes

You've seen plenty of check boxes in Windows and Macintosh dialog boxes; they look just the same on HTML forms. The name and value attributes are required (see Table 17.2). When a user checks the check box, the check box's value becomes active, and is submitted along with the rest of the data in the form. (If it is not checked, the data is not submitted.)

You can set up the check box so that it is already checked, by default; to do this, you use the checked attribute.

```
<INPUT type = "checkbox" name = "update" value =
"yes" checked>
```

If the user leaves the box checked (it is checked by default), here's what is uploaded to the forms-processing program:

```
update/yes
```

Table 17.2 INPUT attributes for check boxes

Attribute	Use and example
checked	Places a check mark in the check box. `checked`
name	Names the field. `name = "update"`
value	Specifies the value to be uploaded if the user checks the box. `value = "yes"`

Laying Out Check Boxes with Tables

Use tables to lay out check boxes and other controls attractively. Here is an example:

```
<TABLE border = "1" cols = "2" width = "25%" align =
"center">
      <TR>
          <TD align = "left">Would you like
          to know when this site is updated?
          <TD align = "center"><INPUT type =
          "checkbox" name = "update" value =
          "yes" checked>
      <TR>
          <TD align = "left">May I sell your
          e-mail address  to junk mail
          companies?
          <TD align = "center"><INPUT type =
          "checkbox" name = "spam" value =
          "yes">
</TABLE>
```

Creating a Group of Check Boxes

In well-designed dialog boxes, you often see a group of check boxes. Within the group, users can check more than one option. You can do this with HTML forms, too.

To group check boxes, you create two or more check boxes that share the same name, as in the following example:

```
<P>Please check the type of music you like:
<P>African Pop <INPUT type = "checkbox" name =
"music" value = "african-pop">
<P>Techno <INPUT type = "checkbox" name = "music"
value = "techno">
<P>Rap <INPUT type = "checkbox" name = "music" value
= "rap" >
<P>Lilith Fair <INPUT type = "checkbox" name =
"music" value = "lilith" >
<P>Elevator <INPUT type = "checkbox" name = "music"
value = "elevator" >
```

If the user checks Techno, Rap, and Elevator, here's what gets uploaded:

```
music/techno
music/rap
music/elevator
```

Radio Buttons

Radio buttons are like check boxes, in that their values do not get uploaded unless the user checks them (or you've checked them by default). They also use the same attributes (checked, name, and value).

But radio buttons differ from check boxes in one very important way (besides being round, not square): Users are accustomed to seeing radio buttons in an area where they can make only one choice. You can use radio buttons singly, but it makes much more sense to use a check box for that purpose.

Radio buttons should be used in a panel of options where only one out of a number of options can be selected. You set this up by creating a series of radio buttons that all share the same name.

Here's an example:

```
How often do you access the Internet?:
<P>A few times per month <INPUT type = "radio" name
= "access-frequency" value = "infrequent">
<P>A few times per week <INPUT type = "radio" name =
"access-frequency" value = "seldom">
<P>A few times per day <INPUT type = "radio" name =
```

```
"access-frequency" value = "daily" >
<P>All day <INPUT type = "radio" name = "access-fre-
quency" value = "all-day" >
<P>Constantly <INPUT type = "radio" name = "access-
frequency" value = "addicted" >
```

When the user selects one of these options, only one name/value pair goes out with the form (for example, access-frequency/seldom).

File Uploading Boxes

If you would like to request users to upload files, you can do so by creating a special text box that is designed to contain the name of a file. When the user clicks the Submit button, the browser uploads the file as well as the rest of the information. (This only works, of course, if the browser supports it.)

It is easy to set up a file uploading box; they are very similar to text input boxes, except that they have a different type.

```
<INPUT type = "file" name = "upload" size = "20">
```

A file uploading box may be easy to set up, but it is fraught with peril: It provides the perfect opportunity for someone to play a prank on you by uploading a virus-infected file. You'll be wise to solicit only plain ASCII text or graphics files, which cannot contain viruses.

If you plan to ask users to upload files, you can add an accept attribute to the FORM tag to specify which types of files can be uploaded. You do this by supplying a comma-separated list of valid MIME types. (MIME, short for Multipurpose Internet Mail Extensions, is a standard for naming file types.) For example, the following accept attribute limits uploading to GIF and JPEG files: accept = "image/gif, image/jpeg".

Hidden Input Fields

Sometimes you may want to send information without the user's knowledge. For example, suppose you are creating a form to upload users' queries to a database program. Generally, these programs need some initial information before they can carry out the search. Hidden input fields provide a way to supply this information without having to bother your users. Here's an example of a hidden input field:

```
<INPUT type = "hidden" name = "search-type" value =
"simple-search">
```

This input field doesn't appear in your form, but its name/value pair is submitted when the user clicks Submit.

Drop-Down Menus and List Boxes

To create drop-down menus and list boxes, you use the SELECT and OPTION elements. SELECT sets up the list box, while OPTION enables you to specify the options that are listed in the drop-down menu. Here's an example:

```
<SELECT name = "favorite-food">
     <OPTION selected>Potato chips
     <OPTION>Broccoli
     <OPTION>Carrots
     <OPTION>Gruel
     <OPTION>Mush
     <OPTION>Pumpkin
     <OPTION>Squash
</SELECT>
```

This displays a drop-down menu showing the selected option, potato chips. The other options are hidden within the drop-down menu.

Creating the List Box with SELECT

To create a list box (showing all the options), you use the multiple attribute, which enables the user to select more than one option. With most browsers, this automatically displays the list as a list box rather than a drop-down menu. Here's an example of the multiple attribute used in a SELECT list:

```
<SELECT multiple name = "favorite-food">
     <OPTION>Broccoli
     <OPTION>Carrots
     <OPTION>Grits
     <OPTION>Potato chips
     <OPTION>Pumpkin
     <OPTION>Squash
</SELECT>
```

This displays a list box showing all the options, and enables the user to select more than one option.

Here's the SELECT element definition:

ELEMENT	SELECT
PURPOSE	In a form, creates a drop-down menu.
TYPE	Inline
NESTED WITHIN	FORM
START TAG	Required
END TAG	Required
CONTENT	OPTGROUP or OPTION elements
ATTRIBUTES	core attributes (id, class, style, title) language attributes (lang, dir) name = "CDATA" size = "number" (optional) multiple (optional) disabled (optional) tabindex = "number"

EXAMPLE	`<SELECT name = "hull-length">`
	     `<OPTGROUP label = "Hull Length">`
	          `<OPTION selected value =`
	          `"34'">34'`
	          `<OPTION>36'`
	          `<OPTION>40'`
	     `</OPTGROUP>`
	     `<OPTGROUP label = "Year">`
	          `<OPTION selected value =`
	          `"1988">1988`
	          `<OPTION>1989`
	          `<OPTION>1990>`
	     `</OPTGROUP>`
	`</SELECT>`

TIP	Insert menu items with OPTGROUP and OPTION.

The following explains what the SELECT element's attributes do.

Table 17.3 Attributes for SELECT drop-down lists

Attribute	Use and example
disabled	Disables the text entry area. `disabled`
multiple	Enables users to select more than one option and displays the control as a list box rather than a drop-down menu. `multiple`
readonly	Makes the list read-only. `readonly`
size	Specifies the number of rows to display, in lines. The default is 1 line. `size = "3"`
tabindex	Specifies the tabbing order for accessing this field with the tab key. `tabindex = "2".`

Creating List Box Items with OPTION

In order to create options within the SELECT list box, you use the OPTION element.

Here's the OPTION element definition:

ELEMENT	OPTION
PURPOSE	In a form, defines an item in a drop-down menu created with SELECT.
TYPE	Inline
NESTED WITHIN	FORM
START TAG	Required

END TAG	Optional
CONTENT	Text
ATTRIBUTES	core attributes (id, class, style, title) language attributes (lang, dir) selected (optional) disabled (optional) label = "text" (optional) value = "CDATA" (optional)

EXAMPLE	`<SELECT name = "hull-length">`
	  `<OPTGROUP label = "Hull Length">`
	    `<OPTION selected value =`
	    `"34'">34'`
	    `<OPTION>36'`
	    `<OPTION>40'`
	  `</OPTGROUP>`
	  `<OPTGROUP label = "Year">`
	    `<OPTION selected value =`
	    `"1988">1988`
	    `<OPTION>1989`
	    `<OPTION>1990>`
	  `</OPTGROUP>`
	`</SELECT>`

TIP	Define the items to appear in the menu by using OPTGROUP and OPTION.

The OPTION element does not require an end tag, as you can see from the above examples. By default, it takes the value of the element's content, which is fine for most purposes; if you wish, you can define your own value using the value attribute.

Table 17.4 lists the attributes you can use with OPTION.

Table 17.4 Attributes for OPTION drop-down lists

Attribute	Use and example
disabled	Disables the text entry area. `disabled`

selected	Selects this value and displays the selection in the drop-down menu window. `selected`
value	Specifies a value for this option other than the element's content. `value = "junk-food"`

Text Entry Areas

If you would like to solicit more than one line of text, use the TEXTAREA element. This element creates a text entry box containing a specified number of rows and columns. Here's the element definition:

ELEMENT	TEXTAREA
PURPOSE	In a form, creates a multi-line text entry box.
TYPE	Block
NESTED WITHIN	FORM
START TAG	Required
END TAG	Required
CONTENT	Text
ATTRIBUTES	core attributes (id, class, style, title) language attributes (lang, dir) name = "CDATA" (optional) rows = "number" (required) cols = "number" (required) disabled (optional) readonly (optional) tabindex = "number" (optional) accesskey = "character" (optional)
EXAMPLE	<TEXTAREA rows = "16 cols = "65" name = "comments">
TIP	Use <INPUT type = "text"> to create a one-line text box.

To create the text entry area, you need to give the control a name, and specify the number of columns (in characters) and rows (in lines). Here's an example:

```
<TEXTAREA name="autobiography" cols = "45" rows =
"25"></TEXTAREA>
```

Note that users can enter more than the specified number of rows and columns. Browsers ought to provide some means of scrolling within the text entry area, as well as of wrapping long lines of text; unaccountably, though, many fail to do the latter, forcing users to press Enter at the end of each line (and making a mess out of the uploaded data). If you wish, you can place some text between the tags; this will appear as default but editable text within the text area, as in the following example:

```
<TEXTAREA name="autobiography" cols = "45" rows =
"25">Please tell us a little about
yourself.</TEXTAREA>
```

Table 17.5 Attributes for TEXTAREA text boxes

Attribute	Use and example
cols	Specifies the number of columns to display, in characters. `cols = "45"`
disabled	Disables the text entry area. `disabled`
name	Names the text area. `name = "comments"`
readonly	Makes the text entry area read-only, so that users can't modify the text contained there. `readonly`
rows	Specifies the number of rows to display, in lines. `rows = "25"`

tabindex	Specifies the tabbing order for accessing this field with the tab key.
	`tabindex = "2"`

Creating Submit, Reset, and Other Buttons

To add the finishing touches to your form, you need to add buttons that enable the user to submit the completed form (or clear it if the user wants to start over). You can do this in several ways. The simplest involves creating INPUT elements with the type attribute set to submit or reset. You can also use the image type, which enables you to use a graphic instead of a button. Even more possibilities arise with the BUTTON element. The following sections discuss these options.

Creating Simple Submit and Reset Buttons

You add the Submit and Reset buttons by using the INPUT element, as in the following examples:

```
<INPUT type = "submit">
<INPUT type = "reset">
```

That's all you need to insert the Submit and Reset buttons in your document. If you would like to show your own text on the buttons, use the value attribute, as shown in these examples:

```
<INPUT type = "submit" value = "Send">
<INPUT type = "reset" value = "Clear">
```

Note that the contents of the value attribute must be a string, that is, a contiguous series of characters with no spaces. However, you can still display two or more words on the button, if you wish: Just use the   entity, as in the following example: <INPUT type = "submit" value = "Tell us about it">.

Using a Graphic Instead of a Button

If you would like to use a graphic instead of a submit button, you can do so by using the INPUT element, and setting the type to image.

Here's an example:

```
<P>Click the rocket to send the form!  <INPUT type =
"image" src = "launch.gif" alt = "Submit">
```

The src attribute enables you to name the graphic that's used in place of the Submit button, while the alt attribute specifies alternate text for people who are not using graphical browsers.

When you use a graphic instead of a submit button, the browser uploads the mouse coordinates as well as the form data. This means that you can implement client- or server-side imagemaps here, but you should do so with caution: If the user has switched off graphics, or is using a text-only browser, the various options will not be available.

Using the BUTTON Element

Yet another way to implement Submit and Reset buttons is available, thanks to the BUTTON element. This is a new element that is not recognized by most browsers yet, but it will provide richer presentation possibilities than the INPUT buttons.

Here's an example of the BUTTON element. It displays an image instead of that boring old pushbutton:

```
<BUTTON type = "submit"><IMG src =
"rocket.gif"></BUTTON>
```

Browsers that fully support BUTTON will display the named image, just as <INPUT type ="image"> does, but with a neat twist: The graphic is displayed as a three-dimensional button, not as a flat image. Additionally, you can use BUTTON to define reset buttons (you can't do that with INPUT). Here's the BUTTON element's definition:

ELEMENT	BUTTON
PURPOSE	Creates a button with definable text on the button face.
TYPE	Inline

NESTED WITHIN	FORM element
START TAG	Required
END TAG	Required
CONTENT	Text (displayed on button face)
ATTRIBUTES	core attributes (id, class, style, title) language attributes (lang, dir) name = "CDATA" (optional) value = "CDATA" (optional) type = "(button, submit, reset)" (optional) disabled (optional) tabindex = "number" (optional)
EXAMPLE	\<BUTTON type = "submit" name = "submit">Send It!\</BUTTON>
TIP	Use this element to specify button text.

Table 17.6 lists the attributes you can use with BUTTON.

Table 17.6 Attributes for the BUTTON element

Attribute	Use and example
disabled	Disables the text entry area. `disabled`
name	Names the button (useful for scripting). `name = "submit"`
type	Defines the button as a Submit or Reset button, or as a button for launching a script. `type = "submit"`
tabindex	Specifies the tabbing order for accessing this field with the tab key. `tabindex = "2"`
value	Specifies a value for this button (useful for scripting). `value = "123"`

Providing Easier Access to Form Fields

Forms are great for interactivity, but many people have complained, justifiably, that they are too hard to use. For example, with previous versions of HTML, you could not select a field by clicking its label text. You had to actually click within the field. That makes things all that much more difficult for people with disabilities.

HTML Version 4 adds a lot of usability to forms, as discussed in this section. You'll learn how to define labels so that users can click on them to select the field. You will also learn how to create keyboard shortcuts for form fields, and also how to set up the tabbing order so that users can navigate forms by means of the TAB key.

Creating Labels

The LABEL element enables you to enter form field labels that are associated with a control, so that the control becomes active when the user clicks on the label text. Here's an example:

```
<LABEL>Type your first name <INPUT type = "text"
name = "firstname" size = "40"></LABEL>
```

Note that the LABEL tags enclose the control as well as the label text.

It's easy to set up labels in the way just described, but there is a problem: You cannot put the label text and input field in different table cells. If you would like to create your form using a table, as suggested earlier in this chapter, you need to explicitly associate the label and the control by means of the for attribute (LABEL element) and id attributes for each control.

Here's an example:

```
<TABLE>
   <TR>
      <TD><LABEL for "f-name">Type your first
      name:</LABEL>
      <TD><INPUT type = "text" name = "firstname"
      size = "40" id = "f-name">
</TABLE>
```

Note that the id must differ from the control's name.

Creating Shortcut Keys

You can create shortcut keys for form fields, just as you can with hyperlinks. To do so, though, you must use the LABEL element to enter the control's explanatory text.

To create the shortcut key, choose a prominent letter within the explanatory text (such as the L in "Last Name"), and make sure it is not used as a shortcut key anywhere else in the document. Then use the accesskey attribute to define the shortcut key.

Note that the accesskey attribute is case-insensitive; it doesn't matter whether the user presses the uppercase or lowercase version of the letter.

```
<LABEL accesskey = "l">Please type your last name:
<INPUT type = "text" size = "40"></LABEL>
```

Browsers should automatically display the shortcut key using some sort of distinctive formatting, such as underlining. Users will have to enter the key using a command key appropriate to their system (such as the Alt key in Windows and the Command key in Mac OS).

Tabbing Around: Determining TAB Order

In this chapter's element definitions, you may have noticed the tabindex attribute, which enables you to define a tab order for the controls in your form. You specify the sequence by adding a unique number to each tabindex attribute, as in example shown on the following page.

```
Type your name: <INPUT type = "text" name = "name"
size = "20" tabindex ="1">
Type your favorite color: : <INPUT type = "text"
name = "color" size = "20" tabindex ="2">
```

You can also specify the tab order in LABEL elements, and there is a good argument for doing so: It makes the selection easier to see.

Grouping FORM Elements

In HTML Version 4, FORMS get their own version of the DIV element discussed earlier in this book: FIELDSET. In brief, FIELDSET enables you to group form elements. You can then assign each FIELDSET group a distinctive style using a style sheet.

Here's an example (it is simplified down to the essentials). Note that there are two FIELDSET groups:

```
<FORM>
        <FIELDSET id = "contact-info">
                <LABEL>What's your name?<INPUT type =
                "text" name = "name">
                <LABEL>What's your e-mail address?<INPUT
                type = "text" name = "email">
        </FIELDSET>
        <FIELDSET id = "preferences">
                <LABEL>What's your favorite color? <INPUT
                type = "text" name = "color">
                <LABEL>What's your favorite sport?
                <INPUT type = "text" name = "sport">
        </FIELDSET>
</FORM>
```

The new LEGEND element enables you to specify a caption for each FIELDSET element. You can use the align attribute to position the caption in relation to the FIELDSET group, as in the following example:

```
<FIELDSET id = "contact-info">
        <LEGEND align = "top">Information about
        you</LEGEND>
        <LABEL>What's your name?<INPUT type =
        "text" name = "name">
        <LABEL>What's your e-mail address?<INPUT
        type = "text" name = "email">
</FIELDSET>
```

Using style sheets, you can give each FIELDSET group a surrounding border, a distinctive color, or other distinguishing characteristics. The gain? Your form is much easier to use.

Summary

Forms add interactivity to your Web pages, but you must route the form output to a program that is capable of processing the data. Fortunately, this is easy to do, and your service provider will be glad to help. The simplest forms-processing programs strip the form output of garbage characters and send the data to your mailbox in a neatly formatted letter. Before you design your form, think about what kind of data you want to collect, and then choose the right controls to collect it. Consider placing your controls within tables so that your form looks neat on-screen. Also, consider using all the accessibility improvements possible with HTML Version 4, including shortcut keys.

In the next chapter, you'll learn how to enable users of Microsoft Internet Explorer Version 4 to subscribe to your site and receive updates.

18

Getting Pushy with the Channel Definition Format

In this chapter, you will learn the following skills:

- Understanding how subscriptions work
- Creating a CDF channel
- Specifying a schedule
- Directing output to the desktop or a screen saver
- Creating a Netcaster channel

How would you like your Web page to be positioned on the Windows desktops of hundreds or even thousands of visitors, so that changes to your Web page are automatically downloaded and displayed for them to see? That's what you can do with push publishing. In contrast to pull publishing, where people have to find your page and go to it deliberately, push publishing brings your page to users' desktops. Once they have subscribed, they don't need to do anything to see site updates. It's all automatic. What's more, changes are downloaded in the background, and in their entirety, so users can browse your page while they are offline, if they wish.

This sounds great, doesn't it? The only catch is, at this writing, the two major browser publishers have seen fit to develop two entirely different push media technologies. To push your content to users of both major browsers, you will need to learn both methods. We'll start with Microsoft Internet Explorer's Channel Definition Format (CDF) and then go on to take a brief look at Netscape's competing push technology, Netcaster, which requires that you modify a JavaScript program and insert this into one of your documents.

How CDF Channels Work

Microsoft's Channel Definition Format (CDF) requires users to create a separate file (with the CDF extension) that is written using the special CDF elements. CDF closely resembles HTML, so it is easy to learn. What's more, CDF is more technically advanced than Netcaster in that it can randomize downloading. The down side is that browsers must know what to do with CDF; currently, the only one that does is Microsoft Internet Explorer (MSIE) 4.0.

When visitors access a page with push capabilities, they can click a link that enables them to initiate and configure the subscription. After clicking the link, they see the dialog box shown in Figure 18.1. They can choose from the following options:

- **Adding the page to the channel lists, without subscribing** The channel lists appear in the Channel Explorer (a special window that appears when users click the Channels button on the standard toolbar, the Channels folder within the Favorites menu, and the Channel Guide, a window that appears on the desktop when the Active Desktop is enabled.
- **Subscribing with notification of updates** Users see a flag next to the page's title, but Internet Explorer doesn't automatically download the page. If users choose this option, they can also choose to receive notifications via e-mail. (This doesn't require any effort on your part; the mail originates from within Internet Explorer once it detects that your site has changed.)

- **Subscribing with notification of updates and automatic downloading of new content** As in the previous option, they can, if they wish, receive notifications via e-mail. Users can choose to download only the page to which they subscribed (the default option), or all the content specified by the channel. By default, the downloads take place at the publisher's recommended schedule, or the user can choose other downloading times (daily, weekly, or monthly). Users can also determine how much to download; for example, they can choose to download all the pages linked to the subscribed page up to a link depth they specify. This feature is especially attractive to Web users who would like to download extensive amounts of content at night when they are not using their computers, and then view the content offline during the day.

After users subscribe, they will see your page in the Channel Explorer, as well as the other channel lists. Clicking the page brings it up very quickly if the user chooses to download the content.

In addition to inserting content within the various channel lists, you can also direct content to windows on the user's desktop and to the user's screen saver.

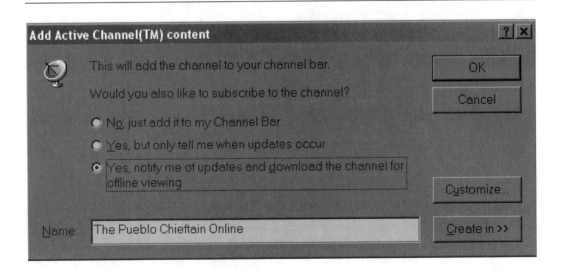

Figure 18.1 Initiating the subscription

To write CDF, Microsoft used XML, a new, simplified version of SGML. When you learn CDF, you get your first experience with an XML-developed markup language.

Creating a CDF Channel

To transform an existing Web page into a channel to which MSIE Version 4 users can subscribe, you need to create a logo, an icon, and a CDF file, and upload all of these to your server. In addition, you need to add a link to the page you want to "push." In this section, you will do this the easy way, without worrying about the many available options. As you'll see, it is really easy to do this—try it!

Creating the Logo

To display your page properly within Internet Explorer's various channel-related lists and dialog boxes, you need to create two graphics. The first, sized 80 by 32 pixels, is your channel's logo. This doesn't have to be elaborate, but it does have to be exactly 80 by 32.

You can create this graphic with any graphics program, such as Paint Shop Pro, that can save the file in the GIF or JPEG format.

Creating the Icon

Next, you need to create an icon that is exactly 16 by 16 pixels. This is not a lot of space, so don't try to cram in too much detail.

Creating the XML Channel File

The last file you need is the channel definition file, which is written in XML, which closely resembles HTML (except that the elements are different, and there are a couple of syntax differences to watch out for).

But don't worry about learning XML. You can easily modify the following file to create your subscription. Edit and save the file, naming it channel.cdf. (You can use any filename you want besides "channel," but you must use the cdf extension.)

```
<?XML VERSION="1.0" ENCODING="UTF-8"?>
<CHANNEL HREF="URL of your page">
<TITLE>Your Title Here</TITLE>
<ABSTRACT>Your Abstract Here</ABSTRACT>
<LOGO HREF="URL of your 16 x 16 icon" STYLE="icon"/>
<LOGO HREF="URL of your 80 x 32 logo"
STYLE="image"/>
</CHANNEL>
```

This looks like HTML, doesn't it? Here's how to modify the above code, line by line:

- On Line 1, just copy the example exactly (<?XML VERSION="1.0" ENCODING="UTF-8"?>). This tells the browser that the file to follow conforms to XML Version 1.0.
- On Line 2, modify the CHANNEL element to contain the URL of the Web page you are offering for subscription.
- In the TITLE element (Line 3), type a brief title. There is room for about 40 characters in MSIE's channel bars, so don't exceed this amount.
- In the ABSTRACT element (Line 4), type a description of your site: what it is about, what it has to offer, why people should subscribe. You can type two or three sentences here. It will show up in an extended tool tip box.
- On Line 5, type the URL of your icon.
- On Line 6, type the URL of your logo.
- Don't forget the CHANNEL element's end tag.

That's all there is to it!

Carefully check your work to make sure you have typed everything correctly. Note the XML syntax for close tags: />. Don't forget the slash!

Adding a Link

To enable users to subscribe to your site, just create an ordinary hyperlink (using the A element) on the page you want to push. Link to the CDF file you created.

Be sure to tell users that the link works only if they are accessing the page with Microsoft Internet Explorer Version 4.

Uploading the Channel Information

To test your CDF file, you must upload the following to your server:

- Icon
- Logo
- CDF file
- New version of page with hyperlink to the CDF file

You must upload all of these in order to test your work, unless you are running a Web server on your computer. CDF requires a Web server.

Testing the Channel

After you have uploaded the CDF file, use MSIE Version 4 to access your page and click the link you inserted. You should see the dialog box shown in Figure 18.1. If you don't, there is an error in the file. Carefully check your typing, upload the corrected file, and try again.

Specifying the Schedule with CDF

The easy-to-use CDF file just introduced does not specify a schedule. This means that your page will not get updated unless the user deliberately updates the content. That's not likely to happen very often. To specify an update frequency, use the SCHEDULE element.

Introducing the SCHEDULE Element

This element is designed to avoid a potentially huge problem. If you could specify an absolute update time, what would happen if your page became popular and thousands of browsers tried to update at the same time? Your server would go down. So the SCHEDULE element specifies a time frame within which updates can occur; a single update will occur within this period. You can also specify an earliest time within the time frame, as well as a latest time, to gain some control over the update timing; nevertheless, the browser is free to choose a random update time within these constraints.

The SCHEDULE element must appear directly beneath the first CHANNEL element, as shown here:

```
<?XML VERSION="1.0" ENCODING="UTF-8"?>
<CHANNEL HREF="URL of your page">
        <TITLE>Your Title Here</TITLE>
        <ABSTRACT>Your Abstract Here</ABSTRACT>
        <LOGO HREF="URL of your 16 x 16 icon"
STYLE="icon"/>
        <LOGO HREF="URL of your 80 x 32 logo"
STYLE="image"/>
<SCHEDULE>
        <INTERVALTIME day = "1">
</SCHEDULE>
</CHANNEL>
```

Specifying the Time Interval

To define the time interval, you use the intervaltime attribute. Valid values are day, hour, and min (minute). If you set the interval time to day = "7," you are telling the browser to update the page once per week. If you set the interval time to day = "1," you are telling the browser to update the page once per day.

You can also define hourly schedules. If you set the interval time to hour = "6," you are telling the browser to update the page four times per day. Beginning at midnight, there are four periods within which updates will occur: midnight to 6 AM, 6 AM to 12 noon, 12 noon to 6 PM, and 6 PM to midnight.

Minute schedules work the same way: They establish the number of minutes during which an update occurs once. If you specify a time interval of min = "90," one update will occur within each 90-minute period.

If you specify an earliest time or latest time, you can control the earliest time and the latest time within which an update will occur during the interval. You can do this with the EARLIESTTIME and LATESTTIME elements, which are nested within the SCHEDULE element. For example, suppose you have created a 24-hour interval. If you specify an earliest time of hour = "2" and a latest time of hour = "6," you've told the browser to update the page only between 2 AM and 6 AM each day. (This is not a very good idea, though, because most people don't leave their computers running all night.) If you leave out the EARLIESTTIME and LATESTTIME elements, the browser chooses a time at random within the interval you have specified.

Specifying the Beginning and Ending Dates

Optionally, you can specify the beginning and ending dates for the subscription. You do this by using the startdate and enddate attributes of the SCHEDULE element, and specifying a date using the following syntax:

```
YYYY-MM-DD (example:  1998-02-20)
```

Sample Schedules

The first sample schedule establishes a daily interval, with an update occurring sometime between 9 AM and 6 PM. The updates run from January 1, 1998 to December 31, 1998, with no further updates after that time.

```
<Schedule StartDate="1998.01.01 EndDate="1998.12.31">
     <IntervalTime DAY="1" />
     <EarliestTime HOUR="9" />
     <LatestTime HOUR="18" />
</Schedule>
```

Here's a weekly schedule:

```
<Schedule>
     <IntervalTime DAY="7" />
</Schedule>
```

Note the following:

- There is no beginning or end date, which means that the schedule begins when the user subscribes and does not end at any particular time.
- There is no earliest or latest time specified, which means that the update takes place at a random time during the week.

Creating Subpages with CDF

If you would like to give users direct access to pages within your site (other than your welcome page), you can define subpages. These appear as indented items within the Channel Bar and as submenus within the Favorites list.

To create subpages, you simply nest CHANNEL elements within the main page's CHANNEL element, as in the following example:

```
<?XML VERSION="1.0"?>
<!-- The main channel-->
<CHANNEL
        HREF="index.html"
        BASE="http://watt.seas.virginia.edu/~bp/c34/" >
        <TITLE>Catalina 34 Home Page</TITLE>
        <ABSTRACT>Headquarters for Catalina 34 owners
        and the Catalina 34 National Association.
        </ABSTRACT>
        <LOGO HREF="caticon.gif" STYLE="icon"/>
        <LOGO HREF="shortlogo.jpg" STYLE="image"/>
<!--Schedule information -->
<SCHEDULE StartDate="1997.06.10T12:00-0800" End-
Date="1998.12.31T12:00-0800">
        <INTERVALTIME day="1" />
        <EARLIESTTIME hour="9" />
        <LATESTTIME hour ="18" />
</SCHEDULE>
<!—Subpage 1: FAQ -->
  <CHANNEL href="faq.html">
        <TITLE>FAQ</TITLE>
        <ABSTRACT>Frequently-asked questions about the
        Catalina 34</ABSTRACT>
        <LOGO HREF="caticon.gif" STYLE="icon"/>
  </CHANNEL>
<!—Subpage 2: Owners database -->
  <CHANNEL href="owners.html">
        <TITLE>Owners Database</TITLE>
        <ABSTRACT>Get involved in the C34 community by
        listing your C34 here</ABSTRACT>
        <LOGO HREF="http://watt.seas.virginia.edu/
        ~bp/c34/caticon.gif" STYLE="icon"/>
  </CHANNEL>
<!—Subpage 3: Technical notes index -->
  <CHANNEL href="techdex.html">
        <TITLE>Technical Notes Index</TITLE>
        <ABSTRACT>Informative abstracts of Mainsheet
        technical notes (1987-present)</ABSTRACT>
        <LOGO HREF="caticon.gif" STYLE="icon"/>
  </CHANNEL>
</CHANNEL>
```

Note that there are three subpages, each within its own CHANNEL element, and these three are nested within the main page's CHANNEL element. A few other things to note:

- **You can add comments to your CDF file, just as you do within HTML** (use <!—to begin your comment and --> to end it). It's a good idea to add comments when your CDF file gets large, as this one is.
- **Each subpage can appear with your site's icon, included with the LOGO element.**
- **To avoid retyping lengthy URLs, use the base attribute of the CHANNEL element to define the base URL for your site.** You can use relative URLs in the rest of the file.

After you've created subpages, you see the subpages in the various lists that Internet Explorer constructs.

Adding Items with CDF

To make your site even more accessible, you can add items within subpages. These could be additional pages of your site, or targets within pages. In Internet Explorer's Channel Explorers and Favorite lists, these appear as submenu options under a subpage.

To create items, you add ITEM elements within the subpage's CHANNEL tags, as shown in this example:

```
<!—Subpage 1: FAQ -->
<CHANNEL href="faq.html">
    <TITLE>FAQ</TITLE>
    <ABSTRACT>Frequently-asked questions about the
    Catalina 34</ABSTRACT>
    <LOGO HREF="caticon.gif" STYLE="icon"/>
    <!— First item under FAQ -->
    <ITEM href="faq.html#anchors">
        <TITLE>Anchors</TITLE>
        <ABSTRACT>Anchors for the C34</ABSTRACT>
        <LOGO href="bullet.gif" STYLE="icon"/>
    </ITEM>
    <!— Second item under FAQ -->
    <ITEM href="faq.html#tallrig">
        <TITLE>Tall vs. Standard Rig</TITLE>
```

```
        <ABSTRACT>Which rigging option is
        best?</ABSTRACT>
        <LOGO href="bullet.gif" STYLE="icon"/>
    </ITEM>
    <!— Third item under FAQ -->
        <ITEM href="faq.html#keels">
        <TITLE>Fin vs. Wing Keel</TITLE>
        <ABSTRACT>Which keel option is
        best?</ABSTRACT>
        <LOGO href="bullet.gif" STYLE="icon"/>
    </ITEM>
</CHANNEL>
```

Note the three ITEM elements, nested within the FAQ subpage's CHANNEL tags. Each ITEM element needs a distinctive bullet, to set it apart from the subpages.

Directing CDF Content to the Desktop, Screen Saver, or E-mail

If you've decided to go the CDF route, you can easily direct one of the documents contained by a CHANNEL or ITEM element to the desktop, the user's screen saver, or e-mail. Just add a USAGE element within the CHANNEL or ITEM tags, as follows:

```
<ITEM href="screensaver.html">
    <USAGE value = "ScreenSaver"></USAGE>
</ITEM>
```

The ScreenSaver value directs the item of USAGE which directs the document to the user's screen saver, where (unlike ordinary screen savers) it can be manipulated and clicked like an ordinary HTML document. You can also use the following instead of ScreenSaver:

- **E-mail** Downloads the document to the user's e-mail account when the document is updated.
- **DesktopComponent** Installs the document on the user's Active Desktop.

Users will have an opportunity to confirm these choices before completing the subscription.

Creating a Netcaster Channel

In contrast to Microsoft's implementation of push media, Netscape chose to implement channels by means of JavaScript. If you would like to offer Netscape Netcaster users the opportunity to subscribe to your site, you will need to modify a JavaScript and add it to your page.

Netcaster is part of the Netscape Communicator package, but Netcaster is not well integrated with the browser or the desktop, as Internet Explorer is. Channels appear in a "webtop," which is actually a large Communicator window that covers everything else.

To create a Netcaster channel, you would need to be very good at JavaScript. Happily, Netscape has created a Web-accessible wizard, which enables you to go through a series of wizard windows that prompt you for the necessary information. The result is a rather lengthy JavaScript that you can add to your page.

To access the wizard, visit the following URL:

```
http://developer.netscape.com/library/examples/index.
html?content=netcast/wizard/index.htm.
```

Be aware that the JavaScript created by the Netcaster Wizard has a grave technical limitation which should make you think long and hard about using it. Unlike CDF, Netcaster requires you to specify an exact downloading time. If your page is very popular, you may face a situation in which hundreds or even thousands of browsers are trying to access your server simultaneously, which could very well bring it down. You should use Netcaster only if you suspect that your subscriptions will not be very numerous.

Summary

Push media enlarges the range of options with which users can interact with your site. The down side is the lack of compatibility of push media formats. Of the two competing formats, Netscape's Netcaster technology has a serious technical limitation that makes it risky to use. Dozens of lines of JavaScript are needed to implement push sites with Netcaster. Microsoft's Channel Definition Format (CDF) is better conceived and easier to implement.

In the next chapter, you'll learn how to add active content to your Web page by means of Java applets and more.

19

What's Your OBJECT?

In this chapter, you will learn the following skills:

- Adding applets, plug-ins, and ActiveX controls to your pages
- Adding multimedia objects to your pages
- Defining user-adjustable settings (parameters) for Java applets
- Inserting Java applets so that older browsers can use them

You can add many goodies to your Web page besides graphics, such as videos, Java applets, ActiveX controls, Microsoft Office documents, Adobe Acrobat files, and data for plug-ins. In the past, this was handled by means of various oddball extensions, but now there's a standard way: The OBJECT element. This element provides all the tools you need to add a huge variety of active content that will really make your pages come alive.

Note that this chapter is not about creating active content, such as GIF animations, Java applets, ActiveX controls, and MPEG movies. That's beyond the scope of this book. Here, you'll find out how to insert these objects into your page. If you are not a programmer or graphics designer, don't despair; on the Web, you'll find lots of animations, applets, controls, and multimedia files that you can incorporate into your documents with the OBJECT element.

If There's No OBJECT, What Are You Missing?

Here's a quick overview. You can add plug-ins (the least desirable of these options), Java applets (cool), ActiveX controls (for Windows users only), and native multimedia (animations, sounds, and movies that the browser can display without outside help).

Plug-Ins

The first method of bringing active content to the Web, called plug-ins, was introduced by Netscape. Modeled after the plug-in architecture of programs such as Adobe Photoshop, Netscape plug-ins are stand-alone programs that, when downloaded and installed, extend Netscape's functionality. Specifically, plug-ins give Netscape the ability to deal with data types that the browser does not specifically support. Examples are sounds, animations, movies, three-dimensional worlds, and much more. Since version 3.0, Internet Explorer has supported Netscape's plug-in architecture, but only for plug-ins that specifically support both programs.

Plug-ins have not exactly been a rip-roaring success. Of the hundreds developed, only a few have gained widespread use (examples are Adobe's Acrobat document-viewing plug-ins, RealAudio streaming sounds, and Macromedia's animation plug-ins). Worse, most users regard even these to be a major pain. If you run into a site that offers plug-ins, you cannot view the plug-in data unless you've downloaded and installed the plug-in software. Do you really want to stop everything, spend an hour downloading six megabytes of plug-in code, run through a lengthy installation program, and then reboot your computer, which forces you to lose your place on the Web?

I don't recommend using plug-ins; users dislike them. You are better off with Java applets, ActiveX controls, or multimedia that browsers natively support.

Java Applets

Before Java came along, programs had to be written for a specific type of computer. The incredible thing about Java is that, as Sun says, you can write the program once, and run it anywhere. Java programs will run on any computer that is running the Java support software—and that includes almost all of the computers hooked up to the Internet. In contrast to plug-ins, Java programs can be embedded in a Web page, download much more quickly than plug-ins, and don't force the user to reboot the computer. It is no wonder that Java has replaced plug-ins as the method of choice for bringing active content to Web pages.

Java programs are of two types, applications and applets. Applications are designed to run on their own, like any other program. Applets, in contrast, are designed to be run by a Web browser. They are embedded in Web pages. Java applets make all sorts of interesting things happen, such as displaying a scrolling banner.

To prevent rogue Java programs from damaging Internet computers, Java does not include features that would enable Java applets to access a computer's file system. (To put it another way, Java applets run in a sandbox.) This is nice, because it prevents people from doing mischievous things to your computer. What is not so nice is that this restriction limits Java to doing fairly trivial things. To deal with this, the people who created Java—Sun Microsystems—are extending Java's functionality and creating a way to display digitally-signed certificates of authenticity, which users can approve before they download and run the applet. Currently, though, only Netscape Navigator supports this. But both Navigator and Internet Explorer can run the more limited Java programs, which don't pose a danger to Internet computers.

It is fairly easy to include Java applets on your Web page, but you will need to check the program's documentation. Chances are you'll need to choose some settings, called parameters, such as the size of the block that the applet occupies within your page. You can do this with the OBJECT element, as you'll see.

ActiveX Controls

If you are sure that your users will be accessing your page with Microsoft Windows 95 or NT, you can consider including ActiveX controls on your page. ActiveX controls are packaged programs, which can be written in a variety of programming languages, including Java, Visual Basic, C++, and many more. The key thing about ActiveX is that it is a means of packaging programs so that they function as objects in Windows' object linking and embedding (OLE) system.

Without going into the details, this is basically a set of standards that enable Windows programs to communicate with each other and exchange data.

Be aware that Microsoft Internet Explorer is currently the only browser that fully supports ActiveX. If you include ActiveX controls, you are essentially limiting your audience to Internet Explorer users.

Is limiting your audience to Internet Explorer users such a bad thing? Not if you are developing content for an internal network (an intranet) in which you know that everyone is using Windows and Internet Explorer. Under such circumstances, ActiveX has significant advantages over competing technologies, such as Java, for the following reasons:

- **ActiveX controls are written in code that is native to the machines people run them on.** For this reason, they run much faster than Java applets.
- **ActiveX controls have full access to the computer's file system and memory, so they can do more interesting things.** They're also more dangerous. That's why ActiveX technology involves a security system that enables users to preview certificates (digitally-signed certificates of authenticity) prior to running the controls.

You can use the OBJECT element to add ActiveX controls to your page, but it is tedious to do so manually. There are lots of strange settings and numbers to type. Happily, Microsoft has created a program called the ActiveX Control Center, which generates the code you need.

You can get the ActiveX Control Center by downloading it from ActiveX.com, located at www.download.com/PC/ActiveX/. This site also offers many ActiveX controls that you can download and use on your pages.

Native Multimedia

Native multimedia refers to the forms of multimedia that the two leading browsers know how to deal with directly.

Table 19.1 presents a quick rundown of the most widely-used multimedia formats on the Web..

Table 19.1 Native multimedia formats

Format	Description
GIF animations	For simple animations, you can't beat the GIF89a standard. As explained in Chapter 16, this GIF format enables you to embed a whole series of GIF images within a file, together with instructions concerning how they're supposed to be displayed in a sequence. You can specify the speed, looping (and other forms of iteration), repeats, and other options. For most of the animations you will want to place on the Web, there is generally no need to resort to a huge, downloaded plug-in format (such as Macromedia Shockwave) when it is so easy to create animated GIFs. What's more, users do not need any special software to view them, and the files can be very compact. You add a GIF animation the same way you add a GIF—with the IMG element, discussed in Chapter 16.
AU sounds	The AU sound format is mainly used for mono sounds of fairly poor quality. It is OK for voice or to give a sample of what music would sound like if it had been saved using a decent sound file format.
MIDI sounds	These are very compact text files that tell the computer's sound card how to simulate real music. The sound is unmistakably artificial; it is simulated music, not the real thing. However, MIDI files are so compact that you can actually consider using them as background sounds for a page; doing so will not lengthen the download to intolerable levels, as would be the case for other sound formats.
WAV sounds	This is the native Windows sound format, which is well supported on other platforms. Quality is

	good, but unfortunately, compression isn't. WAV sounds should not be used unless they contain only a second or two of content.
AVI movies	This is the native Windows movie format. Quality is good, and AVI movies can contain sound. However, the files are ridiculously large and not very well suited to Internet downloading, even under the best of circumstances (a direct network connection).
MPEG movies	A movie format defined by the Motion Picture Expert's Group, MPEG movies are compressed using a "lossy" compression format, but they are still too darned big to be downloaded conveniently over a modem connection. To show more than a few seconds of video, you'll be asking visitors to download files of 500K, 1MB or more. Not too many people are willing to do this.
QuickTime movies	This is the Apple movie format, which is well supported on most computer platforms nowadays. Combining stereo sound with compressed video, it has the same demerits as MPEG—the movie files are just too big.

Take a Sip of Java

To understand how to use the OBJECT element, try embedding a Java applet in your Web page. There are lots of freebie Java applets available for download on the Internet; snag one for this experiment. Be sure to get the documentation that goes along with it.

A great place to find Java applets is Gamelan.com (www.gamelan.com). You'll find hundreds of Java applets that you can download and use on your Web pages (as long as you are not doing so for commercial purposes).

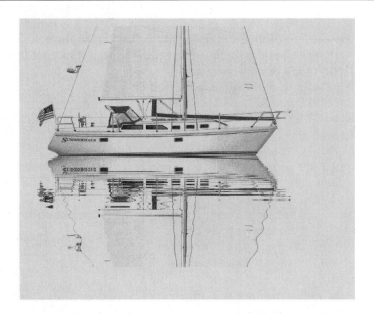

Figure 19.1 The LAKE applet displays a graphic with shimmering water

After you have downloaded an applet, carefully read the documentation (this might be on the applet's home page on the Web, or in a README file that accompanies the software). You need to find out the following:

- **How much space does the applet need on your Web page?** You will need to use the OBJECT element's width and height attributes to specify a rectangular block (in pixels).
- **Do you have to set any parameters?** If so, what kind of values can you specify?

Here's an example. David Griffith, an English programmer, has created a simple and beautiful applet called Lake (Figure 19.1). Basically, this applet displays a GIF or JPEG graphic with a simulated water reflection. It is very beautiful, and very compact.

If you would like to obtain a copy of Lake, access Mr. Griffith's interesting site at http://www.demon.co.uk/davidg/spigots.htm.

To use Lake, you must specify:

- The size of the rectangular frame that the applet will occupy. The rectangle should have the same width as the graphic, but it must be a little less than twice its height.
- The URL of the graphic file that Lake uses.

Here's the OBJECT code that's needed to add the Lake applet (called Lake.class) to your Web page.

```
<OBJECT codetype="application/octet-stream"
classid="java:Lake.class" width = "516" height =
"450">
        <PARAM name="image" value="summercrop.jpg"
        valuetype="ref">
        Sorry, your browser isn't set up to run Java.
</OBJECT>
```

There are a few attributes and other points to notice:

- **codetype** This specifies what the browser is about to download, using a recognized MIME type. For Java, it's "application/octet-stream."
- **classid** Here, you specify the URL of the applet you are adding. To specify the location of a Java applet, you need to use "java:" instead of "http://", but what follows can be a relative URL (as is the case here).
- **width and height** These specify the size of the rectangular box that's created for the Java applet. You specify the width and height in pixels.
- **PARAM** This element lives within the OBJECT element, and it is used to pass information to the Java applet. You must specify the name and value; if you are telling the applet about a URL, you must also include the valuetype ("ref" means "URL").
- **"Sorry, your browser isn't set up to run Java."** This text is displayed if the browser cannot run the applet for some reason.
- **Don't forget the close tag (</OBJECT>).**

The stuff just discussed is just about all you really need to know in order to add Java applets to your pages. In the next section, you will learn more about how to use some of the attributes I've mentioned, but you have got the basics.

OBJECT—In Its Element

The OBJECT element is designed to handle a wide range of programs and multimedia, so it has a lot of attributes.

Let's take a look at the element definition first, and then look at the most commonly-used attributes in closer detail.

ELEMENT	OBJECT
PURPOSE	Inserts a type of data that is not natively supported by the browser, such as a Java applet, script, or font data. For images, use IMG.
TYPE	Block
NESTED WITHIN	BODY
START TAG	Required
END TAG	Optional
CONTENT	Contains inline elements and text; cannot contain block elements.
ATTRIBUTES:	core attributes (id, class, style, title) language attributes (dir, lang) title = "CDATA" (optional) tabindex = "number" (optional) classid = "url" (optional) codebase = "url" (optional) declare (optional) data = "url" (optional) type = "MIME type" (optional) codetype = "MIME type" (optional) archive = "url" (optional) standby = "text" (optional) height = "length" (optional) width = "length" (optional) usemap = "url" (optional) name = "CDATA" (optional) tabindex = "number" (optional) border = "pixels" (optional) hspace = "length" (optional) vspace = "length" (optional) align = "(bottom, middle, top)" (optional)

EXAMPLE	<OBJECT classid= = "stupid.applet.class"> <PARAM name = "spin" value = "fast"> Your browser doesn't support Java. </OBJECT>
DON'T FORGET	Between the tags, place text that will appear only in browsers that don't support the data type.

Table 19.2 lists the attributes used with the OBJECT element.

Table 19.2 OBJECT element attributes

Attribute	Description and example
classid	Specifies the location of the program that displays the object. If you are adding a Java applet, you need to precede the URL (relative or absolute) with java: (java followed by a colon). If you are adding an ActiveX control, precede the URL with classid: `<OBJECT classid="java:Lake.class">`

codebase	Specifies a base URL for URLs given to the object. By default, this is the URL of the object.
	
	`<OBJECT codebase = "http://`
	`www.rivendell.org/applets/>`

data	Specifies the location of data needed by the object, if any.
	
	`<OBJECT data = "http://www.`
	`rivendell.org/rings/locations.dat">`

type	Specifies the MIME type of the data cited in the data attribute. This helps the browser decide whether it can handle the data. You can omit this. `<OBJECT data = "text">`

codetype	Specifies the MIME type of the program that displays the object. This helps the browser display whether it can handle the program. You can omit this.
	`<OBJECT codetype = "application/octet-stream">`
standby	Displays a message while the object is loading.
	`<OBJECT standby = "Loading Java applet…">`
height	Specifies the height of the rectangular space to be occupied by the object, in pixels.
	`<OBJECT height = "410">`
width	Specifies the width of the rectangular space to be occupied by the object, in pixels.
	`<OBJECT width = "520">`

What's Your PARAMeter?

Many Java applets have user-adjustable settings, called *parameters*. You can define these settings using the PARAM element.

To find out which settings you can adjust, consult the applet's documentation.

Here's the PARAM element's definition:

ELEMENT	PARAM
PURPOSE	Defines run-time settings for an object.
TYPE	Inline
NESTED WITHIN	OBJECT
START TAG	Required
END TAG	Forbidden

CONTENT	Empty
ATTRIBUTES:	id = "name" (required)
	name = "CDATA" (optional)
	value = "CDATA" (optional)
	valuetype = "(data, ref, or object)"
	type = "MIME type"
EXAMPLE	<OBJECT classid= = "example.applet.class">
	<PARAM name = "spin" value = "3">
	Your browser doesn't support Java.
	</OBJECT>
DON'T FORGET	Check the applet's documentation to find out how to set the run-time settings (parameters).

The choices available for the name and value attributes are determined by the programmer. Again, consult the applet's documentation to find out whether any user settings are available, and if so, what name and value pairs you should use.

Inserting ActiveX Controls

You can add ActiveX controls with the OBJECT element, but don't try to do it manually. To add an ActiveX control, you need to know the class ID number of the control—and you can find this out only by hunting around in the Windows Registry. It is much better to use the ActiveX Control Center, a freebie (you can obtain this by downloading it from www.activex.com). To use the ActiveX Control Center, you need to download and install the control on your system—the Control Center cannot otherwise access the information you need. Using the Control Center is simplicity itself: It automatically detects which parameters the control needs, prompts you to supply them, and generates the OBJECT element that inserts the control into your document.

Using Plug-Ins

To include plug-ins on your page, consult the plug-in program's documentation to determine just how you should proceed. Since plug-ins are a Netscape thing, chances are that the plug-in requires the EMBED element, a Netscape extension that is deprecated in HTML Version 4. Happily, most browsers support the EMBED element.

Using EMBED is fairly simple; it is very much like the IMG element—you just specify the source using the SRC attribute. You can also specify the height and width of the rectangular space created for the embedded object. Here's an example:

```
<EMBED src = "chapter1.pdf" height = "320" width =
"400">
```

If you include a link to plug-in data, be sure to add a link to the place where users can download the plug-in itself. For example, if you are including links to Adobe Acrobat documents, include a link to Adobe's Acrobat download page.

Adding Multimedia

You can add sounds and movies to your Web pages in two ways:

- **OBJECT element** If you do this, the sound or movie will download and begin playing automatically, or at least will display the browser's controls that enable the user to start playing the sound or movie. This isn't a very good option for most sounds or movies, which tend to be very large. You should use the OBJECT element to add short sounds (with file sizes of less than 20K or so).
- **A element** For lengthier sounds and all movies, use the A element, referencing the sound or movie's URL just as you would a Web page. This gives the user the option of clicking on the link to begin downloading the data. Be sure to indicate the file size.

Here's an example of sound added with the A element:

```
<A href = "seagulls.au">Seagulls at the beach
(60K)</A>
```

When you're including links to sounds or movies, it's good manners to specify how large the file is. Users can then decide whether they want to spend the time needed to download the file.

Adding Applets with the APPLET Element

If you want to make sure that users of Netscape Version 3 can access your Java applets, you may wish to insert applets with the deprecated APPLET element and the PARAM element, which was introduced earlier in this chapter. Here's the element definition of APPLET:

ELEMENT	APPLET (deprecated)
PURPOSE	Incorporates a Java applet.
TYPE	Inline
NESTED WITHIN	BODY element
START TAG	Required
END TAG	Required
CONTENT	None
ATTRIBUTES	core attributes (id, class, style, title) archive = "CDATA" (optional) code = "CDATA" (required) codebase = "url" (optional) object = "CDATA" (optional) alt = "text" (optional) name = "CDATA" (optional) width = "length" (required) height = "length" (required) align = "(top, middle, bottom, left, right)" hspace = "pixels" vspace = "pixels"
EXAMPLE	\<APPLET code= "tic-tac-toe.class" width="500 height = "500"> \<PARAM name = "snd" value = "hello"> Play tic-tac-toe! \</APPLET>
TIP	As you can see from the element definition, the APPLET element is very similar to the OBJECT element. Use the code attribute to specify the location of the applet, and use width and height to define the applet's space.

Summary

You can add Java applets and other objects (including ActiveX controls) with the OBJECT element, but you will get broader usability if you add multimedia objects using the A element. To get the most out of Java applets, learn how to set user-adjustable parameters with the PARAM element. For compatibility with older browsers, consider adding Java applets with the APPLET element (deprecated in the strict flavor of HTML 4).

Why not try a little JavaScript programming yourself? It's easy, as the next chapter explains, and the results are great, thanks to the new HTML Version 4 support for element-related events.

20

Stick to the SCRIPT

In this chapter, you will learn the following skills:

- Understanding what scripts are and what they do
- Adding a pre-written script with the SCRIPT element
- Understanding the essentials of object-oriented programming (OOP)
- Writing simple scripts that do really interesting things on your pages
- Writing scripts that display text when the user moves the mouse pointer over an element

Your Web page is being viewed by Web browsers, and most of them are much more than mere programs for viewing text and graphics. They are also *interpreters,* which means they can follow programming language instructions that are actually embedded in the Web page itself. These short, simple programs are called scripts. As browsers interpret the scripts they find in a Web page, the programs perform actions that give your pages much more interactivity than they would have had with static HTML. At the end of this chapter, for example,

373

you'll see how you can use the new capabilities of dynamic HTML to create an interactive table of contents for your site. When you move the mouse pointer over a list item, a hidden paragraph of text springs into view, giving the reader more information about the item.

You don't need programming experience or weeks of spare time to learn how to make these exciting features work for you. Many Web authors borrow public domain scripts and plug them into their pages, even though they do not know enough to write the scripts themselves. This chapter shows you how to do this, but it does much more. You will also learn how to take advantage of the powerful, built-in capabilities of JavaScript, the scripting language that is preferred by most Web authors. Although this chapter doesn't try to teach you everything there is to know about JavaScript—that is a subject for a separate book—you will learn enough to add a very impressive dimension of interactivity to your pages. Specifically, I will teach you the 20 percent of JavaScript that gives you 80 percent of the scripting language's functionality.

Warning: If you enjoy experimenting with computers at all, you need to know that you are probably going to enjoy this chapter tremendously, to the tune of staying up all night and playing with scripts. Do yourself a favor and read it when you don't have to be at an early-morning commitment the next day! I'm not kidding!

Introducing Scripting

If you are new to scripting, you would probably like to know what it's all about. This section is for readers who are new to scripting. If you know your way around a scripting language, skip to the next section.

What is Scripting?

A script is a mini-program that is embedded within the HTML of your Web page. Scripts are written in scripting languages, which are much easier to learn and use than full-fledged programming languages. When somebody downloads your page, the browser detects the scripts, and interprets the instructions they contain. Some computer programs are *compiled*, which means that they can run on their own as an executable program. Compiled programs run fast. Others, like scripting languages, are interpreted, which means that your computer must be running a program that is capable of reading the instructions and figuring out what they mean.

Interpreted programs are much slower than compiled programs, but that does not really matter because almost all scripts are very short. Scripts don't slow down your page very much, much less than those big, memory-hogging Java applets discussed earlier in this book. What is more, scripts bring impressive benefits that more than compensate for the processing time they consume. They can pack so much interactivity into a page, for example, that the user does not need to download an additional page in order to accomplish something. For example, you can write scripts that check form input. These scripts make sure that the user fills out all the necessary information and does so by supplying reminders if anything is missing. Without these scripts, the user might submit a page to the server, only to get a message back—after the usual lengthy delay —stating that key information is missing. Scripts consume only a little processing time and can produce a huge payoff in overall efficiency.

In order to process a script, the user's browser must be able to interpret the scripting language. The leading browsers can interpret JavaScript, which goes a long way toward explaining why this chapter focuses on this scripting language and not others.

Although scripting languages are easy to learn, they have some great properties. In keeping with cutting-edge programming languages, they are event-driven— that is, they spring into motion when something happens, such as a mouse click. As you will see later in this chapter, one of the most amazing things about HTML Version 4 is that it greatly expands the number of possible events and enables you to assign them to any HTML element. This opens up a huge number of possibilities for making your Web pages come alive.

What Scripting Languages Are Available?

Basically, you've got three choices:

- **JavaScript** Originally developed by Netscape Communications, this scripting language superficially resembles Java, but lacks many of Java's advanced capabilities. The language has recently been standardized by an independent standards body, the European Computer Standards Association (ECMA); the standardized version is called ECMAScript. It is supported by the two leading browsers (Netscape Navigator and Microsoft Internet Explorer), as well as by many others. The scripts run on any computer that can run a JavaScript-enabled browser.

- **VBScript** Developed by Microsoft Corporation, this scripting language is great for people who already know Visual Basic, but it has a huge limitation: It is supported only by Microsoft Internet Explorer, and the scripts only run on Windows systems.
- **Tcl** Developed by Sun Microsystems, this scripting language isn't very widely used or supported yet, but some have high hopes for it.

This chapter draws its examples from JavaScript, which I personally prefer because it is cross-platform, unlike VBScript. Also, JavaScript is not a bad choice for a first programming language. Although JavaScript differs in important respects from Java, it does incorporate some of the basic principles of the "New Age" of programming, which is revolutionizing the way programmers approach their tasks. This is called Object Oriented Programming—or OOP, for short.

What Can Scripts Do?

There are basically two kinds of scripts that you can add to your HTML documents:

- **Some scripts execute automatically when the document loads.** They can generate HTML on the fly. For example, there is a simple script that inserts today's date in your page. This makes it look like you are updating your page all the time—a white lie in code, so to speak.
- **Other scripts spring into motion when the user does something, such as click a button.** For example, you can write scripts that evaluate form input to make sure users are typing the right kind of data. With the new capabilities of HTML Version 4, this can lead to an awesome amount of interactivity, including pull-down menus. This enables users to download a page that has a lot of hidden material that can be quickly accessed—much more quickly than the time that would be required to retrieve a document from the network.

Just what's so new and spiffy about HTML's support of JavaScript? The answer becomes clear when you bring CSS into the equation. As you will learn later in this chapter, you can write scripts that dynamically rewrite styles on the fly. The implications of this are fantastic. It means, essentially, that the pages you write are not static entities with a fixed appearance. Whole regions can spring into view when the user clicks something. With just one download, you can distribute a ton of information that is dynamically accessible to the user with nearly instantaneous speed; additional units of information spring up like lightning, rather than being retrieved at molasses speed from the network.

Is There a Down Side to Scripts?

Scripting has a number of disadvantages:

- **Other people can see your code—and steal it.** There is no way to hide your script. It is visible to anyone who knows how to use the browser's View Source command. From there it can be copied, and you can be pretty sure somebody will do this, even if you include a copyright statement.
- **Scripting languages cannot do a lot of the things you would like to do.** Basically, you cannot write scripts that would harm somebody's computer . The necessary commands have been left out of the scripting languages, for obvious reasons. Still, this means that scripting languages lack the power to do many of the things you'd most like to do with scripts. That's why people use ActiveX controls and other techniques that do not have these restrictions.

Neither of these shortcomings should deter you. Chances are you don't make your living as a professional programmer, so it is not going to put you out of business if somebody steals your scripts. As for the limitations of scripting languages, they are very real, but they don't keep you from doing interesting things, as this chapter explains. In the sections that follow, you will learn how you can apply JavaScripts to introduce compelling interactivity to your Web pages.

Adding Scripts with the SCRIPT Element

In HTML Version 4, as in previous versions, you can add scripts using the SCRIPT element. (You can also add them with event handlers, discussed in the following section.) However, HTML Version 4 introduces some changes from previous HTML practices, so be sure to read this section carefully if you think you already know how to do this.

Defining the Script Language

HTML does not specify a particular scripting language. For this reason, you need to tell the browser which language you're using. In HTML Version 4, you can define the scripting language by means of the following generic META tag, which goes in the HEAD:

```
<META http-equiv="Content-Script-Type" content =
"MIME type">
```

For "MIME type," you need to specify the official MIME designation of the scripting language you're using. For JavaScript, it is text/javascript. Here's what this META statement looks like if you are using JavaScripts in your document:

```
<META http-equiv="Content-Script-Type" content =
"text/javascript">
```

You can also identify the scripting language by using the type attribute of the SCRIPT element, which is discussed in the next section. This enables you to add scripts written in more than one type of scripting language, should you wish to do so.

The SCRIPT Element Definition

The SCRIPT element enables you to insert scripts within your HTML document. Here's the element definition:

ELEMENT	SCRIPT
PURPOSE	Contains a script.
TYPE	Inline
NESTED WITHIN	BODY
START TAG	Required
END TAG	Required
CONTENT	A script in a language such as JavaScript.
ATTRIBUTE:	**Strict DTD:** type = "MIME type" (required) charset = "character set" src = "url" defer
	Transitional DTD (deprecated): language = "scripting language"
EXAMPLE	<SCRIPT type = "text/javascript"> <!-- hide your script within HTML comment tags--> </SCRIPT>
TIP	Hide your script within comment tags so that it will not be displayed by older browsers.

Specifying the Scripting Language

If you haven't specified the default scripting language, use the type attribute as follows:

```
<SCRIPT type = "text/javascript">
</SCRIPT>
```

Referencing an Externally-Stored Script

You can reference a script stored externally by using the src attribute:

```
<SCRIPT type = "text/javascript" src="form-
update.js">
</SCRIPT>
```

Enclosing the Script within the SCRIPT Element

Within the start and end tags, you place your script, as in the following example:

```
<SCRIPT type = "text/javascript">
     document.write ("Your Web page shows the
     script's output, but not its source code.");
</SCRIPT>
```

Try typing this little script into a text editor, and open it with your browser. You won't see the script; you'll just see the script's output, the text that's enclosed within the quotation marks.

Hiding the Script from Script-Challenged Browsers

To make sure your script doesn't show up as text in browsers that can't process scripts, enclose the entire script (but not the SCRIPT tags) within an HTML comment, as shown in this example:

```
<SCRIPT type = "text/javascript">
<!-- This is the beginning of a JavaScript
     document.write ("Your Web page shows the
     script's output, but not its source code.");
//This line closes the comment-->
</SCRIPT>
```

Note the double slashes at the beginning of the closing comment line. This is a JavaScript comment identifier. It's needed so that the JavaScript interpreter can tell that the closing HTML comment line is indeed a comment that it should ignore.

OOPs! Where's My Object?

Before you get started with JavaScript, you will find it helpful to understand the basic concepts of object-oriented programming (OOP). That's because JavaScript resembles HTML Version 4. Just as you need to understand the HTML Version 4 way, you need to understand object-oriented programming in order to learn and apply JavaScript quickly.

The Old, Bad Way

To understand the new way, you must understand the old way. In the dark ages of programming, people used procedural languages, which told the computer what to do, step by step. The programs acted on data, which was separate. The programs were difficult to write and test, and what was worse, the various components of the program could not be re-used without having to modify them significantly. Taking a part of these programs out was extremely detrimental.

The object-oriented way is totally different. Instead of painstakingly writing procedural programs that act on data, programmers create objects. And what, you ask, is an object?

Objects: Properties and Methods

There are lots of objects in daily life—we trip over them all the time. In object-oriented programming, the term object has a special meaning. The term refers to a unit of computer code that includes a bunch of data (called *properties*) as well as the procedures (called *methods*) needed to make this data useful. In Table 20.1, you see a list of the predefined objects in JavaScript. You can define all the new objects you want, but this chapter concentrates on using the predefined ones. As you'll see, there is an amazing world of functionality in these objects, and you can make use of it without spending the time needed to master all the ins and outs of JavaScript programming.

So what's the big deal about the object-oriented way? Each of these objects embodies a lot of knowledge about something, such as forms or history lists or windows. They also contain information (properties) and what is more, methods for accessing those properties or doing things. You can stick these objects into any code you like. By combining them, you can create a complex program in very short order. If you were to try to do the same thing with procedural programming languages, it would take you days.

Table 20.1 Pre-defined objects in JavaScript

Object name	Description, property, and method
button	Buttons in a form. Property: button.value (the current value of a button). Method: button.click(). Same as clicking the button.
date	Dates and times. Property: No properties (they are defined by the user's system). This object does not exist unless it has been specifically created by a script and initialized with the system's current date and time settings. Method: date.getDate(). Finds out the current date by looking at the system date.
document	The current document. Property: document.title () (the title of the document). Method: document.write. Writes text to a new HTML file and tells the browser to display it.
form	The form that appears in a document. Property: form.name (the name of the form as defined by the NAME attribute). This object does not exist unless the current document contains a form. Method: form.submit(). Same as clicking the Submit button.
history	The user's browser's history list. Property: history.length (the number of items currently in the user's history list). Method: history.go(x). Tells the browser to go forward or backward in the user's browser's history list; -1 is the same as clicking the Back button, while +1 is the same as clicking Forward.
input	Input fields in a form. Property: form.value (the current contents of an input field). This object

	does not exist unless the current document contains a form. Method: No methods.
location	The document's source location. Property: location.href (contains the current window's URL). Method: location.toString (). Gets the current value of location.href.
window	The window in which the document is displayed. Property: window.location() (the source URL of the document displayed in the current window). Method: window.alert("Message"). Displays an alert box with the message enclosed in the quotation marks.

Object Hierarchies

Just one more quick point about objects, and then we will look at some examples. They are named in a way that reflects a hierarchy, in which the "parent" objects rule over the "child" ones. For example, the location object is the "mother" of the href object; the proper name of the object is location.href. This is important because the "mother" object passes its properties down to the "child" object. What this means is that the href object knows everything that the location object does. In OOP parlance, this is called inheritance.

Some Simple Examples

OK, now that you know what objects are, why not experiment a bit? You can use object properties and methods to enter information into your document automatically. These are some really neat tricks and they are easy.

All of the following examples make use of the document.write method to create new HTML documents. If you put them into an existing page, the script will generate output text on the fly, and insert the text at the script's location. So you may want to think about where you want this text to appear, and how you want it formatted. To do this, you can enclose the SCRIPT tags within HTML markup. (It's much trickier to put the markup within the SCRIPT tags, as you'll see later in this chapter.)

For example, the following script's output would appear within a <P> element and its surrounding text:

```
<P style = "font-family: Times-Roman, Serif">Today's
date is <SCRIPT> [JavaScript code] </SCRIPT>.<P>
```

The script's output will appear within the surround text, just as if you had typed it, and it will take on the formats you have assigned to the current element. The bad thing about this, though, is that the script output will not appear if the user is not browsing with a JavaScript-enabled browser, or has turned JavaScript off for some reason.

If you are having trouble getting scripts to work, remember that JavaScript is case-sensitive; be sure to copy the capitalization patterns exactly. Also, remember that every statement must be followed by a semicolon (;). JavaScript is fussy about spaces, too; don't put spaces in willy-nilly. Be sure to check the parentheses, too. You need to have exactly the same number of opening and closing parentheses.

Indicating the Document's URL

If you would like to include your document's URL on your page somewhere, don't type it manually. What if you moved the page, and forgot to change it? Here's a script that automatically inserts your document's current location.

```
<SCRIPT type = "text/javascript">
      document.write(location.toString());
</SCRIPT>
```

The output of this script is a URL. Embedded in surrounding text, it could look something like this:

```
If you'd like to return to this document, the URL is
http://www.rivendell.com/elrond.
```

Echoing the Document's Title

The following script looks at the current document's TITLE element, and returns the text that it finds there. You can use this script to echo the document's title anywhere in the document. This can save some retyping time if you would like to refer to this title more than once.

Here's the script:

```
<SCRIPT type = "text/javascript">
        document.write(document.title);
</SCRIPT>
```

Try enclosing this script in H1 tags and placing it at the beginning of your document.

Indicating the Date of Last Modification

You have probably noticed that thoughtful Web authors indicate when they last modified the pages they publish. But it's a pain to do so—I often forget, and as a result the page looks older than it really is. Here's a little JavaScript that automatically enters the date on which you last modified the file.

```
<SCRIPT type = "text/javascript">
        document.write(document.fileModifiedDate);
</SCRIPT>
```

You can embed this in an ADDRESS element, such as the following:

```
<ADDRESS>This file was last modified on <SCRIPT
type="text/javascript">document.write(document.file-
ModifiedDate);</SCRIPT> by Arwen (<A
HREF="mailto:arwen@rivendell.org>arwen@rivendell.org<
/A>).
```

This code will generate something like this:

```
This file was last modified on November 8, 1997, by
Arwen (arwen@rivendell.org).
```

More Advanced Examples

You have learned the basics of JavaScript—more than enough, really, to copy some scripts from public domain sources and include them in your page. A bit more knowledge will give you the tools to start writing your own scripts. Here, you will learn more about objects and some arcane matters such as string concatenation, but the payoff's big: You'll learn a couple of snazzy scripts for inserting dates and times into your Web page automatically.

Accessing Dates and Times

The Date object is really useful, but unfortunately it doesn't exist until a JavaScript gives it life. That is because the Date object's properties have to be pulled out of the user's system. To make Date objects work, you have to include some extra information that pulls and initializes the object's properties.

Let's start with a simple version of the script, although it is unsatisfactory, for reasons you will see when you try it:

```
<SCRIPT type = "text/javascript">
      chronos = new Date();
      document.write(chronos.getHours())
</SCRIPT>
```

This script creates a new object, called chronos, and tells JavaScript to define this object by constructing a new Date object.

Don't leave out the empty parentheses after Date. In a JavaScript instruction, these parentheses indicate that you are referring to a method.

Here's a little taste of the object-oriented way for you: When you create chronos, you are creating an object. And since the chronos object you have created is identical to the Date object, the chronos object knows everything that the Date object does. What is more, it inherits all of the Date object's methods, such as date.getHours. That is why chronos.getHours is such a knowledgable object. Little chronos got everything it knows from its "mother," Date.

But the script isn't very satisfactory. If it's 11:58, the script returns nothing more than "11." How about the minutes? To do this, you'll have to do a little string concatenation.

Concatenating Strings

Don't let this scare you off. Concatenation just means "tying together." With string concatenation, you can create more interesting output from document.write. Here's an example that fixes the problems with the time script just given:

Here's a script that produces nice output by using string concatenation:

```
<SCRIPT type = "text/javascript">
     chronos = new Date();
     document.write((chronos.getHours()) + ":" +
     (chronos.getMinutes()));
</SCRIPT>
```

Remember, chronos knows all. (Everything its Date knows, anyway.) So we can include chronos.getMinutes. Note that, within the document.write parentheses, each object has to live in its own parentheses. The output of getHours and get-Minutes is tied together with the plus sign (+), which just happens to be the concatenation symbol. Also, notice that it is possible to stick some text in the midst of all this. The colon, surrounded by quotation marks, separates the hours and minutes, like this:

```
11:58
```

Putting Today's Date Into Your Page

Here is a variation on the above script that takes advantage of the very knowledgeable chronos. It's sort of a symphony of string concatenation, so type it carefully.

```
<SCRIPT type = "text/javascript">
     chronos = new Date();
     document.write((chronos.getMonth() + 1) + "/" +
     (chronos.getDate())+ "/" +
     (chronos.getYear()));
</SCRIPT>
```

Be sure to type this script carefully. There are lots of parentheses, and they all have to be typed in correctly. Also, note the +1 after getMonth. Without this, your date will be one month behind.

This script's output looks like this: 2/20/98. By moving the elements around, you can indicate the date in non-North American formats.

Hiding HTML within SCRIPT Elements

Earlier, I pointed out that people who don't have JavaScript will not be able to see the output of your scripts. That is bad if you have put some text in your document that assumes document.write will be putting something in. For example, your document could wind up looking like this:

```
Hi! Welcome to . The time is . The date is .
```

Looks dumb, huh? What's missing? The output from document.title, date.getHours, date.getMinutes, and all the date stuff.

The solution to this problem? Hide everything within the SCRIPT tags, and use string concatenation within document.write to contain the text you want to display. That way, if the user's browser doesn't have JavaScript, the user doesn't know there's anything missing. Here's the last-modified-date script presented earlier, with incorporated text:

```
<SCRIPT type = "text/javascript">
     document.write("This file was last modified on
     " + (document.fileModifiedDate));
</SCRIPT>
```

Great! This works fine. And to hide this from non-JavaScript browsers, you can use the HTML comment tags, as explained earlier in this chapter.

```
<SCRIPT type = "text/javascript">
<!--Hide from non-JavaScript browsers…
     document.write("This file was last modified on
     " + (document.fileModifiedDate));
//this is the end of the comment-->
</SCRIPT>
```

Incorporating HTML Markup

You are probably wondering how to add markup to the text within the document.write parentheses. You can, but you need to learn a trick. This is needed because, when JavaScript runs into a forward slash in HTML, it thinks the script is over. HTML end tags need the forward slash. If you put an HTML end tag within your string, users will see an error message.

Here's an example:

```
document.write("<B>This won't work.</B>");
```

There's a pretty simple way around this. You just include an escape character within the HTML end tag. The escape character tells the JavaScript interpreter to ignore the very next character. In JavaScript, the escape character is a back-slash.

To tell JavaScript to ignore a forward slash character, just put a backward slash character in front of it. So this version works:

```
document.write("<B>This will work!<\/B>");
```

See the "\ /" in the close tag? That's the ticket. I know, it's ugly, but nobody will see it.

Try this:

```
<SCRIPT type = "text/javascript">
        document.write ("<SPAN style=\"font-family:
        Arial\">It's nice to see script output in
        something other than the default document
        font.<\/SPAN>");
</SCRIPT>
```

This example shows how to prevent JavaScript from getting bollixed up by the quotation marks it encounters within HTML. The backslash tells JavaScript to ignore the quotation mark that comes right after it.

The Function Junction

Are your scripts getting a bit long? Would you like to access them more than once in a document? These are both good reasons for creating your own functions. In brief, a function is a user-defined procedure for doing something.

What Functions Look Like

It's easy to write a function that you can use to check for form input.

You will delve into the form details later; for now, let's examine the syntax.

```
function filledIn(input) {
      return(input.value.length != 0);
}
```

This function is called "filledIn," and it deals with a HTML element: an INPUT element. The curly braces contain the function's JavaScript, which consists of a return function. This function examines the expression contained within its parentheses, and decides whether this expression is true or false. The expression looks at an object called input.value.length, and sees whether it is unequal (!=) to zero. If it is unequal to zero, the expression is true, and the function returns a value of true. If the user has not typed anything in the field, then the length does equal zero, and the expression is false. In this case, the function returns the value of false. By itself, returning a value does not mean much; there have to be other scripts that deal with this. We'll get to that later.

Where Functions Go

Functions go in the document's header, within the SCRIPT element. Putting the functions in the HEAD makes them accessible to later scripts incorporated within the document's BODY, since the HEAD is evaluated before the BODY. Here's how the filledIn function looks, properly stored:

```
<HEAD>
      <SCRIPT type = "text/javascript">
            function filledIn(input) {
                  return(input.value.length != 0);
            }
      </SCRIPT>
</HEAD>
```

What triggers functions? An event does. What is an event? Read on.

Handle This Event, Would You?

Among the most powerful capabilities of JavaScript is the language's ability to spring into action when something happens, such as a mouse click. Look first at a simple event, and then you'll learn how to link events to functions.

Try This

Type the following into a Web page, save it, and open it with your browser. Open your browser and surf around for a bit, and then open this page. Click the link, and see what happens.

```
<A HREF="#" onClick="history.go(-1);">Return to the
previous page</A>
```

What gives? There's is no SCRIPT element. But there is a script.

If you typed everything correctly, you will see the Web page you previously visited. Why?

- The A element contains an attribute called an intrinsic event handler (here, onClick). The JavaScript that follows the event handler comes into play when the user clicks on the highlighted text ("Return to the previous page"). The script is a method: history.go(-1).
- Although HTML is not case-sensitive, JavaScript is. Within the JavaScript, be sure to type capital and lower-case letters exactly as you see them in the script you are copying (for example, you must type go, not Go).
- The HREF attribute has a value that functions essentially as a placeholder (empty).
- The JavaScript that follows onclick ("history.go(-1);") references one of JavaScript's built-in objects. You will learn more about objects subsequently. For now, just note that this code says, "in the browser's history list, identify the Web page that was just viewed (that is, -1 in the history list), and display it."
- The JavaScript statement ends with a semicolon. Without the semicolon, the statement will not work.

Introducing Event Handlers

The key to the rather impressive functionality of this simple JavaScript is the event handler that's used—here, onClick. One of the coolest things about HTML Version 4 is the inclusion of many more event handlers than previous versions of HTML offered. As you'll see, the new event handlers open up all kinds of possibilities for building interactive pages.

In HTML Version 4, you can distinguish among three different types of event handlers: standard event handlers, forms event handlers, and special-purpose event handlers. Tables 20.2, 20.3, and 20.4 list these event handlers and briefly explain how they work.

Table 20.2 Standard event handlers

Event handler	Launches an action when
onclick	The left mouse button is clicked when the pointer is positioned over an element.
ondblclick	The mouse button is clicked twice when the pointer is positioned over an element.
onmousedown	The mouse button is depressed while the pointer is positioned over an element.
onmouseup	The mouse button is released while the pointer is positioned over an element.
onmouseover	The mouse pointer is positioned over an element.
onmouseout	The mouse pointer is moved away from an element.
onkeydown	Any key on the keyboard has been depressed.
onkeyup	Any key on the keyboard has been released.
onkeypress	Any key on the keyboard has been both depressed and released.

The following table summarizes the event handlers for forms.

Table 20.3 Forms event handlers

Event handler	Valid elements and action
onfocus	LABEL, INPUT, SELECT, TEXTAREA, BUTTON Launches when the element receives focus by means of the pointing device or tabbing.

onblur	LABEL, INPUT, SELECT, TEXTAREA, BUTTON
	Launches when the element loses focus because the user has moved the pointer away from the element or has tabbed away from it.
onsubmit	FORM
	Launches when the user clicks the Submit button.
onreset	FORM
	Launches when the user clicks the Reset button.
onchange	INPUT, SELECT, TEXTAREA
	Launches when the user changes the current value in the selected field.

In addition to the event handlers just presented, there are a couple of special-purpose ones, described in the following table.

Table 20.4 Special purpose event handlers

Event handler	Valid elements and action
onload	BODY, FRAMESET
	Launches when browser finishes loading a window (or all frames in a FRAMESET document).
onunload	BODY, FRAMESET
	Launches when browser removes a document from a window or frame.

Using Event Handlers in Forms

You can use events to trigger functions. Let's see how an event handler can trigger a form function. (If you have not read the chapter on forms, do so before proceeding.) You've placed the following function in the HEAD of your document:

```
<HEAD>
    <SCRIPT type = "text/javascript">
    function filledIn(input) {
    return(input.value.length != 0);
    }
</SCRIPT>
</HEAD>
```

Suppose you have created an INPUT field called last-name, using the following HTML:

```
<FORM>
    <INPUT type = "text" name = "last-name">
</FORM>
```

OK, simple enough. This displays a text box.

Now you want to make sure that the user has filled this out. Add this to the INPUT element:

```
<INPUT type="text" name="lastname"
    onblur=" if (!filledIn(form.lastname))

    {
    alert('Please fill in your last name');
    form.lastname.focus();
    } " >
```

What's up here? The onblur event kicks in the filledIn function. The exclamation point says that what follows should be ignored if the script is true—that is, if something is filled in. If filledIn returns false, the script displays an alert box that says "Please fill in your last name," and it returns the focus (cursor) to the last-name field.

Note, too, that this script contains a control; specifically, if. This control sets up a test. It checks to see whether the value of filledIn is true or false. There are other controls you can use in JavaScript. I have included this example to whet your appetite. JavaScript is a complete programming language that enables you to set up a variety of control structures, which can do amazing things that this book doesn't have the space to cover. Let's move on now to look at the cool new possibilities of using JavaScript to manipulate CSS styles.

Isn't It Dynamic?

The term *dynamic HTML* refers to the use of JavaScript to make HTML documents more interactive. As you'll see in this section, Cascading Style Sheets (CSS) multiply the ways you make your documents come alive with interactive features. In this section, you will look at the display property, and learn how to modify a document so that explanations pop on screen when you move the mouse over some text.

Here's an example. In Figure 20.1, the text shown below the "In this issue" list changes depending on which of the list items you've positioned the mouse on (it's

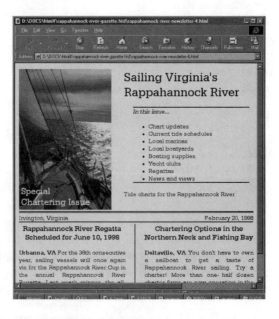

Figure 20.1 "Tides" item description appears only when mouse is over item

not necessary to click the items for the message to appear). Notice the text that says "Tide charts for the Rappahannock River." This text appears only when the user places the pointer over "Current Tide Schedules." It's very easy to implement this, as the following sections explain.

The Display Property

The Display property is part of the CSS.1 specification, and it is simple. In an inline style, it looks like this:

```
<P style = "display: hidden">This text doesn't
appear.</P>
```

What's the point of Display? There wouldn't be much point if it were not for scripts that know how to interact with your style sheets. Basically, from the point of view of JavaScript, your document's style sheet is a "mother" object with lots of little child objects, and the whole thing can be dynamically rewritten based on events.

Try This

To see what dynamic HTML can do for your documents, try creating a list of "In this issue" items such as the one to follow.

```
<P><I>In this issue...</I></P>
<UL>
<LI onmouseover="document.all.chart.style.display=''"
onmouseout="document.all.chart.style.display='none'">
Chart updates</LI>
<LI onmouseover="document.all.tides.style.display=''"
onmouseout="document.all.tides.style.display='none'">
Current tide schedules</LI>
<LI onmouseover="document.all.news.style.display=''"
onmouseout="document.all.news.style.display='none'">
News and views</LI>
</UL>
```

What's up here? Each of the LI elements includes an event handler (onmouseover) followed by a style object (such as "document.all.tides.style.display"). These objects refer to SPAN elements with specific ids (such as "regattas") that are defined later in the document. As you will see, each of these elements has its Display property set to "hidden." And each of these style objects is set to a blank value ('').

Basically, what this event does is to rewrite the current object's setting so that it is blank (which removes "hidden" and kicks in the default value). Magically, the element appears. But of course, you want the element to go away when the user moves the mouse away from the list item. So the onmouseout event handler kicks in, and rewrites the style again so that it's once again set to "hidden."

Here's what the hidden text looks like. Put this where you want the individual items to appear when the user puts the mouse over them:

```
<SPAN id="chart" style="display: none">Up-to-date
charts of the Rappahannock River</SPAN>
<SPAN id="tides" style="display: none">Tide charts
for the Rappahannock River</SPAN>
<SPAN id="news" style="display: none">The latest news
concerning Rappahannock River sailing.</SPAN>
```

Figure 20.2 shows what happens when you select "Boating Supplies."

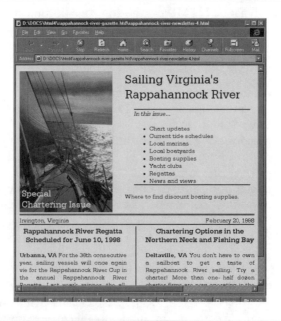

Figure 20.2 Text displayed when mouse cursor is over "Boating Supplies"

> *Be aware that this script works with Internet Explorer version 4, but it doesn't work with earlier versions of Internet Explorer, or with any version of Netscape. There's a pressing need for the World Wide Consortium's Document Object Model (DOM), which will standardize the list of accessible objects that a browser provides. Just as this book was going to press, the Consortium announced a DOM recommendation—and that's good news for HTML authors.*

Summary

Scripts add a wonderful dimension of interactivity to your Web pages. It is easy to learn how to use JavaScript for simple tasks. As this chapter has explained, you can easily learn enough about JavaScript to pull off some amazing stunts, even if you have not mastered all the details of JavaScript syntax.

You have come to the end of *Discovering HTML 4*, and you know enough now to create a first-class Web site. If you would like to extend your knowledge, consider learning XML (eXtensible Markup Language), which many people believe will define the next generation of Web technology, and learn more about JavaScript. This chapter has given you a taste of this great scripting language.

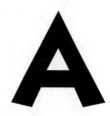

HTML Entities Quick Reference

Character name	Entity code	Mnemonic
ampersand	&#3;	&amp;
angle quotation mark, left	&#17;	&laquo;
angle quotation mark, right	&#18;	&raquo;
broken vertical bar	&#16;	&brvbar;
capital A, acute accent	&#19;	&Aacute;
capital A, circumflex accent	&#19;	&Acirc;
capital A, dieresis or umlaut mark	&#19;	&Auml;
capital A, grave accent	&#19;	&Agrave;

Character name	Entity code	Mnemonic
capital A, ring	&#19;	&Aring;
capital A, tilde	&#19;	&Atilde;
capital AE, diphthong (ligature)	&#19;	&AElig;
capital C, cedilla	&#19;	&Ccedil;
capital E, acute accent	&#20;	&Eacute;
capital E, circumflex accent	&#20;	&Ecirc;
capital E, dieresis or umlaut mark	&#20;	&Euml;
capital E, grave accent	&#20;	&Egrave;
capital Eth, Icelandic	&#20;	&ETH;
capital I, acute accent	&#20;	&Iacute;
capital I, circumflex accent	&#20;	&Icirc;
capital I, dieresis or umlaut mark	&#20;	&Iuml;
capital I, grave accent	&#20;	&Igrave;
capital N, tilde	&#20;	&Ntilde;
capital O, acute accent	&#21;	&Oacute;
capital O, circumflex accent	&#21;	&Ocirc;
capital O, dieresis or umlaut mark	&#21;	&Ouml;
capital O, grave accent	&#21;	&Ograve;
capital O, slash	&#21;	&Oslash;
capital O, tilde	&#21;	&Otilde;
capital THORN, Icelandic	&#22;	&THORN;
capital U, acute accent	&#21;	&Uacute;
capital U, circumflex accent	&#21;	&Ucirc;
capital U, dieresis or umlaut mark	&#22;	&Uuml;
capital U, grave accent	&#21;	&Ugrave;
capital Y, acute accent	&#22;	&Yacute;
cent sign	&#16;	&cent;
circled R registered sign	&#17;	&reg;
copyright sign	&#16;	&copy;
currency sign	&#16;	&curren;
degree sign	&#17;	&deg;

Character name	Entity code	Mnemonic
division sign	&#24;	&divide;
feminine ordinal indicator	&#17;	&ordf;
fraction 1/2	&#18;	&frac1;
fraction 1/4	&#18;	&frac1;
fraction 3/4	&#19;	&frac3;
greater-than sign	&#6;	&gt;
inverted exclamation mark	&#16;	&iexcl;
inverted question mark	&#19;	&iquest;
less-than sign	&#6;	&lt;
masculine ordinal indicator	&#18;	&ordm;
micro sign	&#18;	&micro;
middle dot	&#18;	&middot;
multiplication sign	&#21;	&times;
negation sign	&#17;	&not;
non-breaking space	&#16;	
paragraph sign	&#18;	&para;
plus-or-minus sign	&#17;	&plusmn;
pound sign	&#16;	&pound;
quotation mark	&#3;	&quot;
section sign	&#16;	&sect;
small a, acute accent	&#22;	&aacute;
small a, circumflex accent	&#22;	&acirc;
small a, dieresis or umlaut mark	&#22;	&auml;
small a, grave accent	&#22;	&agrave;
small a, ring	&#22;	&aring;
small a, tilde	&#22;	&atilde;
small ae, diphthong (ligature)	&#23;	&aelig;
small c, cedilla	&#23;	&ccedil;
small e, acute accent	&#23;	&eacute;
small e, circumflex accent	&#23;	&ecirc;
small e, dieresis or umlaut mark	&#23;	&euml;

Character name	Entity code	Mnemonic
small e, grave accent	&#23;	&egrave;
small eth, Icelandic	&#24;	&eth;
small i, acute accent	&#23;	&iacute;
small i, circumflex accent	&#23;	&icirc;
small i, dieresis or umlaut mark	&#23;	&iuml;
small i, grave accent	&#23;	&igrave;
small n, tilde	&#24;	&ntilde;
small o, acute accent	&#24;	&oacute;
small o, circumflex accent	&#24;	&ocirc;
small o, dieresis or umlaut mark	&#24;	&ouml;
small o, grave accent	&#24;	&ograve;
small o, slash	&#24;	&oslash;
small o, tilde	&#24;	&otilde;
small sharp s, German (sz ligature)	&#22;	&szlig;
small thorn, Icelandic	&#25;	&thorn;
small u, acute accent	&#25;	&uacute;
small u, circumflex accent	&#25;	&ucirc;
small u, dieresis or umlaut mark	&#25;	&uuml;
small u, grave accent	&#24;	&ugrave;
small y, acute accent	&#25;	&yacute;
small y, dieresis or umlaut mark	&#25;	&yuml;
soft hyphen	&#17;	&shy;
spacing acute	&#18;	&acute;
spacing cedilla	&#18;	&cedil;
spacing diaresis	&#16;	&uml;
spacing macron	&#17;	&hibar;
superscript 1	&#18;	&sup;
superscript 2	&#17;	&sup;
superscript 3	&#17;	&sup;
yen sign	&#16;	&yen;

B

Color Codes

Basic Color Palette

Color code	Color
#FFFFFF	white
#FF0000	red
#00FF00	green
#0000FF	blue
#FF00FF	magenta
#00FFFF	cyan
#FFFF00	yellow
#000000	black

216 Color "Netscape" Palette

Color code	Color
#70DB93	aquamarine
#5C3317	baker's chocolate
#9F5F9F	blue violet
#B5A642	brass
#D9D919	bright gold
#A62A2A	brown
#8C7853	bronze
#A67D3D	bronze II
#5F9F9F	cadet blue
#D98719	cool copper
#B87333	copper
#FF7F00	coral
#42426F	corn flower blue
#5C4033	dark brown
#2F4F2F	dark green
#4A766E	dark green copper
#4F4F2F	dark olive green
#9932CD	dark orchid
#871F78	dark purple
#241882	dark slate blue
#2F4F4F	dark slate grey
#97694F	dark tan
#7093DB	dark turquoise
#855E42	dark wood
#545454	dim grey
#856363	dusty rose

#D19275	feldspar
#8E2323	firebrick
#F5CCB0	flesh
#238E23	forest green
#CD7F32	gold
#DBDB70	goldenrod
#545454	grey
#856363	green copper
#D19275	green yellow
#8E2323	hunter green
#F5CCB0	indian red
#238E23	khaki
#CD7F32	light blue
#DBDB70	light grey
#545454	light steel blue
#856363	light wood
#D19275	lime green
#8E2323	mandarian orange
#F5CCB0	maroon
#238E23	medium aquamarine
#CD7F32	medium blue
#DBDB70	medium forest green
#EAEAAE	medium goldenrod
#9370DB	medium orchid
#426F42	medium sea green
#7F00FF	medium slate blue
#7FFF00	medium spring green
#70DBDB	medium turquoise

	#DB7093	medium violet red
	#A68064	medium wood
•	#2F2F4F	midnight blue
•	#23238E	navy blue
•	#4D4DFF	neon blue
	#FF6EC7	neon pink
•	#00009C	new midnight blue
	#EBC79E	new tan
	#CFB53B	old gold
	#FF7F00	orange
	#FF2400	orange red
	#DB70DB	orchid
	#8FBC8F	pale green
	#BC8F8F	pink
•	#EAADEA	plum
	#D9D9F3	quartz
•	#5959AB	rich blue
	#6F4242	salmon
	#8C1717	scarlet
	#238E68	sea green
	#6B4226	semi-sweet chocolate
	#8E6B23	sienna
	#E6E8FA	silver
	#3299CC	sky blue
	#007FFF	slate blue
	#FF1CAE	spicy pink
	#00FF7F	spring green
	#236B8E	steel blue

#38B0DE	summer sky
#DB9370	tan
#D8BFD8	thistle
#ADEAEA	turquoise
#5C4033	very dark brown
#CDCDCD	very light grey
#4F2F4F	violet
#CC3299	violet red
#D8D8BF	wheat
#99CC32	yellow green

Index

A

A element: 72
  adding sounds and movies: 369
  anchor: 203
  attributes: 198-199
  href attribute: 73-74
  mailto URL: 204
  new window: 202
  purpose: 72, 197
  rel and rev: 200
  target: 202
ABBR element: 183
absolute positioning: 230-232

  current positioning context: 232
  offsets: 233
  properties: 232-233
absolute URL: 42, 73, 120
ACRONYM element: 183
active link color: 131
ActiveX: 358-360, 358
ADDRESS element: 214, 384
Adobe Systems: 18
advertising: 7, 18
alignment: 144, 159
alternate text: 293

anchor: 196, 203
Andreesen, Marc: 17
angle bracket: 74
animated GIF: 300, 306, 361
anonymous FTP: 93
APPLET element: 214
approach: 106-107
ASCII: 52
ASCII transfer mode: 94, 98
asterisk: 270
attributes
  accesskey: 198, 199
  action: 322

409

align: 159, 245, 309, 370
alt: 78, 370
archive: 370
bgcolor: 245
border: 245
borders: 309
cellpadding: 246
cellspacing: 246
charset: 198
checked: 326
cite: 148
class: 142-143, 157, 167,
    192
classid: 366
code: 370
codebase: 366, 370
codetype: 367
cols: 246, 335
content: 210
core attributes: 61
data: 366
datetime: 187
deprecated: 61
dir: 57
disabled: 332, 333, 335,
    338
frame: 246
frameborder: 274, 275
height: 309, 367, 370
href: 73, 197, 198
hspace: 309, 370
id: 143, 157, 368
lang: 57
language attributes: 57
marginheight: 274
marginwidth: 274
maxlength: 325
media: 80
method: 323
multiple: 330, 332
name: 198, 210, 273, 325,
    335, 338, 368, 370
noresize: 274
object: 370
profile: 58
readonly: 325, 332, 335

rel: 198, 200
rev: 198, 200
rows: 335
rules: 246
scrolling: 274
selected: 334
size: 325, 332
src: 78, 274
standby: 367
tabindex: 198, 202, 325,
    332, 336, 338
target: 198, 202
type: 80, 325, 338, 366
value: 326, 334, 339, 368
valuetype: 368
vspace: 309, 370
width: 66, 246, 309, 367,
    370
AU sound: 361
audience: 106
authorial privilege: 5, 7
auto detect: 94
automatic "we've moved"
    page: 215
AVI movies: 362

B

B element: 181
background color: 116-125,
    134
background images: 119-120,
    134
background shorthand prop-
    erty: 132
background-attachment prop-
    erty: 123
background-color property:
    117
background-image property:
    119-120
background-position proper-
    ty: 121-122

background-repeat property:
    120-121
BASE element: 204
base URL: 43, 204
Berners-Lee, Tim: 9, 10
bgcolor: 41
BIG element: 181
binary transfer mode: 94, 98
bitmap: 296
bitmapped graphic: 296
    distortion
    quality: 297
blank lines: 71
blink: 190
block elements: 27, 142-144
BLOCKQUOTE element: 148
BODY element: 60
body text color: 130
body type: 115
boldface: 181, 189
boolean data type: 35
border shorthand property:
    150, 155
border-bottom-color property:
    150
border-bottom-width proper-
    ty: 152
border-color shorthand prop-
    erty: 151
border-left-color property:
    150
border-left-width property:
    152
border-right-color property:
    150
border-right-width property:
    152
border-style shorthand prop-
    erty: 155
border-style-bottom property:
    154

border-style-right property: 154

border-style-top property: 154

border-top-color property: 150

border-top-width property: 152

border-width shorthand property: 153

borders
  color: 150-152
  CSS border properties: 150-156
  style: 152
  table: 248
  width: 152-153

bottom property: 233

BR element: 70

browser: 10, 26, 54, 58, 60

bullet type: 169
  small graphic as bullet: 169

bulleted list: 75

BUTTON element: 338

C

CAPTION element: 255

Cascading Style Sheets (CSS): 21
  absolute positioning: 230-232
  alignment: 144
  background color: 117-118
  background image: 119-120
  background position: 121-122
  backgrounds: 116-125
  borders: 150-156
  box formatting model: 220-222
  browser support: 81
  class attribute: 142-143
  dynamic rewriting: 376
  font color: 144-145

fonts: 126-132
  indentation: 145
  inheritance: 140-141
  JavaScript: 394
  Level 1: 220
  Level 2: 220
  line spacing: 146
  newspaper columns: 236-237
  specifying URLs: 119
  styles for character cmphases: 187-191
  syntax: 81

case
  element names: 52
  specifying with CSS: 191

case sensitivity: 42

CDATA data type: 36

CENTER element (deprecated): 159

CERN: 9, 13, 15

CERN HTTPd: 17

Channel Definition Format (CDF): 343-356
  Active Desktop: 353
  beginning and ending dates: 350
  channels: 344-346
  creating a channel: 346-348
  e-mail notification: 353
  items: 352
  schedule: 348
  screensaver output: 353
  subpages: 350
  subscription options: 344
  testing: 348
  time interval: 349
  update frequency: 348

channels: 344-346

character data type: 36

character encoding: 33

character formatting: 180-182
  boldface: 181
  emphasis: 181

italics: 181, 187
  oblique: 187
  small caps: 188
  strikethrough: 185
  subscript: 181
  superscript: 181

character set: 199

charset data type: 36

check boxes: 326-328
  group: 327-330

CITE element: 182

class attribute: 61

clear attribute: 70

clear property: 230

client-side imagemaps: 311-315

closing tag: 12

CODE element: 182

COL element: 258-262

COLGROUP element: 261

color: 40
  active hyperlink: 130, 134
  code: 130
  data type: 36
  depth: 297-298
  document text: 129, 134
  font-color property: 130
  hyperlink: 129, 134
  mnemonic code: 40
  name: 130
  numbers: 40
  property: 144
  RGB code: 40
  scheme: 113, 114
  sixteen basic: 41
  visited hyperlink: 129, 134

comma-separated list of lengths: 268

comments: 45, 387

Common Gateway Interface (CGI): 91

compression: 299

container: 241-242

content model: 28, 29
coordinates: 234
copyright: 295-296
core attributes (id, class, style, title): 61
curly braces: 81
current positioning context: 232, 234
Cute FTP: 96, 97, 98, 99

D
daemon: 17
data types: 35-39
database searches: 86
date and time: 187
   ISO 8601 format: 187
date/time data type: 37
dates: 46-47
DD element: 173
default page: 98
definition lists: 172
DEL element: 185
deprecated attributes: 60
   align: 78
   alink: 62
   background: 61
   borders: 78
   center: 63, 68
   clear: 70
   compact: 75
   height: 77
   hspace: 77
   justify: 63, 68
   left: 63, 68
   link: 62
   right: 63, 68
   text: 62
   type: 75, 76
   vlink: 62
   vspace: 77
   width: 77
deprecated elements: 31
   BASEFONT: 125, 135

CENTER: 158-160
DIR: 164
FONT: 31, 125, 160-161
MENU: 31, 164
destination: 196
DFN element: 182
digital cameras: 294
dir attribute: 57
directories: 98-99
Display type: 116
distributed hypertext system: 9
DIV element: 156-158, 229, 235-237
DL element
   element definition: 172
   purpose: 172
Document Object Model (DOM): 397
Document Type Definition (DTD): 11, 54
domain name: 85
   registration: 89
drop-down menus: 330-334
DT element: 172
DTD. See Document Type Definition (DTD)
Dublin Core: 211-216
dynamic HTML: 394

E
e-mail: 45
e-mail address: 203, 215
Early Mosaic: 75
element: 25
   attributes: 28
   block: 27
   content: 28
   defined: 27
   empty: 28
   end tag: 28
   floating: 229

   height: 227-228
   inline: 27, 179-194
   intrinsic height: 233
   intrinsic width: 233
   name: 28
   nested: 32
   percentage widths: 237
   start tag: 27
   value: 28
   width: 228
element definition: 29
elements
   A: 72
   ABBR: 183
   ACRONYM: 183
   ADDRESS: 214, 384
   APPLET: 214
   B: 181
   BIG: 181
   BLOCKQUOTE: 148
   BODY: 60
   BR: 70
   BUTTON: 338
   CAPTION: 255
   CENTER: 159
   CITE: 182
   CODE: 182
   COL: 258-262
   COLGROUP: 261
   DD: 173
   DEL: 185
   DFN: 182
   DIV: 156-158, 229, 235-237
   DT: 172
   EM: 181
   EMBED: 368
   FIELDSET: 341
   FONT: 160-161
   FORM: 322
   FRAME: 272-274
   FRAMESET: 270
   H1-H6: 62-63
   HEAD: 58
   HR: 149
   HTML: 56

IFRAME: 279
IMG: 77, 309-310
INPUT: 324-325, 393
INS: 185
KBD: 182
LABEL: 340
LEGEND: 341
LI: 164
META: 209-310
OL: 164-165
OPTION: 332-336
P: 67-68
PARAM: 364-368
PRE: 65
Q: 184
SCRIPT: 378
SELECT: 331-332
SMALL: 181
SPAN: 192
STRONG: 181
STYLE: 79-81
SUB: 181
SUP: 181
TABLE: 244-246, 248
TBODY: 256-258
TD: 251
TEXTAREA: 334
TFOOT: 256-258
TH: 256
THEAD: 256-258
TITLE: 58
TR: 249-251
TT: 181
UL: 75
VAR: 182

EM element: 181
EMBED element: 368
embossing: 124
end tag: 28, 29, 68, 74, 77
Enter key: 65
entities: 32, 33, 59
   character encoding: 33
entity: 71
error message: 99

escape character: 388
European Computer Stan-
   dards Association
   (ECMA): 375
event handler. See intrinsic
   event handler
extension: 16,19, 20, 21, 31,
   53
external: 135-136

F
face attribute: 125
Fetch: 97, 98, 99
FIELDSET element: 341
file name: 98
File Transfer Protocol (FTP):
   92-95
file uploading boxes: 329
flavors of HTML: 22
float property: 229
floating elements: 229-230
FONT element (deprecated):
   160-161
font shorthand property: 133
font size: 128-129, 160-161
   decreasing: 181
   specifying: 129
font size property.: 128
font-color property: 130
font-family property: 127
font-style property: 187-188
font-variant property: 188
font-weight property: 189
fonts
   color: 129-131, 134, 144-
      145
   CSS font properties: 187-
      191
   CSS Level 1 support: 125-
      132
   downloading: 125, 131

FONT element (deprecat-
   ed): 160-161
generic font names: 126
intellectual property concerns: 125
listing font names: 126-127
monospace: 66, 181
sans-serif: 115-116
serif: 115-116
TrueType: 125
forced march: 284
forcing a line break: 70-71
foreign language characters:
   32, 71
FORM element: 322
form input controls
   check box: 326-328
   drop-down menu: 330-334
   file uploading box: 329
   hidden input fields: 329-
      330
   list box: 330-334
   password text box: 326
   radio button: 328-329
   reset button: 336-339
   single-line text box,: 324-
      326
   submit button: 336-339
   text entry box: 334-336
FormPost: 319
forms: 317-342, 393
   accessibility: 338-339
   element groups: 341-342
   event handler: 393
   FormPost: 319
   get method: 323
   keyboard shortcuts: 339-
      341
   name/value pairs: 323
   new features in HTML 4:
      318
   output: 317, 318
   post method: 323
   processing form output:
      319

single-line text boxes: 324-326
style sheets: 342
tabbing order: 339-341
table layout: 327
forward link: 200
fragment URL: 42, 43
FRAME element: 272-274
frames: 55, 61, 265-280
 alternatives: 278
 correct order: 275
 disadvantages: 265
 element definition: 267-270
 inline: 279-280
 layout: 276-277
 master document: 266
 nested: 271, 275-276
 numbering: 271, 275
 targets: 277-280
Frameset DTD: 55
FRAMESET element: 270
frameset flavor: 22, 55
frameset version statement: 56
FTP: See File Transfer Protocol (FTP)
FTP client: 92, 95, 97, 98
FTP server: 94, 96, 99
FTP server address: 92

G

generic font names: 126
GIF. See Graphics Interchange Format
GIF 89a: 299, 361
GIF animations: 300, 361
global structure: 30, 50
graphical browser: 17
graphics
 alternate text: 78, 293
 browsers: 293
 clip art: 295
 color depth: 297
 compression: 297, 299

copying from Web: 294
copyright: 295-296
file size: 293
imagemaps: 310-315
IMG element: 78
obtaining: 293-295
positioning for non-CSS-capable browsers: 309-310
positioning with CSS: 306-308
processing: 303-306
resolution: 298-299
graphics file formats
 GIF: 299-301
 JPEG: 301
 PNG: 301-302
Graphics Interchange Format (GIF): 299-301
 animation: 300
 guidelines for use: 303
 interlacing: 300
 patent: 299
 popularity: 299
 transparency: 300
guestbooks: 86
guided cloud: 285

H

H1 element: 62
H2 element: 63
hash mark (#): 40
HEAD element: 58
height property: 227
Hewlett Packard: 18
hexadecimal: 40
hidden input fields: 329-330
hiding a script: 379
Hot Dog Professional: 14
HR element: 149
HTML
 editors: 14
 versions: 11

HTML element: 56
hyperlink errors: 74
hyperlinks
 internal: 203
 link types: 200-201
 mailto URL: 204
 shortcut keys: 199
 terminology: 196
hypertext: 4
Hypertext Transfer Protocol (HTTP): 15
hyphens
 ordinary hyphens: 71
 soft hyphens: 71

I

I element: 181
IBM: 18
id attribute: 61
IFRAME element: 279
imagemaps: 310-315
 appropriate graphic: 311
 border: 315
 creating with MapEdit: 312-315
 editor: 311
images subdirectory: 44
IMG element: 77, 309-310
indentation: 145, 223
 nesting structure: 52
 outdent: 224
index.html: 98
inheritance: 79, 118, 140
 background color: 118
 block vs inline elements: 142
 DIV element: 158
 examples: 141-144
inline elements: 27, 142
inline styles: 167, 191-192
INPUT element: 324-325, 393
INS element: 185

insertions and deletions,
  marking: 185
interlaced GIF: 300
interlacing: 125
Internet Explorer. See
  Microsoft Internet
  Explorer
InterNIC: 89, 100
interpreter: 373
intrinsic event handlers: 391
ISO 8601: 46-47, 187
italics: 181, 187

J
Java
  advantages: 359
  applets: 359
  applications: 359
  parameters: 359
  security: 359
Java applet: 370, 375
  documentation: 362-364
  downloading: 362-364
  embedding with OBJECT
    element: 362-364
  memory consumption: 375
  OBJECT element: 365, 368
  PARAM element: 367
  run-time settings: 368
JavaScript
  browser support: 375, 397
  button object: 381
  case-sensitive: 383
  comment identifier: 380
  cross-platform: 376
  date object: 381, 385
  document object: 381
  ECMAScript: 375
  escape character: 388
  form object: 381
  hiding: 379
  history object: 381
  input object: 381
  location object: 382

objects: 381
  resembles Java: 375
  semicolon: 390
  string concatenation: 385
  window object: 382
Joint Photographic Experts
  Group (JPEG): 301
  compression: 301
  guidelines for use: 302
  progressive display: 301
JPEG. See Joint Photographic
  Expert's Group (JPEG)
JPEG File Interchange Format
  (JFIF): 301

K
KBD element: 182

L
LABEL element: 340
lang attribute: 57
language attributes (lang, dir):
  57
language code data type: 37
language codes: 39
Latin-1: 33
left property: 232, 233
LEGEND element: 341
length data type: 37
letter-spacing property: 189-
  190
LI element: 164
  element definition: 76
  purpose: 76
line
  breaks: 65, 69-71
  spacing: 146
line-height property: 146
line-through: 190
link. See hyperlink
LINK element: 136, 206
link types: 200-201

linking element: 196
list boxes: 330-334
list-style-type property: 166
  use with class atrribute:
    167
lists
  combined: 170-171
  definition: 172-174
  deprecated attributes: 174-
    176
  explanatory text: 171
  nested: 168
  ordered: 164-167
  style sheets: 174
  types: 163
  unordered: 169
login name: 92
LZW compression: 299

M
mailto URL: 45, 203, 215,
  322
MapEdit: 312-315
margin shorthand property:
  225
margin-bottom property: 224
margin-left property: 224
margin-right property: 224
margin-top property: 224
margins
  CSS box properties: 224-
    225
  cumulative: 224, 228
  outdent: 224
  parent element: 223
markup languages: 9, 27
marquee: 19
master document: 266-267
media descriptor data type:
  37

META element: 209-210

metainformation: 208

metalanguage: 10

methods (JavaScript), 381-382

method of development: 109-110

Microsoft Front Page: 14

Microsoft FrontPage: 240

Microsoft Internet Explorer: 19, 22, 54, 231-232
  Active Desktop: 353
  Channel Definition Format (CDF): 344-356
  Channel Explorer: 344-356
  CSS Level 2 support: 220, 231
  deprecated watermark property: 123
  subscription options: 344
  support for FACE element: 125

Microsoft Internet Information Server (IIS): 91

Microsoft Windows: 53

Microsoft Windows NT: 91

Microsoft Word: 52

MIDI sounds: 361

MIME type: 38, 39, 368, 278

Mnemonic code: 40

mood: 114

Mosaic: 17, 75

movie file formats
  AVI: 362
  MPEG: 362
  QuickTime: 362

moving files: 99

MPEG movies: 362

multi-level guided cloud: 286

multi-page site designs
  forced march: 284
  guided cloud: 285

multi-level guided cloud: 286

semantic cloud: 282-284

style sheet: 286-287

multimedia: 360

N

name: 37

name data type: 37

native multimedia formats: 361-371

navigation aids: 243

Nelson, Ted: 8

nested element: 31

nesting structure

NetCaster: 19, 354

NetObjects Fusion: 14

Netscape Communications: 17, 18, 368, 370

Netscape Navigator: 19, 22, 54, 368, 370

Netscape Page Composer: 14

newspaper columns: 236-237

non-breaking space: 69

non-CSS-capable browsers: 61

Notepad: 13

Novell: 18

numbered lists. See ordered lists

O

object
  defined: 380

OBJECT element: 357-372

Object Oriented Programming (OOP)
  basic concepts: 380-382
  efficiency: 381
  inheritance: 382, 385
  methods: 380
  objects: 380

properties: 380

oblique: 187

obsolete elements: 31

offset: 233

OL element: 164-165

opening documents
  in full window: 278
  in new window: 202, 278
  in previous frame: 278
  in same frame: 278

opening tag: 12

OPTION element: 332-336

ordered lists: 164-167
  combining with unordered lists: 170
  default appearance: 165
  default numbering scheme: 176
  initial value: 175-176
  manual numbering: 175-176
  nesting: 168
  numbering types: 165

overlining: 190

P

P element: 67-68

padding: 226-227

padding shorthand property: 226

padding-bottom property: 226

padding-left property: 226

padding-right property: 226

padding-top property: 226

page design
  audience analysis: 107
  method of development: 109

Paint Shop Pro: 303-306

paragraph breaks ignored: 65

PARAM element: 364-368

parser: 56
password text box: 326
path: 16, 42
perl: 85
PICS. See Platform for Internet Content Selection (PICS)
pixels data type: 38
plain text: 52
Platform for Internet Content Selection (PICs): 213-214
plug-ins: 358
  inserting: 368
PNG. See Portable Network Graphics (PNG)
Portable Network Graphics (PNG): 301
  browser support: 302
  compression: 301
  transparency: 301
position property: 232
positioning context: 235
pound sign (#): 203
PRE element: 65
presentation: 10, 18, 21
printing: 282
programs
  compiled: 374
  executable: 374
  interpreted: 374
progressive JPEG: 301
  creating: 305
proofreading: 52, 63, 74
properties (JavaScript): 381-382
protocol: 15, 16
protocol name: 42
publishing
  company or school server: 84
  cost: 87, 88-91
  data transfer fees: 91

  intentions: 105
  on your computer: 87-91
  purposes: 103
  service provider's computer: 84-85
  Web hosting service: 85-86
pull publishing: 343
push publishing: 8, 18, 19, 343-344
  browser support: 343

Q
Q element: 184
QuickTime movies: 362
quotation marks: 29, 74, 81, 148
quotations
  long (BLOCKQUOTE element): 184
  short (Q element): 184

R
radio buttons: 328-329
real-time chatting: 86
relative positioning: 233-236
relative URL: 43- 44, 93, 119, 204
renaming files: 99
repetitive stress injuiries (RSI): 199
replacable elements: 222, 223, 229, 306
reserved target names: 278
reset button: 336-339
resolution: 298-299
resolving the URL: 43
resource: 16, 42, 43
Resource Description Framework (RDF): 209
RGB code: 40
right property: 233
RSACi rating service: 214

rules: 149
  CSS border properties: 150
  HR element: 149

S
Safe for Kids rating service: 214
SafeSurf rating service: 214
SAMP element: 182
scanner: 293
script: 373
  automatic execution: 376
  benefits: 375
  browser interprets: 374
  date of last modification: 384
  debugging: 383
  defined: 373-374
  disadvantages: 377, 383
  ease of use: 374
  echoing title: 383
  efficiency: 375
  enclosing within SCRIPT element: 379
  events: 389-390
  form input: 375
  function: 388
  hiding: 387
  hiding scripts: 379
  incorporating markup: 387
  indicating URL: 383
  inserting date: 386
  output: 383
  rewriting CSS styles: 395
  scripting language: 374
  short: 375
  specifying scripting language: 379
  styles: 376
  user initiated: 376
SCRIPT element: 378
scripting languages
  JavaScript: 375-376
  Tcl: 376
  VBScript: 376

search engines: 59, 209, 210
  increasing retrievability: 59
secure server: 86
SELECT element: 331-332
semantic cloud: 282-284
server-side imagemaps: 311-315
SGML: See Standard Generalized Markup Language (SGML)
shopping cart: 86
shortcut keys: 199, 340
shorthand properties
  specifying borders: 152
site managers: 14
slash mark: 12, 74
small caps: 188
SMALL element: 181
smart quotes
SoftQuad: 18
sound file formats
  AU: 361
  MIDI: 361
  WAV: 361-362
source anchor.: 196
spaces: 36, 42, 65
SPAN element: 192
Spyglass: 18
Standard Generalized Markup Language (SGML): 10
standardization process: 20
start tag: 27, 29, 68
strict DTD: 55
strict flavor: 22, 55, 61, 240
strict version statement: 55
strikethrough: 190
string concatenation: 385
STRONG element: 181
structure: 10, 18, 21
style attribute: 61
style data type: 38

STYLE element: 79-81
style sheet: 21
style sheets
  external: 206, 223
  in-line: 223
styles
  inline: 191-192
SUB element: 181
subdirectory: 97, 99
submit button: 336-339
subscript: 181
subscription: 344
Sun Microsystems: 18
SUP element: 181
superimposed text and graphics: 231
superscript: 181
suppressing line breaks: 69
syntax: 26, 79

T

Tab key: 67
tab order: 340-342
tabbing order: 202
TABLE element: 244-246, 248
tables: 239-264
  alignment: 247, 250, 253
  border: 248
  caption: 241
  cell spanning: 243-246, 253-256
  columns: 241, 247, 258
  container: 241-242
  data: 242
  examples: 242-244
  header cells: 254
  layout: 240
  navigation aids: 243
  row and column grouping: 256-262
  rows: 241, 249-251
  style sheets: 263

  tables: 254-255
  width: 248
tags: 10, 12
targets: 42, 43, 278
TBODY element: 256-258
Tcl: 376
TD element: 251
template: 53
tessellation: 124
text boxes: 325-326. See form input controls
text direction: 57
text editor: 13, 65
text entry: 64-68
text entry areas: 334-336
text-align property: 144
text-decoration property: 190
text-indent property: 145
text-only browser: 36
text-only browsers: 78
text-transform property: 191
TEXTAREA element: 334
TFOOT element: 256-258
TH element: 256
THEAD element: 256-258
timeout: 94
times: 46-47
title attribute: 61
TITLE element: 58
titling your page: 59
top property: 232, 233
TR element: 249-251
transitional DTD: 55
transitional flavor: 22, 31, 55, 60, 61, 133, 240
  alignment: 159
  deprecated BASEFONT element: 135
  deprecated BODY attributes: 133

transitional version statement: 56

transparent GIFs: 142, 300, 305

TT element: 181

typing errors: 53-54

typography: 115-116

U

UL element: 75

underlining: 190

Unicode 2.0: 32

Uniform Resource Locators (URL): 15-16
    absolute URL: 73
    base URL: 204
    CSS syntax: 119
    fragment URL: 42, 43
    proofreading: 74
    relative URL: 43- 44, 93, 119, 204

Universal Character Set (UCS): 32

Unix: 16

unordered lists: 75
    combining with ordered lists: 170
    deprecated type attribute: 169
    small graphic as bullet: 169
    specifying bullet type with CSS: 169

unvisited link color: 131

unwanted document retrieval: 208

uploading files: 93

uploading graphics: 93

URL: See Uniform Resource Locator (URI)

URL data type: 38

usage statistics: 86

V

validation checker: 56

values: 29, 30, 35-39, 43 , 52

VAR element: 182

VBScript: 376

version statement: 50, 54-56, 62

visited link color: 131

W

W3C: 18, 20

watermark: 20, 123

WAV sounds: 361

Web hosting service: 85-86

Web server: 16-17

Web-based newsgroups: 86

white space: 75

WHOIS Web gateway: 100

width attribute: 67

width property: 228

word processing program: 52, 65

World Wide Web: 9

World Wide Web (WWW): 8

World Wide Web Consortium (W3C): 18, 20, 26, 31, 40

WYSIWYG editor: 13, 14

X

Xanadu: 8, 13, 16

XML: 346, 397